Thc Art of Discussion-Based Teaching

The Art of Discussion-Based Teaching

Opening Up Conversation in the Classroom

JOHN E. HENNING

Routledge
Taylor & Francis Group

NEW YORK AND LONDON

First published 2008
by Routledge
270 Madison Ave, New York, NY 10016

Simultaneously published in the UK
by Routledge
2 Park Square, Milton Park, Abingdon, Oxon OX14 4RN

Routledge is an imprint of the Taylor & Francis Group, an informa business

Typeset in Helvetica Neue and Minion Pro by Prepress Projects Ltd

Printed and bound in the United States of America on acid-free paper by Sheridan Books, Inc.

Library of Congress Cataloging in Publication Data
Henning, John E.
The art of discussion-based teaching: opening up conversation in the classroom/John E. Henning.
    p. cm.
Includes bibliographical references and index.
1. Discussion–Study and teaching. 2. Communication in education. 3. Inquiry-based learning. 4. Active learning. I. Title.
LB1032.H45 2008
    371.39–dc22
    2007020946

ISBN 10: 0-415-95633-1 (pbk)
ISBN 10: 0-203-93589-6 (ebk)

ISBN 13: 978-0-415-95633-8 (pbk)
ISBN 13: 978-0-203-93589-7 (ebk)

To Maria
for your passionate and enduring devotion

Contents

Acknowledgments

I would like to thank all of the teachers and students whose contributions made this book possible. I am especially grateful for the cooperation I received from the teachers at the Malcolm Price Laboratory at the University of Northern Iowa, including Megan Balong, Amy Lockhart, Craig Saddler, Sheryl Hoffman, Lynne Ensworth, J. D. Cryer, Curt Nielsen, Dr. Jody Stone, and Dr. Lyn Countryman. For their feedback about the bow tie, I would like to express my appreciation to Eric Schultz, Amy Ludens, Ann Craig, Mary Fliehler, Ted Tauber, Robert Young, Scott Gay, Jessica Kelsey, Valerie Shanley, Melissa McMullen, Shirley Jarzombeck, and Tonya Wilson-Storey. Also, special thanks to my editor, Catherine Bernard, whose support and comments about the manuscript were invaluable.

Finally, I would like to express my gratitude to The Graduate College at the University of Northern Iowa for supporting this work with a Professional Development Assignment.

Introduction

At the dawn of the twentieth century, visitors in an urban high school would have noted that large classrooms of around fifty students were typical. Had they asked, they would have learned the desks were bolted to the floor to promote a quieter and more orderly atmosphere. They would have also seen that interactions between teacher and student followed a highly predictable pattern. At the rate of two or three per minute, students would be called upon to stand and recite the answer to a question. After each student finished giving an answer, the teacher would pronounce it right or wrong, and then ask a question of another student (Cuban, 1984).

Since these early descriptions of teacher and student interactions, many changes have occurred in American education. Desks are no longer bolted to the floor, class sizes are smaller, and students are rarely, if ever, called upon to stand when they answer. Yet despite repeated criticism and the introduction of numerous innovations, the recitation of memorized facts continues to dominate the classroom interactions between teachers and students. (See "For Further Reading" at the end of the book for specific references.)

What are Discussions?

In comparison to a recitation, a discussion is a related but different form of classroom discourse. *Classroom discourse* is a very broad and inclusive term that refers to any and all verbal interchanges among teachers and students in a classroom. Larger patterns of classroom discourse, such as recitations and discussions, are composed of individual *discourse moves.* Examples would include the types of questions asked by the teacher, the types of responses made by the student, and the teacher's follow up moves. Both discussions and recitations engage students in a *dialogue*, or a two-way communication between student and teacher—as opposed to a lecture, which is a *monologue* or one-way communication from teacher to student. However, the discourse moves common to a recitation consist of a very simple form of dialogue: the teacher asks a question to which there is a right or wrong answer, a student responds, and the teacher pronounces the answer to be correct or incorrect.

In contrast, a *discussion* may include some form of recitation, but only as one part of a far more complex discourse. To facilitate participation during a discussion, teachers ask open-ended questions that enable longer, more varied student responses, require more varied teacher responses, and encourage more student-to-student interaction. In addition, the teacher places less emphasis on evaluation, more emphasis on feedback, and casts the student in a more participatory role. What distinguishes expert discussion leaders from novices is the complexity of their classroom discourse. They do not rigidly adhere to a single "best" way of talking but, instead, they use their skills to respond flexibly to students with varying needs (Henning & Lockhart, 2003; Viiri & Saari, 2006).

Why Discussion-Based Teaching?

Discussion-based teaching involves the systematic use of discussions to accomplish curricular objectives. It was initially advocated to promote democratic values in response to the rise of fascism in Europe in the 1930s (Delamont, 1983). Throughout the remainder of the twentieth century, interest in discussion-based teaching spread, partly due to the increasing recognition of the essential role of social interaction for promoting student thinking and partly due to the increasing support for discussion-based teaching in the research literature. Benefits have been demonstrated across multiple subject areas, including social studies, English, science, and mathematics. More specifically, discussion-based teaching has led to gains in general subject mastery, reading comprehension, conceptual understanding, problem-solving ability, moral development, attitude change and development, and communication skills. The acceptance of discussion-based teaching as a sound pedagogy has led to the introduction of numerous instructional approaches for improving the quality of teacher and student dialogue, such as indirect instruction, dialogic instruction, conversational teaching, and instructional conversations. (See "For Further Reading.")

Obstacles to Discussion-Based Teaching

Despite the research-supported benefits and a proliferation of new methods, recitation is still a much more prevalent form of classroom discourse than discussion. Several explanations have been offered for the lack of discussion-based teaching. One suggests that teachers don't value a discussion-based approach. It is thought teachers may not appreciate the beneficial outcomes of discussions, or they simply may prefer avoiding controversial issues by adopting a more autocratic teaching style (Gall & Gillet, 1980; Gall, 1985; Dillon, 1994). A second explanation is that limiting factors in the teaching environment may inhibit discussion-based teaching. Teachers may avoid discussions when their class sizes are too large, or when they feel pressure to raise test scores by teaching the acquisition of facts and skills (Gall, 1985). In a stressful environment, controlling the talk in a classroom can often appear to be the safest and most efficient option.

It's Harder than it Looks

In my own case, I never doubted the benefits of discussions. My high school English teachers were wonderful, and our class discussions had a profound impact on my thinking. So years later, when I began teaching high school English, my first inclination was to duplicate the exciting discussions I had once experienced as a student. Unfortunately, my fantasy of eager students responding enthusiastically to challenging questions didn't materialize. Only in my best classes was that vision even partially realized; in them, I was able to get as many as seven or eight students to participate while the rest listened respectfully. In the other classes, however, either the entire group would remain stonily silent or else everyone would talk—at once and to each other. It wasn't as easy as it had looked.

My experience illustrates a third explanation for the lack of discussion-based teaching—it's hard. Leading a discussion is one of the most difficult and complex tasks in teaching (Greene, 1954). Anticipating, managing, and making sense of the unpredictable and often idiosyncratic responses of a group of highly diverse students can be daunting. Teachers must consider the questions they ask, listen carefully to student responses, and then respond to them spontaneously while keeping the discussion focused on a particular set of curricular objectives. For new teachers, it is even more difficult to plan, anticipate, and manage the direction of discussions. Their lack of experience can inhibit their ability to engage in discussion-based lessons, which in turn prevents them from acquiring the needed experience to become a more effective discussion leader.

A potential further obstacle is the belief that only a few skills or strategies are involved. Often, when I ask my preservice teachers how they would create an effective discussion, they will name one strategy, such as asking good questions or building rapport. But no single strategy can consistently address the complexity of classroom interactions during a discussion. Too many varying factors are at work, e.g., the students' interest and ability, the difficulty of the subject matter, the class size, and other environmental influences. The role that any of these factors plays in any single discussion can vary significantly depending on the context. Therefore, leading a discussion requires multiple strategies that complement and build upon each other.

Another barrier is that teachers are rarely given systematic instruction on how to conduct a discussion (Gall, 1985; Smith, Hardman, Wall, & Mroz, 2004). Most of us learn by gradually accumulating a patchwork of discussion strategies, many of which are understood at an instinctive level. The expertise of those who follow this uncertain path tends to be limited to the specific lesson plans and classroom settings in which it was acquired. Without a grasp of the fundamental principles that lead to successful discussions, teachers are limited in their ability to apply their skills across contexts, and their discussions are bound to specific lesson plans. For these teachers, only a limited number of topics can be discussed productively.

Purpose of the Book

This book is intended to be an explicit guide to understanding and practicing discussion-based teaching. While there are no ready made prescriptions or formulas that can guarantee an effective discussion, a careful and thorough study of the principles of discussion-based teaching can greatly increase your chances of success. Knowing how to create the conditions for a discussion, how to anticipate the students' responses, and how to guide the direction of a discussion reduces the unpredictability of student responses, thus enabling teachers to feel in control while letting students be expressive. As you become a more resourceful and flexible decision maker during discussions, you will be more likely to take greater risks with your students and less likely to view elements of the classroom environment as limiting.

Interested readers might include practicing teachers taking a graduate course or participating in a professional development program; teachers who would like to engage in self-reflection and professional development as part of a collaborative study group; teachers interested in improving their practice on their own; teachers interested in deepening their understanding of classroom interactions in preparation for National Board Certification; or teachers using the book as a text in a graduate or undergraduate education course. For preservice teachers, reflections and transcripts of classroom discussions are included in the book. Reading and discussing them can provide you with insight into the complex decision making of practicing teachers. In addition, the activities at the end of each chapter can be adapted to field experiences.

Organization of the Book

The book is organized into five sections, consisting of twelve chapters. In chapters 1–3, you will learn about all the different types of discourse moves that can take place in a classroom. In general, teachers initiate a classroom interaction by asking a question or in some way eliciting a student response, to which the teacher adds a follow up comment. Each of the three chapters in this section treats one aspect of the three-part cycle of classroom dialogue. Chapter 1 will address teacher questioning, chapter 2 will treat possible student responses, and chapter 3 will examine teacher follow up moves. Learning these discourse moves provides a means for analyzing your discussions and determining where improvement can be made. In addition, the results of your initial analysis can be used as a benchmark to measure future improvement.

After you have mastered the discourse moves associated with discussions in the first section, you will learn how to guide and create discussions in the second section of the book. Chapter 4 will show you how to combine the discourse moves you learned in the first three chapters into larger patterns of discussion. Understanding the patterns described in this chapter will make it easier for you to anticipate student responses, to maximize student participation, and to meet your curricular objectives. Chapter 5 will show you how to create new discussions using four specific approaches: responding to a problem, responding to an observation, responding to a reading, and reflecting on an activity. These four approaches will enable you to generate new discussions with widely varying subject matter and in divergent contexts. Students of any grade level will respond enthusiastically to a discussion that has been well designed.

The third section of the book, which consists of chapters 6 and 7, will show you how to keep students involved with discussions. Chapter 6 will illustrate how to cultivate positive relationships with and among students. Chapter 7 will focus on providing individual support for students whose cultural differences may provide especial linguistic and instructional challenges.

The fourth section of the book uses concepts from the first seven chapters to help teachers redesign existing lessons or plan new ones that incorporate more discussion-based teaching. The position taken in this book is that some opportunities for discussion are better than others. By understanding when discussions are most and least effective, teachers can maximize the amount of discussion and interaction with students. To assist in planning, a conceptual aid referred to as the "bow tie" will be introduced in chapter 8. The bow tie can help teachers discover the most promising opportunities to design and implement more open discussions. It includes three types of discussion: framing, conceptual, and application. Chapters 9, 10, and 11 will fully describe each of these discussions.

The fifth section consists of a single chapter on analyzing discussions. Chapter 12 describes several techniques for videotaping classroom interactions and discussing them in teacher study groups. Analyzing videotapes is one of the most efficacious ways to reflect on practice and could provide added insight into the thinking processes associated with the discourse interactions discussed in this book. This chapter has been included for the benefit of (a) inservice or preservice teachers interested in employing a collaborative, evidence-based approach to improving their classroom discourse, (b) schools that are interested in organizing their teachers in collaborative teams to analyze and expand their instructional strategies, or (c) teacher educators who would like to organize their undergraduate course around a preservice teacher's field experience or an inservice teacher's practice. The opportunity to read, apply, analyze, and then reapply the techniques discussed in this book would make a strong approach to improving your practice. A subsidiary benefit for those who collect videotapes is their potential usefulness as part of a portfolio, professional development plan, or career plan. These videotapes and/or their transcripts can provide compelling evidence of a teacher's ability to meet state and national teaching standards. For these reasons, you may want to turn to chapter 12 sooner rather than later so that you can begin collecting and discussing videotaped classroom interactions as you read through the rest of the book.

Discussions and Activities

At the beginning and end of each chapter, topics will be provided for discussion. Discussions that precede the chapter reading will be referred to as "framing" discussions. Framing discussions are intended to help readers organize their existing knowledge in a way that provides a "frame" for the ideas that follow in the chapter. Therefore, for those who are reading the book with a study group or as part of a class, these questions should be discussed before reading the chapter. It may also be helpful to summarize and record discussion responses as a preassessment that can be compared with later work. In the fourth section of the book, readers will learn how to design and lead framing discussions in their own classes. Framing discussions are useful for maximizing student engagement, assessing their current state of knowledge, and activating prior knowledge.

A second type of discussion will follow the reading of each chapter. These discussions are referred to as application discussions because they provide an opportunity for readers to apply what they have learned during the chapter to the discussion topic. Like framing discussions, the subjects of these discussions will be based on transcripts of teacher and student interactions, written reflections from teachers, and live or videotaped observations of teacher and student interactions. Engaging with framing and application discussions from the very beginning of the book will enhance your understanding of them. The uses and characteristics of framing and application discussions will be explained and illustrated in separate chapters of the fourth section of the book. Also introduced in the fourth section of the book is a third type of discussion called a conceptual discussion.

Taking the time to engage in these discussions as a member of a teacher study group can increase your understanding of the content. The subject of these discussions will be based on transcripts of teacher and student interactions, written reflections from teachers, and live or videotaped observations of teacher and student interactions. In addition to the discussions, activities are also suggested at the end of each chapter. These activities have been written so they can be completed by individual teachers working alone or by teachers working collaboratively as a part of a study group.

How to Use the Book

One of the most poignant experiences in my teaching career occurred when I introduced cooperative learning into my high school English classroom. At that time, there were no teaching models available for me to observe: no one was using cooperative learning in my high school building. The innovation was based solely on my reading of several books urging the adoption of cooperative learning. I took all of my ideas from the books I had read, implemented the ones I felt were most important, and experienced a fair degree of success, probably in part because the students were so hungry for more interaction.

Shortly after introducing cooperative learning, I had an experience that caused me to further refine my approach. To prepare my students for a whole group discussion, I had assigned them to small groups, given them a worksheet with questions to answer, and told them that, after they had finished, we would discuss the questions in a large group. To encourage discussion in small groups, I offered an incentive to the members of the small group who participated the most during the large group discussion. The winning group would be excused from filling out the worksheets the next time we discussed in small groups. That group would be allowed the privilege of discussing the questions without having to write out their answers.

For some students, this proved to be a powerful incentive. Two of the five groups worked industriously to answer the questions. But the other three groups were completely unmoved: they did little more than write down a few perfunctory answers. When I asked them why they weren't working on the questions, they said they had no chance to win my little competition because I had placed all the smart people in two of the groups. Later, during the whole class discussion, the two "smart" groups competed ferociously, waving their hands wildly, grunting, and begging for me to call on them. In short, they disrupted the discussion in their desire to win the competition. The other three groups contributed little or nothing, withdrawing completely from the discussion.

I went back to my books on cooperative learning and found that I had overlooked a fundamental principle of cooperative learning: it is based on cooperation not competition. My belief in motivating students through competition was so strong that it had colored the way that I had understood and implemented cooperative learning. This incident gave me a profound insight into the nature of professional development. My initial readings on cooperative learning had not allowed me a full understanding of the method because I lacked the authors' practice knowledge. I had not fully understood the words I had read. Only after I had tried the method could I fully appreciate what the authors had meant.

Having acquired a deeper understanding of the method, I redesigned the incentive for small group work: now any group whose members participated at least once during the whole group discussion would not have to write out the answers to the worksheets. And if everyone in the class participated at least once – a hundred percent participation – then everyone would receive a few bonus points. This gave everyone an incentive to work in small groups, to participate in the large group discussion, and a reason to value the participation of their classmates. Structuring the discussion this way consistently resulted in an orderly discussion with full or nearly full participation.

My experience fully supports one of the primary tenets of this book: your understanding of the reading must be informed by practice. The template for discussion-based teaching described on the following pages requires understanding the numerous intersecting influences that determine the quality of classroom discussions. Mastering the art of discussion-based teaching involves acquiring multiple and sometimes competing strategies, e.g., eliciting participation from students who are trying to discuss unfamiliar ideas. It is only through practice that you can observe how these complementary strategies mesh together.

To develop your powers of judgment, I would encourage you to reread and revisit the ideas in this book after you have tried them. Your experiences may enable you to understand much more deeply what you thought you understood perfectly well the first time. Another strategy would be to target parts of the book that you find difficult, try some innovations in your classroom, and then revisit those specific sections. In addition to rereading, use the information in chapter 12 to collect data for the purpose of analyzing your classroom interactions. Learning new strategies combined with a thorough examination of your practice can provide the speediest course to innovation. Either one alone is not sufficient.

This book was born from a very similar process. I have taken my own experiences with discussion-based teaching, extended them through my reading or research and through my interactions with practicing and prospective teachers from a variety of grade levels and content areas, and tried to integrate them into a model that will work broadly across a variety of contexts. As you move from reading and discussing discussion-based teaching to implementing changes in your classroom practice, your understanding will inevitably grow and deepen. To better facilitate this process, don't be afraid to think about discussion-based teaching in the way that is most useful for you, to develop short cuts or adaptations that make it fit your practice better, to understand it and practice it in your own unique way. Allowing yourself that freedom is crucial to your understanding and your ability to practice discussion-based teaching. It is through our constant thinking and rethinking, as we continually adapt our practice to changing circumstances, that the art of teaching is perpetually invented and reinvented.

What Teachers Need to Know

In summary, teachers need to understand a complex network of skills and processes in order to conduct an effective discussion. First, they need to understand the types of discourse moves associated with discussions and how to assess their students' responses. This knowledge enables teachers to analyze and improve the effectiveness of their discussions. Second, teachers need to know how to plan and guide discussions. This knowledge can help teachers to encourage more student participation and better anticipate student responses while achieving the learning goals. Third, teachers should also know how to create the appropriate climate for discussions by building relationships, using accountability strategies, and providing support for culturally and linguistically diverse students. Understanding how to build a supportive atmosphere can help assure more consistent success with a discussion-based approach to teaching. Fourth, teachers need to be able to identify the best opportunities for discussion within a teaching unit and which strategies can best help them realize those discussions. Fifth, teachers need to have an understanding of how to collect data and analyze their discussions. It is through this process they can best improve their skill in leading discussions.

part one
Classroom Discourse Moves

The purpose of chapters 1–3 is to define and illustrate the different types of discourse moves made by teachers and students during classroom interactions. Recognizing them is essential to evaluating and systematically improving your discussion skills. These chapters can help you become aware of the discourse moves at which you are already proficient, pinpoint the discourse moves you use infrequently but would like to use more, and introduce some unfamiliar discourse moves that could be added to your repertoire. By understanding a wide array of discourse moves, teachers can better locate their current skill level and identify which additional strategies can best enhance their skill base.

one
Asking Questions

Framing Discussion

Below, you will find a description of a discussion written by a teacher of industrial technology. In the paper, he reflects on his discussion strategies, how his students responded to them, and the adjustments he made based on their responses. As you read his reflection, try to identify the different types of strategies he used. Pay particular attention to his strategies for asking questions. Consider the different ways he uses questions to advance the discussion. Then discuss the following questions:

1. How did this teacher use questions to guide this discussion?
2. What other kinds of strategies did this teacher use to create an effective discussion?
3. Rank these strategies in the order of their importance.
4. Do you think the relative importance of these elements would change if the grade level or ability level of the students changed? Explain.
5. Would the relative importance of these strategies change if the subject matter changed?
6. Based on your own experience, what are the most important strategies necessary to create an effective classroom discourse?

Purpose and Desired Outcomes

The purpose of this analysis is to check for adequate skills in conducting a classroom discussion. Several skills that I would like to focus on are my questioning techniques, my ability to extend student thinking without questions, and my ability to encourage a majority of my students to participate in the discussion.

To analyze proper questioning techniques, I will focus on whether I use questions that appropriately frame the dialogue, ask for supporting evidence, and summarize students' ideas. To analyze my ability to extend student thinking without questions, I will study my ability to use appropriate wait time, to restate students' comments to link together individual comments, and to contribute information to build on previous comments. To analyze whether I encourage the majority of my students to participate, I will study my ability to affirm students' comments, credit individual students for their contributions, and express appreciation for student thinking.

The intended outcome I had for this discussion was to have the students brainstorm ideas for safety features that they would incorporate into their vehicles that they were to create. I wanted the students not only to discuss the obvious ideas of safety such as seatbelts, airbags, etc., but also to analyze the not so obvious features such as a roof or dashboard and how these features enhance safety in a vehicle. I wanted students to state the safety feature and why that feature was important to the safety of the driver or passenger. I then wanted the students to make connections between the safety features discussed and how they would incorporate the features into the car they were going to build. Technological developments have increased our ability to accomplish the feat of traveling farther and faster. But, because of these advancements, we have also created some problems. My introduction question for the discussion was "What type of problems have we created because of the developments in transportation?" With this type of question I was trying to explore student's current understanding. I was also trying to frame the dialogue in such a way that I would receive responses that would guide the discussion toward safety features in a vehicle. The first response by a student was "Usage of fuel." Since this was an adequate answer to the question of problems created by transportation vehicles, I confirmed the students' answer with "That is correct; we now have a fuel shortage." At this point, I thought my initial question was too broad and I had to close down the "frame" of the question. I then asked "Because of our ability to travel long distances in a quick amount of time, what type of problems do we encounter?" Student response: "Accidents." I confirmed with a "That is right." My next question was "What features do we have in our automobiles that are considered safety features that would protect a driver/passenger from injury or death?"

I feel that these two questions gave a dialogue frame that would create discussion toward my main goal of safety features in an automobile. I feel that they are not too closed where students could only respond with one correct answer and the questions were not too broad – such as the initial question about advancements in technology – guiding the students into a discussion that would not address my main goal.

Student responses at this point were along the lines of seatbelts, airbags, and bumpers. With each response, I asked the students to support their answers with evidence. The students responded with statements such as "Seatbelts keep us in the car" or "Airbags cushion us when we get hit." I then wanted the students to think of safety features that were not so obvious. My next question was very simplistic, "What else?" Not a question that would develop a deeper level of thinking. The first response was "Transmission." This answer caught me by surprise. I tried to reformulate the idea into a question, "Does a car's transmission provide safety for the driver/passenger?" The student responded with "The transmission keeps the car from going down a hill too fast." I then restated the student's response by asking, "Do you mean a transmission gives the car the ability to slow down and speed up?" Student response, "Yes." Immediately another student yells out, "A gas pedal is used for safety since it controls the speed of the car." Even though the initial response by the first students seemed totally off the direction of the discussion, by my trying to reformulate and restate the student's response into questions, it triggered another student to think of another related idea.

At this point in the discussion, I knew the students were stuck on the obvious safety features in a vehicle. My next question was "What are the parts of a car that have been part of a car over the last twenty, thirty, forty years?" A student responded with "Steering wheel." I stated, "That is right, steering wheels are a guidance system to help us control vehicles." The next response was "Horn." Once again, I confirmed the answer was correct and then added, "A horn is used as a warning device that is used to prevent accidents." With these types of responses, I feel that I am contributing technical information to a student's response, helping the student shape his thoughts toward the application of the safety device they mentioned.

I still felt at this point the students were not getting to the part of the discussion that I thought was important. I wanted the students to understand that having a closed in vehicle with individual parts such as a roof, dashboards, and compartments for the engine and passengers are all safety features. When the students create their vehicles, there is not much thought about enclosing their vehicles. Many times, students will cut out their patterns traced on their cardboard, fold up the two sides of the vehicle, and call it quits, thinking they have a completed, safe vehicle. They have no roof, no method of keeping the engine from slamming into the egg on point of impact, and no windshield. I started to close down my statements and questions. "Most serious accidents happen when the driver/passenger gets thrown from their car at point of impact. What safety features do we have in our cars that keep us from being thrown out of a car?" Student response, "Seatbelts." My next question was a very closed question, "What part of a car keeps us from being thrown out the top of the car when we are in an accident?" Finally the response was a roof. I then contributed more information by stating how dashboards keep the engine from slamming into the passenger compartment of the car causing injury.

We then ended the discussion and moved on to the designing of the vehicles.

Reflections

When reflecting on this discussion, what comes to mind foremost is the importance of structuring the discussion. The major fault was the fast pace of the discussion with many of the students shouting out answers and other students having side conversations about their cars. This did not change even after I stopped the discussion and told the students if they had something to add then they needed to raise their hands. Much of this could be resolved if I had used a strategy of grouping the students together and had small group discussion first. I feel the grouping of students would organize their responses to my initial questions, and the dialogue would funnel down quicker to the objectives that I was trying to accomplish. Also, small group discussions, with proper evaluation techniques, would make the students contribute to the class discussion in a manner that would prevent side discussion taking place during the whole class discussion. Grouping of students, with guiding questions directing the small group discussion, would also cut down on the initial excitement of a student shouting out answers when they are introduced to the method of whole group discussion.

I also feel that, because we do not have many class discussions, this thirty-minute discussion being the only one for the nine weeks, the students did not know the proper format or discourse for a class discussion. Once again, proper structuring of the class for a group discussion would have taken the initial excitement out of the scenario.

Another area of improvement would be in giving the appropriate class time to having a good open question group discussion. When starting this unit, I always feel that I need to funnel down the discussion quickly in order for the students to have a proper amount of time to design and construct their vehicles. What was once a fifteen- to eighteen-day activity is now an eight- to nine-day activity. Therefore, discussion time is sacrificed for needed construction of the vehicle. Because of what I think is a need to get through the discussion quickly, I do not use adequate "wait time" or proper encouragement of student participation. By slowing down the pace of the discussion, I could improve on giving proper feedback when responding to student answers.

Introduction

Teachers use questions to accomplish multiple purposes. For example, in the reflection paper above, the teacher asked questions to stimulate student interest, to elicit more participation ("What else?"), to structure the discussion, and to guide student thinking. As you read through the reflection, you may have noticed how the nature and the type of questions changed as the discussion unfolded. Near the beginning of the discussion, the questions were broader and invited more student participation. As the discussion progressed, they became more focused on the specific safety features of cars. Finally, you may have also noticed that questions were only one of many potential strategies for that particular discussion. In the teacher's concluding reflections, he indicates that, for future discussions, he needs to consider a number of other strategies.

Unlike the questions asked in the teacher reflection above, most classroom questions occur in the form of recall or recitation questions. Recall questions are so named because they require students to recall previously learned material in order to make a factual statement. Although recall questions can serve a number of useful purposes during a discussion, the research literature consistently indicates that teachers ask a disproportionately high number of them. Therefore, this chapter will begin by showing teachers how to differentiate between recall questions and questions that are more likely to elicit higher level thinking. The sections that follow will show teachers how they can structure questions to increase student participation and to provide more support for higher level thinking. Near the end of the chapter, there will be a discussion of how to lead a discussion without asking questions and of the potential advantages of not asking any questions. Finally, the chapter will outline an approach to analyzing questions for the purpose of evaluating and improving your question asking strategies.

The Benefits of Asking Questions

Asking questions is the most frequent teacher discourse move and therefore plays a highly significant role in facilitating classroom interactions between teachers and students. About forty percent of the teachers' discourse moves can come in the form of questions, on average about one to three questions per minute (Gall, 1971; Appalachia Educational Laboratory, 1994). In a revealing study by Susskind (1979), even teachers were surprised by the number of questions they asked. On average, the teachers in the study estimated they asked fifteen questions and their students asked about ten questions during thirty minutes of a classroom interaction. In fact, however, they had asked 50.6 questions and their students only asked 1.8 questions.

Asking questions has also been shown to positively affect student achievement (Gall, Ward, Berliner, Cahen, Winne, Elashoff, & Stanton, 1978; Redfield & Rousseau, 1981). In a review of the research literature, Gall and Rhody (1987) identified several specific benefits of teacher questions:

1. Questions can motivate students and help keep them focused on the task at hand.
2. They can elicit higher level processing, by encouraging active engagement with text or issues.
3. Questions can activate metacognitive processes, thus helping students to better regulate their own learning. (Metacognition is the ability to think about thinking.)
4. Questions provide further opportunities to practice and rehearse the curriculum content.
5. For students, answering a question correctly is reinforcing, and answering incorrectly offers the teacher an opportunity to reteach.
6. Asking questions during discussions can prepare students for the types of questions they will have to answer on tests.

Types of Questions

The degree to which student learning is enhanced by asking questions depends on a variety of considerations. One of the most important is the type of question asked. Typically, teachers employ a wide variety of questions to achieve an equally wide variety of purposes (Dillon, 1987). Accordingly, questions are often classified by the educational objectives they are intended to serve. These objectives have been classified in taxonomies, which serve as categories of educational objectives or outcomes. Numerous taxonomies for classifying educational objectives have been developed by educators; however, the original and most widely used was developed in the mid-twentieth century with the input of thousands of educators and under the leadership of Benjamin Bloom (Bloom, Englehart, Hill, & Krathwohl, 1956). It is still widely used today and is familiar to most teachers.

One of the reasons for the enduring popularity of Bloom's taxonomy has been its usefulness for practicing teachers. It provides a relatively simple way for teachers to identify whether or not their lesson plans are likely to lead to higher level outcomes.

In the next section, the six levels of educational objectives in Bloom's taxonomy will be briefly summarized. The levels begin with the least cognitively complex level of thinking and move toward the more cognitively complex. Later in the chapter, you will learn how to use Bloom's taxonomy to analyze the questions you are asking. This type of analysis could eventually lead to more extended, thoughtful responses from students.

An Overview of Bloom's Taxonomy

Knowledge

At the knowledge level of Bloom's taxonomy, the student is asked simply to remember, recognize, or recite previously learned information, ideas, and principles. The knowledge level can include a wide range of material located in memory, such as terminology, specific facts, procedures (e.g., conventions, trends and sequences, classifications and categories, criteria, methodology), and universals (e.g., principles, generalizations, theories, and structures). At the knowledge level, the student is only asked to recall what they know from memory; they are not asked to manipulate or transform information in any way. The lack of interpretation or mental manipulation is the key distinction between the knowledge level and higher levels of Bloom's taxonomy. It is also the reason that the knowledge level is considered the lowest level of cognition in Bloom's taxonomy.

Questions constructed at the knowledge level may ask students to recall common terms, specific facts, methods and procedures, basic concepts, and principles. This could include stating or describing the who, what, when, where, and how of a situation. Knowledge questions could prompt students to arrange, define, duplicate, describe, enumerate, identify, know, label, list, match, name, outline, read, recall, recognize, record, reproduce, select, state, or tell.

Examples
1. What is the capital of Iowa?
2. What is the name of the main character in the *Scarlet Letter*?
3. What is the product of 8×7?
4. What are the six levels of Bloom's taxonomy?

Comprehension

At the comprehension level of Bloom's taxonomy, students are asked to demonstrate their understanding of the meaning or significance of ideas. This may be shown by translating material from one form to another (words to numbers), by interpreting material (explaining or summarizing), and by estimating future trends (predicting consequences or effects). The comprehension level represents a higher level outcome than the knowledge level because students are using previously learned knowledge in new situations.

At the comprehension level, students may be asked to interpret facts and principles, interpret verbal material, interpret charts and graphs, translate verbal material to mathematical formulas, estimate the future consequences implied in data, or justify methods and procedures. Comprehension level questions might prompt students to cite, classify, compare, convert, describe, differentiate, discuss, distinguish, estimate, exemplify, explain, extend, generalize, give examples, indicate, infer, interpret, locate, paraphrase, predict, restate, retell, review, or summarize.

Examples
1. Who can summarize the events leading to the Civil War?
2. What is another way to express $4x/2$?
3. Can anyone explain photosynthesis in your own words?
4. What is the purpose of Bloom's taxonomy?

Application

At the application level of Bloom's taxonomy, students are asked to apply their previous learning in new situations. They may select, transfer, and use data and principles for the purpose of completing a problem or task, or for applying concepts, rules, methods, principles, laws, and theories. Examples of learning objectives at this level include applying concepts and principles to new situations, applying laws and theories to practical situations, solving mathematical problems, constructing graphs and charts, and demonstrating the correct usage of a method or procedure. Since the application level of Bloom's taxonomy requires both understanding and application, it is considered a higher level of cognition than the comprehension level.

Questions at the application level could prompt students to act, administer, apply, articulate, assess, chart, choose, collect, compute, construct, contribute, control, demonstrate, determine, develop, discover, dramatize, employ, establish, extend, illustrate, implement, include, inform, instruct, modify, operate, participate, predict, practice, prepare, preserve, produce, project, provide, relate, report, schedule, show, solve, teach, transfer, use, utilize, or write.

Examples
1. How is Lincoln's decision to free the slaves an example of executive power?
2. How can Boyle's Law help predict the movement of electrons?
3. How can your knowledge of subordinate clauses help you punctuate the topic sentence in the sample essay correctly?
4. Why is Bloom's taxonomy helpful in analyzing the effectiveness of teacher questions?

Analysis

At the analysis level of Bloom's taxonomy, students are asked to divide and organize concepts, ideas, examples, theories, or other information or materials into their component parts to better understand its organizational structure. Students may use this analysis to better understand the organizational structure of such information by identifying motives or causes, by making inferences, or by finding evidence to support generalizations. This may include looking for patterns, recognizing hidden meanings, analyzing the relationship between parts, and recognizing guiding organizational principles. The analysis level is considered cognitively higher than the application level because it requires an understanding of both the content and the structure of an idea.

Examples of learning objectives at this level include recognizing unstated assumptions, recognizing logical fallacies in reasoning, distinguishing between facts and inferences, evaluating the relevance of data, and analyzing the organizational structure of a work (art, music, writing). Questions may include verbs such as analyze, appraise, break down, calculate, categorize, compare, contrast, criticize, correlate, diagram, differentiate, discriminate, distinguish, focus, illustrate, infer, limit, outline, question, point out, prioritize, recognize, separate, test, or subdivide.

Examples
1. What are the steps of your revision process when writing an essay paper?
2. What were Scarlett's motives when she married Frank Kennedy in *Gone with the Wind*?
3. What features distinguish a bird from a mammal?
4. What is the difference between the knowledge and analysis levels of Bloom's taxonomy?

Synthesis

At the synthesis level of Bloom's taxonomy, students are asked to originate, integrate, and combine ideas into a product, plan, or proposal that is new to him or her. They may be engaged in writing an essay, composing a speech, designing an experiment, creating a classification scheme, or generating any kind of project that requires the formulation of new patterns or structures.

Questions may prompt students to adapt, anticipate, arrange, assemble, categorize, collaborate, collect, combine, communicate, compare, compile, compose, construct, create, design, develop, devise, express, facilitate, formulate, generate, hypothesize, incorporate, individualize, initiate, integrate, intervene, invent, model, modify, negotiate, plan, prepare, progress, propose, rearrange, reconstruct, reinforce, reorganize, revise, structure, substitute, validate, or write.

Examples

1. How would the United States be different had we not declared our independence from England?
2. What kind of life forms could exist on Mars?
3. How could the two methods for solving the problem be combined?
4. Which levels of Bloom's taxonomy could be combined in order to make a simpler classification system for both educational objectives and asking questions?

Evaluation

At the evaluation level of Bloom's taxonomy, students are asked to make value decisions about issues, resolve controversies or differences of opinion, or develop opinions, judgments, or decisions. Examples would include judging the value of ideas, statements, written work, works of art, musical compositions, projects, products, performances, or processes. Learning outcomes in this area are highest in the cognitive hierarchy because they incorporate elements of the previous five categories, plus conscious value judgments based on clearly defined criteria.

Questions at the evaluation level may prompt students to compare and discriminate between ideas, assess the value of theories or presentations, or make choices based on reasoned argument and the value of the evidence. Questions may include verbs such as appraise, argue, assess, attach, choose, compare, conclude, criticize, critique, decide, defend, estimate, frame, grade, interpret, judge, justify, rate, rank, recommend, or support.

Examples

1. Which of the following four paragraphs uses transition words most effectively?
2. What is our most important national problem?
3. What is the best measure of success: personal happiness, recognition from peers, or monetary rewards?
4. How useful is Bloom's taxonomy for classifying questions?

Recall or Recitation Questions

It is important to remember that Bloom's taxonomy is only one of many taxonomies used for categorizing educational objectives and their related questions. (See Anderson and Krathwohl (2001) for a summary of different taxonomies.) The differences among taxonomies suggest that there is no single "right" way to classify questions. Furthermore, taxonomies of educational objectives may be more or less useful depending on the context in which they are applied. So, rather than investing a lot of energy in memorizing a single set of classifications, it may be better to focus your attention on a few important insights supported by all of the taxonomies.

For example, most taxonomies make a primary distinction between the knowledge level and higher level thinking levels. In Marzano's taxonomy (1993), questions asked at the knowledge level are referred to as *recitation* questions; in Aschner, Gallagher, Perry, and Afsar (1961) and Walsh and Sattes (2005) taxonomies, they are referred to as *recall* questions, and in Bloom's revised taxonomy (Anderson & Krathwohl, 2001), they are referred to as *remember* questions. Several benefits accrue from asking recall questions. Asking a high frequency of recall questions has been shown to benefit student achievement in elementary settings, particularly when basic skill acquisition is the primary objective (Gall, 1984) or with students of low socioeconomic status (Wilen & Clegg, 1987). For the purpose of discussion, recall questions can be used effectively to find out what students know and to establish a factual basis for a sequence of higher level questions to follow (Wilen, 1990; Wells, 1993). Thus, recall questions clearly serve an important role in the classroom when used appropriately.

Despite these demonstrated benefits, the original impetus for creating Bloom's taxonomy was the concern that more advanced cognitive outcomes were being neglected (Bloom et al., 1956). Since then, a number of studies have demonstrated that teachers rely much too heavily on recall questions. As many as seventy-five to eighty percent of teacher questions are on the recitation level, and only twenty to thirty percent call for higher level thinking (Gall, 1971, 1984; Goodlad, 1984; Klinzing & Klinzing-Eurich, 1988; Swift, Gooding & Swift, 1988). Several reasons may explain their overuse. First, they are relatively easy to generate. Second, assessment practices often tend to emphasize the importance of recall knowledge over higher level thinking skills. Third, it may be that some teachers are not practiced in asking higher level questions because they do not see the value of students explaining or elaborating on their ideas.

During discussions, recall questions usually invite a brief response that provides few opportunities for students to extend their thinking. There is usually little elaboration or justification of an idea on the part of a student. The student's response is usually followed by an evaluative comment made by the teacher, i.e., she says whether the answer was right or not. Usually, interaction is limited to an exchange between the teacher and a single student, followed by another exchange between the teacher and another student. There is little student-to-student interaction. This has been referred to as the Inquiry–Response–Evaluation (IRE) cycle in the research literature. The transcript excerpt below illustrates a typical IRE cycle during a teacher and student interaction. It is taken from a videotape of a vocabulary lesson, in which a fifth grade language arts teacher was asking her students to provide definitions of vocabulary words.

Ms. Lowell:	What does that mean if you were to *peer* around the corner? [*Recall question*]
Jared:	Look. [*Student response*]
Ms. Lowell:	Yes, to look. [*Teacher evaluation*]

Beyond Recitation: Create and Use Questions

In an attempt to simplify Bloom's taxonomy, some authors have tried to reduce their descriptions of higher level thinking into fewer categories. For example, Walsh and Sattes (2005) propose only two categories of questions beyond the knowledge level: *use* and *create* questions. *Use* questions ask students to apply knowledge they have already learned to new situations, as illustrated in the examples below:

1. How could we use the communicative property to explain why each side of the equation is equivalent?
2. Does the First Amendment guarantee the right of students to protest in schools?

Like the application level of Bloom's taxonomy, students are required to apply their understanding of a concept, idea, theory, process, or other information to a new situation. In contrast, *create* questions ask students to use what they already know to construct new knowledge, as illustrated in the examples below:

1. How could *Romeo and Juliet* have ended differently?
2. How could you redesign your experiment to eliminate the extra variable?

Create questions can be viewed as a combination of the analysis and synthesis level of Bloom's taxonomy. Analysis is the process of breaking down information into its parts; synthesis creatively combines those parts into new relationships, which lead to new conceptualizations. Create questions ask students to analyze, synthesize, or both to create new knowledge. Since their emphasis is on the construction of new knowledge, they are considered cognitively more complex than use questions.

Working with two categories of questions above the recall level may make it easier to compose new questions or to analyze existing questions. It simplifies higher level thinking into one of two formulations: applying previous knowledge to a new situation or using previous knowledge to create a new idea. In the former, a concept is applied to an example or application; in the latter, case examples or applications are used to create new concepts. Both help students connect their academic learning to their experience. Creating these connections can help students view previously learned ideas in new ways, thus strengthening their understanding of the relationship among ideas.

Increasing Student Participation

As shown in the teacher reflection at the beginning of the chapter, teachers often ask questions to stimulate student interest and participation. In the following sections, two question asking strategies for eliciting more participation will be discussed: providing cues and asking divergent questions.

Providing Cues

Asking questions that require higher level thinking skills can pose quite a challenge for students, thus making it more difficult for them to participate. To better facilitate student participation, teachers often embed cues into their questions. A cue provides information or direction in regard to how a question should be answered. This additional information can be provided either nonverbally or verbally. Nonverbal cues include pointing, facial expressions, or body language. For example, the teacher may point or gesture toward a book or painting, may indicate approval or disappointment with their facial expression, or could suggest enthusiasm or receptiveness with their body language.

Verbal cues often involve giving additional information in the form of a clue. For instance, a teacher could ask the question, "What is the subject of this sentence?" then add, "Before you answer, think back to the sentence diagramming you did yesterday."

The cue can also be embedded in the original question. For example, asking the question, "In how many ways did Henry reveal he was shy?" By asserting that Henry was shy, part of the answer is contained within the structure of the question, providing impetus and direction to the student's thinking.

Convergent vs Divergent Questions

Adding information not only provides support, it also tends to further structure the question and thus narrow the range of possible acceptable answers. Questions with a relatively narrow focus have been termed convergent questions by Aschner et al. (1961). Convergent questions require students to analyze and integrate their previous learning within a tightly structured framework that necessarily leads to a response that is deemed correct or incorrect. Convergent questions can focus the discussion on the learning goals for the unit; they can move the discussion toward the curricular goals more quickly; they can facilitate student insights into the subject matter; and they can elicit student answers that can be assessed in relation to the curricular goals. However, the narrower focus may limit the participation of students, who may be reluctant to risk an incorrect answer. It may also limit the creativity of their responses. The following are examples of relatively convergent questions:

1. What is the capital of Tennessee?
2. Can you explain your experimental observations of heat and pressure using Boyle's Law?
3. How does *Macbeth* illustrate the structure of a Shakespearean tragedy?

In contrast, a divergent question, or more open-ended question, allows for a greater variety of responses that are acceptable to the degree they can be supported or justified by the student. For example, a more divergent form of the question "In how many ways did Henry reveal he was shy?" would be "How would you describe Henry?" The latter is more divergent because it allows for a greater variety of student responses. Following are some other examples of divergent questions:

1. Show your students a work of art and ask: "What do you notice in this painting?"
2. After demonstrating an experiment, ask: "What did you see during the experiment?"
3. After the students complete a reading assignments, ask: "What interested you about the reading assignment?"

Divergent questions tend to increase student participation because they allow a greater variety of answers that can be considered appropriate. They can also facilitate more creativity and higher level thinking on the part of students, partly because increased participation in and of itself may stimulate student thinking. Two potential disadvantages of asking divergent questions are the risk that student responses may not address the topic satisfactorily and the additional time needed to reach the learning objectives.

How Much Guidance is Appropriate?

Both convergent and divergent questions can elicit higher level thinking from students. There are two schools of thought regarding which is better. Convergent questions more directly address the educational objectives of the discussion; thus teachers can move the discussion toward the objectives through their questions. In addition, convergent questions can help teachers make a rapid assessment of student knowledge. This enables the teacher to quickly assess what her students know and track their progress in relation to their learning goals. Providing more guidance is supported by Vygotsky's (1978, 1986) theories of learning. According to Vygotsky, teaching should anticipate the development of students by engaging with them at a level that is just beyond their capacity to work independently, what he called the Zone of Proximal Development (ZPD). By providing support in the ZPD, teachers are helping their students function at a higher cognitive level that is just beyond their current ability. Students will eventually internalize these higher level processes and use them independently. As the child grows increasingly competent and independent, the teacher gradually withdraws her support.

The counterargument is that convergent questions may focus the topic too narrowly. Thus, student creativity is limited, student initiative is discouraged, and students are less responsible for discovering and defining the problem, an important thinking skill in its own right. Teachers who rely too heavily on convergent questions may eliminate unexpected or creative student answers, may fail to recognize the potential depth of student thought, and may make their students chronically dependent on the teacher's approval. In contrast, more divergent or open-ended questions stimulate student participation, creativity, and self-reliance. With less guidance, students are more likely to take the initiative and responsibility for both formulating the problem and finding a solution. By not specifically delineating all the elements of a problem, teachers are granting both freedom and increased responsibility for framing the problem, thus leading students to think more deeply (Jonassen, 1997).

The decision to either provide more structure or allow more freedom requires expert judgment to know what is appropriate at a particular moment in a classroom. Ideally, teachers should provide a wide range of thinking experiences for students in order to achieve multiple outcomes, e.g., introducing an ill structured problem and then scaffolding student thinking as needed. Factors influencing the teacher's decision could include the curricular goals, the difficulty of the subject matter, the ability levels of the students, their level of motivation, and the inherent interest of the subject matter. Any or all of these may shift in importance as a series of discussions unfolds over the course of a unit. For instance, student interest may increase, thus reducing the need for motivational strategies. Or the content may increase steeply in difficulty, thus increasing the need for scaffolding. Even within a single discussion, the teacher's goal may shift from encouraging participation to providing more guidance. Effective discussion leaders are able to recognize student needs at a particular moment and employ a wide range of alternative strategies that enable them to respond flexibly to those needs.

Asking Fewer Questions to Increase Thinking

Another way to encourage more divergent thinking is to ask fewer questions. This approach was first advocated by J. T. Dillon (1990), who challenged long held assumptions about the value of asking questions during discussions. He argued that teacher questions are often very leading, too controlling, and therefore can inhibit student thinking. Reducing the number of questions puts more responsibility for the direction and content of the discussion on students.

As alternatives to asking questions, teachers can use other discourse moves that invite students to speak. A teacher invitation for a student to speak could be as simple as stating a student's name in a questioning tone, "Jerry?", or leaving a sentence unfinished, "I think that could best be accomplished by . . .", or repeating what a student has said in a questioning tone. To begin a discussion without a question, the teacher might invite student response by simply saying, "I would like to hear your comments on the reading." Invitations to speak have been termed "elicitations" by Mercer (2000). They include questions, as well as the other invitations described above.

In place of questions, Dillon has suggested four alternatives to invite student participation:

1. make a statement in relation to what a student has just said (e.g., "I agree. I think it is more likely that X is the cause.");
2. provide for a student question (e.g., "Think of the question that's still bothering you about that.");
3. give a signal indicating interest or comprehension (e.g., "Mm hmmm.");
4. maintain a deliberate, appreciative silence.

Walsh and Sattes (2005) suggest two more possible responses:

5. paraphrase what you heard the student say (e.g., "So you think that . . .");
6. describe your state of mind (e.g., "I'm confused about what you're saying.").

Although it is difficult to consistently sustain a discussion without asking questions, you may find Dillon's approach to be useful for promoting student engagement in specific, well-defined situations during a part of the discussion. The teacher reflection at the beginning of chapter 4 illustrates this approach. The teacher doesn't ask any questions at the beginning of the discussion, but later in the discussion uses questions to elicit ideas overlooked by the students.

To employ this approach successfully requires considerable skill. The teacher must do more than simply refrain from asking questions: she must successfully employ other discussion-based teaching strategies, such as selecting a topic on which students are highly knowledgeable or preparing students for the discussion through activities and small group work (illustrated by the teacher reflection at the beginning at chapter 4).

Analyzing Questions

Taxonomies of educational objectives, such as Bloom's taxonomy, can be used as tools for analyzing the questions you are currently asking. A simple way to begin is by examining the questions written in your lesson plans. The advantage to analyzing questions is that data collection is familiar, relatively easy, and requires no special equipment. Thus, you can immediately begin analyzing your discussion questions in a teacher study group, even as you are learning more complex methods of collecting and analyzing discourse data.

Those not in the habit of writing out their discussion questions ahead of time may want to initiate this practice, not only for the purpose of analyzing data, but also to improve the level of discussion. Creating effective discussions requires careful planning to ensure the discussion questions address multiple levels of student thinking. A second, less laborious alternative is writing a full set of questions for a few key lessons.

There are several different ways you can use the concepts described in this chapter to analyze your questions. Questions could be identified as to whether they are use or create questions or at what level of Bloom's taxonomy they have been asked. They could also be analyzed to determine the degree that they may support or constrain student thinking by examining them for cues or to determine whether they are convergent or divergent. To start, it may be more comfortable using one of the taxonomies with fewer categories of questions, then later moving to Bloom's taxonomy as it becomes easier to identify different types of questions. Or you may want to use these different taxonomies for different purposes to address different concerns. For example, you may only need to know whether your questions are convergent or divergent in order to increase student participation. In other settings or with other lessons, it may be more important to distinguish between use and create questions. Most importantly, it is essential to know the difference between recitation or recall questions and the kinds of questions that promote complex responses and higher level thinking. It is critical to address student thinking skills beyond the recall or recitation level.

What Teachers Need to Know

Many different types of questions are asked in classrooms in order to accomplish a wide variety of purposes. One approach to classifying questions is by educational outcomes. The best known taxonomy for educational outcomes is Bloom's taxonomy, but other taxonomies can be employed, depending on the purposes of the teacher. A feature in common among almost all taxonomies is the distinction between recall questions and higher level thinking questions. While there should not be an inherent negative connotation associated with using recall questions, relying on them too heavily clearly indicates a lack of discussion skills on the part of the teacher.

Your ability to ask a wide variety of different kinds of questions multiplies your choices during a discussion. At times, it will be more important to guide and extend student thinking by asking more convergent questions. However, overreliance on convergent questions may be too controlling, i.e., you are in too much of a hurry to get to the "right" answer. Using more divergent questions can serve as an antidote by encouraging more participation and more independent, creative thinking. Ultimately, how you balance your question asking strategies will depend on your goals, your understanding, your comfort level, and your skill with using them.

Application Discussion

Below is a transcribed excerpt of discussion from Ms. Fletcher's eighth grade middle school mathematics class. The class consists of twenty-two students: six are African American, one is Hispanic, and nine are part of the free/reduced lunch program. On the previous day, students had worked in groups of two and three to generate different ways of finding the perimeter of a rectangular shape. The data gathered from the previous day's activity is displayed on the overhead. The purpose of the discussion is to reconstruct what the students did previously. To accomplish her goal, the teacher used several questioning techniques. Read the transcript and then analyze it for different types of questions.

1. Does Ms. Fletcher primarily use convergent or divergent questions? Convergent questions tend to elicit a limited number of acceptable answers. Divergent questions tend to elicit multiple acceptable answers. Support your answer by citing multiple examples from the transcript.
2. Identify at least three cues (clues) in Ms. Fletcher's questions. Explain how each cue is used to guide and support student thinking.
3. The following four questions have been taken from the transcript. Identify each of them as either "use" or "create" questions. "Use" questions ask students to apply existing knowledge and "create" questions ask students to create new knowledge.
   a. from Ms. Fletcher (1): Can we develop some sort of pattern or process to help us out?
   b. from Ms. Fletcher (3): How could we find out what this would be without making a long table or counting?
   c. from Ms. Fletcher (4): Why are we taking it times four?
   d. from Ms. Fletcher (13): Can you use that same mentality, that same creativity, and come up with other ways to get the same number of total tiles?
4. On what level of Bloom's taxonomy is each of the questions above? Explain and support your answer.

Ms. Fletcher (1):	Right now you're going off of memory, right? And I can't tell you if you're right or wrong. How could we find out? What could we do so we weren't graphing or counting? Can we develop some sort of pattern or process to help us out?
Danny:	This is a pattern. For every foot on your pool you go up 4 on your tiles. Like on 4 (on the table), it will be 20 tiles.
Ms. Fletcher (2):	So you're saying that for each increase on the left, you're adding 4 to the right side of the table. Right?
Danny:	Right.
Ms. Fletcher (3):	Okay, let's find out why. If we set up an equation or an expression, because I didn't want to go through this table and I wanted to go to 12. They didn't ask us to make a 12 by 12 foot pool. How could we find out what this would be without making a long table or counting? Got any ideas?
Tiffany:	Well, you could do 12 times 4 then add 4.
Ms. Fletcher (4):	Ah! 12 times 4 then she says add 4. Okay. Why are we taking it times 4? (Calls on students with hand up.)
Sheila:	Because we're adding for each time and (unable to understand remainder of statement).
Ms. Fletcher (5):	I'm sorry. You lost me. Try again.

Sheila:	(laughs) I don't know. Ask Don.
Ms. Fletcher (6):	I'm sorry. I just didn't hear you.
Sheila:	Call on Don?
Ms. Fletcher (7):	Call on Don?
Sheila:	Yeah.
Ms. Fletcher (8):	Okay, Don.
Don:	(Comment not picked up by video microphone).
Ms. Fletcher (9):	Okay. So here is an s and here is an s and here is an s and here is an s. So in our case, there are 4 of those or 4 twelves. So 4 times 12. Which is probably what you were saying, Sheila, but I just wasn't understanding, right?
Sheila:	Kinda.
Ms. Fletcher (10):	So, Tracy, where is the plus 4 coming from?
Tracy:	The 4 corners.
Ms. Fletcher (11):	These 4 corners, okay. And it works, right? 4 times 12 is 48 plus 4 is 52. Which is why we don't want to do this on grid paper, right? That's a lot of work. How would we turn this into an equation that could be used elsewhere? What part has to change and what part has to stay the same? (Teacher waits briefly).
Danny:	"n" would stand for the length of the pool plus 4.
Ms. Fletcher (12):	So you're saying that this changes to "n" (points to the 12 written on the overhead). Agree or disagree?
Class:	Yeah.
Ms. Fletcher (13):	Okay, this is the neat part. If that is true, and we know it is because we agreed to that and it gets us the right answer, is that the only way to do it? Is that the only way there is to get the correct total? (Teacher waits). Can you personally think of another way to write that to get the total? I'm going to put the picture up here (on the overhead) so we can look at it. Can you think of something? Because we experimented with that with percentages last week. Yesterday we experimented with perimeter and we came up with lots of different ways. Can you use that same mentality—that same creativity, and come up with other ways to get the total number of tiles? Or is that the only possibility in the whole wide world? (Teacher waits).
Karl:	Are you just looking for a different um . . .?
Ms. Fletcher (14):	Expression? Yeah.
Karl:	Yeah. Like you could do 4 divided by 4 plus 4. NO. Um . . . It's . . .4 times, yeah. Wait. I'll stick with my first answer.
Ms. Fletcher (15):	So you want to divide by 4 instead of multiply by 4? Will that get you in the same place?
Karl:	No.
Ms. Fletcher (16):	Jeff is saying no.

Karl:	Well, Jerry's my homie so you can talk to him.
Jeff:	(Unable to hear comment on tape).
Ms. Fletcher (17):	He's saying you could rearrange it. Okay, that works. What else? (Teacher waits).
Don:	n plus n plus n plus n plus one plus one plus one plus one.
Karl:	Oh, yeah. Duh (referring to himself not Don's comment).
Ms. Fletcher (18):	Okay.
Tracy:	n plus 2 then times 2 then n plus n.
Ms. Fletcher (19):	Let's take a look at the picture for a second. She said take the length here plus these ends twice, then take the other two sides. Does it work?
Class:	Yeah.
Ms. Fletcher (20):	Okay, creativity! We're getting there. What else?
Danny:	n plus n times 2 then add 4.
Ms. Fletcher (21):	Okay. Let's check it out.

Activities

1. Create a series of questions for a discussion that addresses all six levels of Bloom's taxonomy. Exchange and discuss your questions in your teacher study group.

Study Group Activity

2. As a team, discuss and create a plan for collecting the discourse data that will serve as a basis for future discussions. Describe how you will accomplish the following:

   1. determine the types of questions you would like to pursue;
   2. determine what forms of data collection interest you;
   3. determine how to acquire videotaping equipment;
   4. select the lessons to be videotaped;
   5. obtain permission and conform to school policies.

two
Student Responses

In the teacher reflection below, a middle school social studies teacher assesses his students' talking. As you read, note the different indicators of student performance he describes. Think about the different ways that student talking can be assessed. What would you say are indicators of student engagement, content knowledge, and higher level student thinking?

Framing Discussion

1. What is the teacher's source of information for this reflection, and how does it inform his thinking?
2. What kinds of observations does he make regarding the students' content knowledge?
3. What kinds of observations does he make regarding their thinking skills?
4. What kinds of observations does he make regarding the way students interact?
5. What kinds of new instructional strategies does the teacher suggest, and on what basis is he justifying his ideas?
6. What kinds of information do you collect to assess students? What kinds of information do you use to improve instructional strategies? Do you currently assess student talking to either evaluate students or inform your instructional decisions? If so, give some examples of how your assessment of student talking has informed your decision making.

What are they thinking? So many times I have punctuated my entrance to the teachers' lounge with those words. This first unit has focused my attention on how teachers can use student dialogue to assess learning and get a glimpse of how they understand a concept. In this first paper, I am analyzing a two-day activity in which my seventh grade geography students worked with a partner and a laptop to explain how animals were able to adapt to the harsh conditions of the Sahara.

As I observed the students in real time, I was focused on looking for on-task behavior and helping the students understand their responsibilities. The five groups that I taped seemed to be on task and had few interactions with me. When I listened to the groups on tape, they take on an entirely different feel. For the most part, they shared few ideas. It is possible that their dialogue was not picked up by the tape recorder or that they were unusually quiet because of the recording device. I suspect, however, that the students, even in a group situation, are focused on completing the task quickly and are not focused on understanding the material. I was left with the feeling that a great learning opportunity was being missed.

Another general observation I made was that the powerful conversation, laden with vocabulary words, examples, and questions, occurred in bursts. My first group of boys illustrates both points. They spent several minutes deciding how to spell a "ten" and explaining to the others that they had to draw because the other student's art sucked. But in the middle of this, I found evidence of synthesis. One of the boys had a lizard at home. When he saw the monitor lizard and was starting to draw the picture, he observed, "this thing has big ears, huge ears, my lizard doesn't have that big of ears." I see this as evidence of integrating previous knowledge with the assignment. The other student didn't verbalize a response to this conversation, but the boy continued on. He repeated the audio from the video clip describing that the lizard was retreating to the shade. "My lizard likes the heat, what's the matter with that lizard . . . is he sick?" Here, he is asking questions about what he is being told and he has observed related to his pet. There was an opportunity here for co-construction, but his partner fails to respond.

The student's dialogue makes it possible to understand what the student is thinking. It also helped me understand how difficult co-construction can be. The other student may not be interested, may be distracted by the activity, or may not have any experiences to draw upon. During the activity, several students asked me for some type of explanation. Because of this assignment, I invited them to work with their partner to explore the idea and see if they could discover the answer. While most groups were resistant at first, I was pleased with the result. I was surprised at the power of talking to clarify a concept or task. The conversation pushed the students deeper into the idea. While they didn't always get all the way to an answer, they were able to ask a better question. It reminded me of a teaching strategy I use, where I give one student a picture and I give the other student the caption. The activity provides a model for how students can use questions to develop a better understanding of their observations.

This activity has led me to believe that, if I could improve the quality of my student discourse, I could improve the quality of their assignments and, more importantly, increase student learning. If I were using student discourse to assess the quality of learning, I would focus on teaching the individual skill. I would work with the students to define the skill and determine what it would look like, then develop a model of the skill. I believe my students are capable of all these skills and have been exposed to them before, but they do not see the skills as a way to get a better understanding of a subject.

For this assignment, the skill of elaboration would have helped the students identify the desert adaptations that help the animal thrive in the desert. When I evaluated the finished projects, I found that several students described what the animal ate or how many animals lived in a certain area. These characteristics did not connect on their own to the idea of desert adaptations. The ability to make an argument for why they thought they had identified an adaptation would have given them and their partner the ability to identify their own errors. I have evidence that this happened in some of the groups that I did not tape. One of the animals on the list was a monkey that lived in the higher elevations of the Atlas Mountains. When they discovered that the monkey had a thick coat of fur to deal with the cold climate and the snow, they realized that the animal did not live in the Sahara and that they had identified an adaptation for living in a highland climate.

A useful and maybe rare example of analysis came from a group toward the end of the day. As the student was looking at the picture of the animal, she seemed to remember that, when we discussed the camel in class, they had a double set of eyelids to protect their eyes from the desert sand. She asked her partner, "Is there anything special with their eyes?" This question led them into a discussion. This connects back to my idea that the conversations were punctuated with bursts of thinking. At this point, the girls were making and distinguishing between their observations and asking questions about what they were observing. This interaction was very brief, and then they went back to drawing or silently looking for info.

For that reason, as an assessment tool, I think I might have students record their dialogue and identify examples of the skill they were focusing on. I would also encourage the students to explain how the use of the skill helped them learn.

Few students seemed to integrate the task into the framework of the current unit or with the themes of the course. Again, I think I would have to focus on teaching this skill for it to become a useful tool for my students.

The skill that seemed to be the foundation of student discourse was disposition. If the students were not enthusiastic about the task or their partner, dialogue was obviously affected. This is an idea I discovered when I first started having students work in groups.

This unit has turned my attention to how my students talk. When my students get stuck, I focus on the idea of elaborating on what they do know so they can co-construct knowledge. But I have also spent more time listening to what my students are saying and trying to identify when they are using one of the discourse skills we identified. I can use what I discover to help them understand what is happening. Finally, I can use what I hear to understand what they are thinking.

Introduction

The focus of the previous chapter was on asking high quality questions. The purpose of this chapter is to assess the quality of student responses and then use that information to further extend student thinking. Several examples of what teachers can assess are present in the teacher reflection above, including observations about student dispositions, their level of engagement, and their cognitive skills. Other indicators included the students' use of vocabulary and examples, their ability to ask questions, and, to a lesser degree, their ability to analyze content information. The teacher also noted specific forms of talk that he did not see but would like to encourage, such as elaboration and justifying answers.

Accurate assessment is essential to increasing the quantity and quality of student talk in the classroom. If you cannot recognize improvement, then you will not be able to determine whether your discussion strategies are working. Therefore, four specific areas of performance related to student talk will be addressed in this chapter. The first is elaboration, which refers to the students' ability to develop and articulate their thoughts. Elaboration is primary because, without extensive student talking, further and more sophisticated assessment is not possible. In addition, your students' ability to speak at length on a subject provides an initial indication that they are knowledgeable (van Boxtel & Roelofs, 2001). Second, the quality of student thinking can be inferred from student talk by applying Bloom's taxonomy, another taxonomy of educational objectives, or some other relevant description of thinking. Specific skills may include their ability to apply, analyze, synthesize, and evaluate. Third, assessing student-to-student interactions can provide an indication of your students' dispositions and listening and thinking skills. Specific skills may include their ability to facilitate talk, their ability to evaluate ideas, and their ability to synthesize the comments of their classmates. Fourth, content knowledge can be assessed by comparing a preassessment of vocabulary and concepts with formative and post assessments.

These four skill areas have been summarized in a sample rubric (see Table 2.1).

Reading through the chapter will provide more detailed information on each of these skill areas, as well as some strategies for developing those skills. You can use this information to create a rubric that serves your specific needs in your classroom. Creating your own rubric can serve as a helpful exercise for carefully targeting discussion outcomes, recording student performance data, and then using that data to determine the effectiveness of their discussions.

Elaboration

Elaboration has been given top billing in the rubric because, unless students express themselves fully and freely, the teacher is not able to access student thinking. The following sections will address strategies for analyzing and encouraging student elaboration.

TABLE 2.1 Rubric for Student Talk

Elaboration
    Gives longer, more coherent answers
    Can make and defend an argument
    Gives explanations, justifications, and supporting evidence

Thinking Skills
    Synthesis
        Makes inferences based on earlier observations or ideas
        Asks questions about the relationship among ideas or observations
        Integrates previous knowledge with current coursework
    Analysis
        Introduces new details, facts, examples
        Distinguishes component parts of ideas or observations
        Asks questions that isolate parts of ideas or observations
        Comments on specific cues that guide thinking
    Flexibility/Creativity
        Responds to ideas from a variety of perspectives
        Introduces new perspectives into the discourse
        Utilizes similes, analogies, metaphors, or other comparisons that encourage fresh perspectives

Student-to-Student Interaction
    Asks thoughtful questions of classmates and the teacher
    Comments on the ideas of other students
    Incorporates the ideas of other students
    Uses verbal and nonverbal cues to encourage the participation of other students

Content Knowledge
    Frames discourse with conceptual ideas from current coursework
    Makes inferences based on conceptual knowledge
    Utilizes conceptual vocabulary from current coursework
    Utilizes conceptual knowledge to synthesize ideas

Mechanics
    Clear delivery
    Projects well
    Maintains eye contact
    Grammatical correctness

Disposition
    Enthusiasm
    Engagement and participation

Calculating the Ratio of Teacher to Student Talk

One approach to measuring elaboration is through informal observation, i.e., paying attention to whether students are talking for increasingly extended periods of time. However, this is a very subjective, very rough approximation of elaboration. A more precise measure of student elaboration can be used if transcripts of the discussion are available. It is easy and often eye-opening to calculate the ratio of teacher to student talk from a transcript. Simply count the number of words spoken by the teacher and the total number of words spoken by the student. Then calculate the number of teacher words per speaking turn by dividing the total number of words spoken by the teacher by the total number of turns. This yields the average number of words spoken per turn.

As an illustration, examine the following excerpt taken from a discussion in a seventh grade mathematics class on calculating surface area. The teacher has spoken a total of 137 words over six speaking turns. Therefore, the average number of words spoken is approximately twenty-three words during each turn.

Ms. Brady:	. . . little ways, yes, okay? Is that what? And this, and this would be divided up four ways. Okay? So, Justin were you able to get this one? How did you do it?
Justin:	Well, what I did was, I took the eighteen inch height and like . . . like . . . well, like I divided it up into four and stuff and . . .
Ms. Brady:	So, did you divide it up like your paper sort of in your mind or on your paper?
Justin:	In my mind. And then (inaudible) that face of it I got fifty-four or just that surface area of that face . . .
Ms. Brady:	Are you talking, which face are you talking about?
Justin:	The one that you have.
Ms. Brady:	This was fifty . . .
Justin:	four.
Ms. Brady:	Okay. Let's check that out. You have eighteen by four. So we're going to take eighteen times four. Eighteen times . . . does that make sense to you, Justin, or did when you divided it up, you could count it? I don't think this is in eighteen parts. Not even close, okay? We'd have to go a lot more than that. So, we're going to do a grid of eighteen by four.
Justin:	That's seventy-two.
Ms. Brady:	Yeah, you've got it. Seventy-two squares.

The same calculation can be performed for student talking. The students in the excerpt above have spoken a total of fifty-two words over five turns; therefore, the average length of their response is 10.4 words per turn. By dividing the teacher's average number of words per turn by the students' number of words per turn, we find the teachers is talking about 2.2 times as much as the students.

Let's try another example from the same seventh grade mathematics class. In this discussion, the students are using their understanding of surface area and volume to compare the relative merits of packages designed for marketing ping pong balls. As you read through the excerpt below, first, make a few informal observations about the differences in this transcript from the previous one. Then, take a few moments to calculate the ratio between teacher and student talk.

Ms. Brady:	Okay. Give Nathan your attention and respect.
Sharon:	Usually you get your ping pong rackets with the . . . with your tables and even if you wanted to play doubles, you could get more but

	if—they'd be different rackets, so it'd be like "oh, this is different that's why you're winning" or something so people could get into an argument or something. But also you could make this—ah, you could make this bigger if you had the same dimensions . . .
Ms. Brady:	Wait, wait, wait. Make sure you're giving Nathan your attention and respect. Go ahead.
Sharon:	If you had the same dimensions, you could make it just as big. Like if I had my diameter the same as maybe her height and then I had my height the same as her, whatever, it would be just more cost efficient. And I know that when you have the balls and you put them together in four, the diameter's going to increase due to the—cuz the—like—should I draw it on the board or something?
Ms. Brady:	Just explain.
Sharon:	Cuz if you have four, it's going to increase because you can't put those things together but that's only going to make it increase by maybe two centimeters and that's not going to add too much—that's not going to add too much surface area—er, volume, so it would still be more cost efficient. But a suh-phere I think would be the most cost efficient. I think we all—or I think we all had this. I think the best design would be a suh-phere. And you could package it, like you could hold it in a ball and like have little shelves just like holding it.
Ms. Brady:	A sphere would actually be the most cost effective. That is the least surface area. This is what I need you to do.
Sharon:	Can I say something real quick?
Ms. Brady:	Very quickly Sharon.
Sharon:	Okay, I know that you guys are debating about Allan's, we're all like going for Larry's a bunch of us. And one thing is what if you might want—what if you want to play doubles but it's not going to be like we're not worrying about everybody arguing who's a better—who's got a better paddle. I mean different brands would still say like, oh yeah, that one's better. And then you could pick her big pack to put on the shelves and his small one to put on the shelves and then you'd get people . . .
Ms. Brady:	So you could get both of them.

A casual inspection of the two transcripts above reveals a marked difference in the ratio of teacher to student talk. Clearly, the students' comments extend much longer in the second example, leading to a much higher ratio of student to teacher talk. The average response length of the teacher turn is 9.3 (56 total words/six turns), and the average length of the student response was 72 (359 total words/five turns). The ratio of student to teacher talk in this example is 7.7 to 1, which indicates that the student talked about eight times more than the teacher.

One explanation for the difference in student elaboration is the location and purpose of the two discussions within the overall unit. The first discussion occurred while students were learning how to calculate surface area and volume. Because these concepts were still unfamiliar, the students required a lot of teacher support to express their ideas. The second discussion occurred after an activity in which students applied those concepts to their package design project. Since the students had learned those concepts earlier and had just finished applying them in an extended activity, they were more knowledgeable and therefore better prepared to make longer comments.

Clearly, there are times when it is appropriate to introduce new and challenging concepts that require more teacher guidance and support. Therefore, it may be best to think about desirable teacher to student talk ratios in relative terms. While it should be within the repertoire of every teacher to elicit a high ratio of student to teacher talk, there are also times when less student talking may be an appropriate means to attaining the learning objectives.

Facilitating Elaboration

You may have noticed that there is an inverse ratio between teacher and student talk, which simply means the more the teacher talks, the less students can talk and vice versa. The research literature clearly indicates that teachers do most of the talking in classrooms. Flanders (1970) found that, even in the most participatory classrooms, the teacher's talk accounted for two-thirds of classroom interactions. More recently, in a study of thirty-four secondary science classes, Newton (1999) found that talk was dominated by teacher lecturing; fewer than half the lessons included deliberative interaction between the teacher and pupils and, when it did occur, it took less than five percent of the lesson time.

Therefore, one key to increasing student elaboration is for the teacher to talk less. Your willingness to speak less, however, must be accompanied by strategies that will help your students elaborate more.

Reflection

Asking students to reflect on their participation is a way for teachers to encourage more elaboration. The teacher can meet with students during a short debriefing session either before or after the discussion to talk about the importance of participation. Then either give them an opportunity to discuss why their engagement is important or ask them to respond in writing to questions like the following (Walsh & Sattes, 2005).

- What did you contribute to this class discussion?
- How, specifically, did your statements affect what your classmates said following your contribution?
- What did you learn about the process of discussion from today's class dialogue?

■ Think about the class as a whole. What can we do to improve the quality of the discussion?

Charting Response Patterns

Encouraging and assessing student participation by recording and analyzing classroom participation patterns can also increase the amount of student talking. The purpose of such an analysis would be to spread participation more equally among students. In a study by Strother (1989), students who participated during discussion performed better on subsequent achievement tests than students who did not participate. However, teachers typically call on volunteers, and these volunteers constitute only a select group of students (Sauer, Popp, & Isaacs, 1984; Sadker & Sadker, 1985). Those volunteers are more likely to be high rather than low ability students (Good, 1970; Good, Slavings, Harel, & Emerson, 1987) and boys rather than girls (Sadker & Sadker, 1985; Patchen, 2006). In addition, where the students sit in the classroom can influence their level of participation. A study of thirty-two mathematics and social studies classes found that most verbal interaction came from students seated in the front row and center seats, a T-shaped area referred to as the action zone (Adams & Biddle, 1970).

Charting student response patterns is a relatively simple way to ensure a more equal distribution of participation. There are several ways that participation could be recorded. A colleague could be invited to tally student responses, or the class could be videotaped and the response pattern charted from the videotape. Simpler yet, use a seating chart, design a participation chart, or create some other type of chart with a list of students' names to keep track of student participation during the discussion. This approach doesn't require any equipment and offers the added advantage of serving as an accountability strategy. Students who are aware the teacher is recording their participation are often more likely to contribute to the discussion (Dallimore, Hertenstein, & Platt, 2004).

The results of your analysis could be used to inform strategies for cold calling, or calling on nonvolunteers. Cold calling can be an effective technique for more equally distributing participation and thereby improving student achievement—if teachers take care to build a supportive environment, give students adequate time to prepare, ask effective questions, and affirm student contributions with constructive feedback. Without these supports, the practice may cause resentment and inhibit rather than enhance discussions (Dallimore et al., 2004).

Several other options exist to further address possible bias regarding the location of students. One is to change the seating arrangements. Move less engaged students into the action zone or rotate seating periodically (e.g., weekly) so that all students have the opportunity to be at the front of the class at some point during a grading period. Or try using a prearranged pattern to call on students, such as calling on students in a diagonal or square pattern, as a systematic way of ensuring equal participation. Another option would be to put students in different grouping arrangements and call on students in their groups (Walsh & Sattes, 2005). Teachers can also shift their perspective by intentionally moving around the classroom and standing in a different position every few minutes.

Assessing Thinking Skills

A variety of tools can be utilized to assess thinking skills. The most familiar is Bloom's taxonomy, which was described in chapter 1. Six levels of thinking were identified and defined, including recall, comprehension, application, analysis, synthesis, and evaluation. Two categories (synthesis and analysis) from Bloom's taxonomy are included on the rubric in Table 2.1. However, you do not have to limit yourself to the classroom thinking skills described in the rubric. There are also numerous other descriptions available to teachers (e.g., Schiever, 1991; Beyer, 1997), which may include thinking abilities such as making generalizations, drawing conclusions, using dialectical reasoning, and clarifying the premise of a problem. Any one of these could be used to modify the rubric in Table 2.1, create a more detailed rubric, or develop an entirely different one.

Your rubric could also include thinking processes associated with a particular subject area, e.g., thinking processes associated with thinking scientifically, mathematically, or historically. Evaluating discipline-specific thinking skills is justified by the increasing recognition that learning to think like a scientist or a mathematician depends on learning to talk like one (e.g., Nelson, Megill, & McCloskey, 1987; Prelli, 1989; Simons, 1989; Gross, 1990; McCloskey, 1998). In science, a rubric might include the ability to make detailed observations, state a testable hypothesis, and draw conclusions based on data. In mathematics, it might include finding multiple solution paths. In history, it might include the ability to make inferences based on historical artifacts or newspaper accounts. Engaging students in the same kinds of discussions and thinking processes as scientists, mathematicians, or historians deepens their understanding, helps them internalize the thought processes related to the discipline, and makes them familiar with the rhetorical tactics of the discipline.

Asking Good Questions is Not Enough

Asking high level questions was introduced in the previous chapter as a way to elicit more thoughtful student responses. This approach is supported by studies that have shown that asking high level questions increases the length and complexity of student responses (Cole & Williams, 1973; Lange, 1982; Klinzing & Klinzing-Eurich, 1988). In addition, the use of higher, cognitive questions has a positive effect on student achievement (Redfield & Rousseau, 1981), "especially in higher grade levels and with students of average and high ability" (Klinzing & Klinzing-Eurich, 1988, p. 217). However, several other studies have indicated that students do not always give high level responses to higher level questions. After reviewing eighteen individual studies on asking questions, Winne (1979) concluded there was no difference between low and high cognitive level questions on student achievement, a finding that was corroborated by Samson, Strykowski, Weinstein, and Walberg (1987). Dantonio and Paradise (1988) found that students were much more likely to answer a low level question with a low level answer than a higher level question with a high level answer. Finally, Mills, Rice, Berliner, and Rousseau (1980) concluded that "the results of their study provided a firm basis for dispelling the belief that there is a high correlation between teacher questions and types of student answers" (p. 200).

These findings seem to indicate that asking a lower level question is almost sure to elicit a lower level response. In contrast, asking a higher level question increases, but does not guarantee, the chances that students will respond with a higher level answer. In fact, "The odds are only about 50-50 that an analysis, synthesis, or application question will be responded to with an answer reflecting analysis, synthesis, or application" (Berliner, 1984, p. 64). This suggests that asking a higher level question is a necessary, but not sufficient, condition for eliciting higher level thinking from students. In other words, asking students good questions is not enough; other strategies are needed as well.

Wait Time

One of the most established and well accepted methods for improving the quantity and quality of student responses is simply to remain silent for a few seconds after asking a question. This brief pause is known as wait time. Lengthening your wait time after asking a question gives students a better opportunity to process the question more thoroughly, thus deepening their thinking and extending their answer.

Rowe (1986) reviewed the research literature and found that substantial benefits accrue when teachers increase their wait time. First, increasing wait time increases the quantity and quality of students' talk. More students participate voluntarily in the discussions, and the number of unsolicited but appropriate contributions also increases. The length of student responses increases between 300 and 700 percent, an effect that was observed across grade levels. In addition, the failure to respond to questions decreases, and classroom discipline improves.

There is also an increase in the quality of student talk. Students appear to gain confidence in their ability to construct explanations and to challenge the logic of a situation. They do more speculating about possible alternative explanations or ways of thinking about a topic. More of their inferences are supported by evidence and logical argument. Achievement on written measures improves, particularly on more cognitively complex test items. Finally, the number of questions asked by students increases, the number of student-to-student exchanges increases, and cooperation among students increases.

Increasing wait time also has a positive impact on teacher behaviors. Because students are talking more and sharing more ideas, teachers ask fewer questions, respond more flexibly to student comments, and increase their expectations for certain students. Despite these benefits, however, teachers rarely (less than twelve percent of the time) allow more than three seconds of wait time (Walsh & Sattes, 2005), typically calling on students less than one second after asking the question, thus preventing enough time for students to think about their response. Furthermore, teachers may allow even less wait time for low achievers.

When asked, teachers gave several reasons for not allowing more wait time, including:

1. they felt pressed for time;
2. they felt like they had to keep things moving;
3. they wanted to keep students actively engaged;
4. they were concerned about classroom management;
5. they were caught up in the excitement of the lesson;
6. they felt uncomfortable with the silence;
7. they were unaware of the importance of wait time (Walsh & Sattes, 2005, p. 18.).

Many of these concerns are very understandable; students can lose their focus very quickly when the teacher stops talking. Newer teachers may feel even more pressure to avoid losing student interest. To fill the uncomfortable void created by silence, it is tempting to resort to verbal habits that interfere with wait time, such as mimicking student responses, giving verbal commands before three seconds have passed, responding with "Right?" or "Don't you think that?" or using "Yes, but, although" constructions.

Assessing Student-to-Student Interactions

Assessing student-to-student interactions provides another approach to assessing the quality of student thinking. A high level of student-to-student interactions serves as an indication that the students are listening to each other and actively analyzing, synthesizing, and evaluating each other's comments (all on the higher levels of Bloom's taxonomy), rather than simply passively awaiting the teacher's approval. During a more teacher centered discussion, the teacher asks a question, the student gives an answer, the teacher responds to it, then moves on to another student. In a more student centered discussion, students are more likely to respond to each other's comments by asking questions, agreeing or disagreeing with previous comments, by elaborating on previous comments, by clarifying, or by summarizing previous comments. Several strategies for increasing student-to-student interactions will be discussed in the following sections.

Teaching Students to Ask Questions

As discussed in the previous chapter, students tend to ask very few questions. So one way to promote more student-to-student interaction is by encouraging students to ask each other questions. Asking questions of each other can reflect an interest in what another person has said, can encourage more elaboration, or can determine the relationship between a cause and an effect, such as "Can you explain why you think it's true that if these things are in place, such and such a thing will occur?" (Brookfield & Preskill, 2005).

With some careful instruction, students can learn how to ask higher level questions. Usually this will involve helping students make some simple distinctions between types of questions they could create. For example, in the following excerpt, Ms. Lowell is asking her fifth grade students about the "fat" and "skinny" questions they have composed based on their reading of *Amos Fortune: Free Man*. Fat questions refer to divergent or more open-ended questions and skinny questions refer to "convergent" or more closed questions. As part of her instruction, Ms. Lowell requires her students to compose their own questions based on the reading assignments and stresses the importance of creating "fat" questions.

Ms. Lowell:	Read over your fat questions and somebody come up with a fat question that they think was their best. What do you think would be your best fat question? Corey, do you have one?
Rasheed:	Do you think Amos lives a good life? Why or why not?
Ms. Lowell:	That is a good fat question. Very good. What did you come up with?
Amy:	Why is it not a good time to make a will?
Ms. Lowell:	What would be your opinion on that? Why wouldn't it be a good time to make a will?
Amy:	He didn't have money to make a will.
Ms. Lowell:	Okay. What do you think he was saving that money for in that special pot?
Amy:	(Inaudible).
Ms. Lowell:	He kind of put all of his coins and the things that he got from getting rid of his leather into that pot. Violet was always saying he's saving that for something special. Do you think it was to free the slaves?
Amy:	Yes.
Ms. Lowell:	Or to buy a slave?
Heather:	I have a fat question here. Do you think there should be a sequel to his book?
Ms. Lowell:	What do you think?
Heather:	I think there should.
Daniel:	I think there should because you don't know what happened to . . .
Ms. Lowell:	So it could kind of pick up with her life and what she did after that. Good thinking. What do you have?
Steve:	What do you think Amos wants to do for God's children?
Ms. Lowell:	Another good fat question. Excellent. Darren, what do you have?

Synthesizing Ideas

A second way to encourage more student-to-student interaction is to encourage students to make statements that integrate ideas, such as linking, clarifying, summarizing, or paraphrasing statements. For example, students could be encouraged to listen and reflect on their classmates' comments in order to make one of the following statements, adapted from Brookfield & Preskill (2005, pp. 99–100):

1. They could make a comment that explicitly links the contributions of two other students.

2. They could make a comment that at least partly paraphrases a point someone else has already made.
3. They could make a summary observation that takes into account several people's contributions and that touches on a reoccurring theme in the discussion.
4. They could also contribute something that builds on what someone else has said. In this case, they should try to be specific about the connection they are making.

Facilitating Discussion

Students can also make statements that encourage their classmates to elaborate. For instance, they could indicate that they found another person's ideas interesting or useful. They should also be encouraged to specifically state what it was that interested or helped them. Using body language (in a slightly exaggerated way) to encourage classmates or to show their appreciation is also appropriate. It is also okay to disagree with someone, as long as it is done in a respectful and constructive way.

Talking in Groups

Another approach to facilitating more student-to-student interaction would be to let students talk to each other in groups. Talking in small groups can lead to improved student-to-student interactions during whole group discussions (Wilen, 2004). It also affords the teacher an opportunity to eliminate herself completely from the dialogue so that all interactions take place among students. This provides students with a more extended opportunity for verbal interactions and an opportunity for the teacher to provide one-on-one support for individual students.

Assessing Content Knowledge

A fourth way to assess student responses is for content knowledge. Content knowledge can be assessed by comparing the changes in student comments from the beginning to the end of the unit. To discern these changes requires conducting discussions throughout the teaching unit, both before and after substantial learning has taken place.

The potential differences between student talk at the beginning and end of the unit are illustrated below by two transcript excerpts taken from Ms. Brady's seventh grade mathematics class. The first was taken from a discussion conducted early in the unit, and the second was taken near the end of the unit. One of the primary learning goals of the unit was to learn how to calculate area and volume. The purpose of this initial discussion was to introduce students to the idea that differently shaped ice cream containers serve different functions. The teacher began the discussion by asking her students why ice cream comes in different containers. As you read through the first excerpt, take note of the vocabulary used by students and the content knowledge embedded in their responses.

Ms. Brady: Okay! A lot of you already have some good ideas, so all I want you to do is share your ideas with each other, okay? Share your ideas with each other. Remember that I would like to hear all of you contributing today. And some of you I've already heard, almost all of you, I didn't talk to each and every one have some idea of why things are shaped . . . are the way they are as far as ice cream containers, so who feels they want to start? Who feels like . . . Tony, go ahead.

Tony: I think they have different containers to fit people's needs because like that one on the end behind, that's like for a person who wants some ice cream on their own and they like have that. And like the gallon, whatever in the box, rectangular prism size is for bigger families or whatever and it's just like . . . yeah . . . different people's needs.

Ms. Brady: So, multiple packages to fit different needs. All right, Chuck, go ahead.

Chuck: Well, those, um . . . like the cylinder boxes and those others um . . . those are used a lot by Haagen-Dazs, and Ben & Jerry's, and Blue Bunny and those are really big and well known companies, but like you'll see Hy-Vee ice cream in the square ones and think the little . . . well, those aren't square . . . the rectangular prism boxes are a little cheaper than just the hard ones. But the circular, well some of these, are easier to use because there's no corners for the ice cream to get stuck on.

Ms. Brady: Oh! I've never thought of the corner things.

In the excerpt above, Tony and Chuck were able to elaborate at some length on the shape of the containers. To do so, they drew on their everyday experience of ice cream containers. No mathematical concepts were used to support their observations, and their use of mathematical vocabulary was limited to the terms "prism" and "cylinder." Other than those references, there is a very limited expression of more formal mathematical relationships.

In contrast, compare the talk above to the transcript excerpt below, which was taken from the last discussion during the unit. Below, the students are explaining the features of a package designed to hold ping pong balls, which they have constructed as part of a project. What differences do you see between the student talk in the first and second excerpt?

Ms. Brady: Okay. Who did I say next? Chuck? Ah, Chuck!

Chuck: Okay, this is my smallest cube. I just made cubes because cubes have small surface areas for their volume so I was worried about cost a lot.

Ms. Brady: Okay.

Chuck: Trying to have a low cost. So then this one holds eight ping pong balls. It costs $3.47. It's 7.6 centimeters by 7.6 centimeters. Its surface

	area is 346 square centimeters. And the volume is 438.976 cubic centimeters.
Ms. Brady:	All right. What questions do you have for Chuck? Okay, Steve?
Steve:	Why did he choose a box and not like a prism?
Chuck:	I chose a cube because they have a really small surface area. Because we were working with the real cube—centimeter cubes and then whenever all the dimensions were all close together then it had the smallest surface area so I did cubes so then it would cost less.
Ms. Brady:	All right. All right. Thanks. Anything else? Um . . . anyone else have a question for Chuck?

In comparison to the first excerpt, the second demonstrates increased content knowledge and associated thinking skills. For instance, Chuck uses more mathematical terms than the first example (cubes, centimeters, volume, surface area, prism), displays his ability to calculate volume and surface area, and uses mathematical reasoning to justify his choice of a cube for his package. ("I chose a cube because they have a really small surface area.")

Pre, Formative, and Post Assessment

Listening to students' talk provides an excellent opportunity to assess what students know and don't know. From student talk, the teacher can learn what the student knows at the beginning of a teaching unit (preassessment), how well they are learning as they move through the unit (formative assessment), and what they have learned by the end of the unit (post assessment).

Preassessment

Teachers can preassess by beginning a teaching unit with a discussion. The information gained can potentially provide important insights about what students already know, and then be used to either evaluate individual students or inform teaching decisions. When evaluating individual students, teachers can compare the comments made during the initial discussion with comments made later or at the end of the unit. By the end of the unit, students may be better able to answer recall questions, they may be better able to compare or contrast two or more different ideas, they may be better able to ask more informed questions about the content, or they may have incorporated new and more technical vocabulary words into their speech.

The insights gained from preassessment can also inform teaching decisions. A discussion conducted at the very beginning of the unit could inform teachers of what the students already know, what they don't know, and what their misconceptions are. It also provides an opportunity to make connections with the students' preexisting knowledge. Connecting new information to previously learned knowledge greatly increases the chances that the new information will be retained.

Formative assessment

Formative assessment occurs as the unit is being taught. As the class moves through the unit, the teacher can continue to monitor student progress through their discussion comments. As the unit unfolds, further discussions can provide insight into how student thinking is progressing. The primary purpose of formative assessment is to inform teaching decisions, regardless of whether the teacher is assessing a single individual or the entire class.

Summative assessment

Summative assessment occurs near the end of the unit and provides a final evaluation of the students' learning. However, it is difficult and somewhat rare for teachers to assess the talk of each individual student as part of a summative assessment. To do so would require that every student in the class participate during the discussion. It is more common to assess the cumulative learning from discussions through another form of assessment, such as a test, essay, or final project.

Assessing Discussions through Student Writing

Student writing—such as essays, essay questions on tests, or research papers—can provide documentation of the thinking skills and content knowledge acquired during discussions. Therefore, student writing can serve as either formative or summative assessment of classroom discussions, for assessing either individuals or the overall impact of the discussion on the whole group. One approach to assessing discussions through writing would be to collect writing samples taken from before (preassessments) and after (post assessments) a series of discussions. Comparing the preassessments with the post assessments would be very much like grading papers using a writing rubric. Two differences will be noted here. First, evaluating writing mechanics such as punctuation and spelling is not influenced by discussions and need not be considered as part of the evaluation. For the purpose of evaluating the impact of a discussion, more useful criteria would include the development of ideas, organization, voice, and word choice. Criteria for assessing sentence fluency and mechanics also could be deemphasized or dropped. Second, when judging content matter, it is important to distinguish between questions that ask students to recall information they heard in the discussion from questions that ask students to construct new relationships. The latter would indicate a greater impact of the discussion method in terms of the students' ability to think constructively.

What Teachers Need to Know

In order to properly assess student learning and the effectiveness of classroom discussions, teachers need to consider four factors when evaluating the quality of student responses. The first is the students' ability to elaborate on a topic. Without elaboration, it is not possible to assess student talk. Student elaboration can be enhanced by asking students to reflect on their participation and by charting participation patterns.

The second is the quality of student thinking. Resources such as Bloom's taxonomy can provide helpful information when trying to construct a rubric. Key indicators of student thinking include the students' ability to make connections with other ideas, including their ability to introduce new facts, to synthesize new relationships, and to see ideas from new perspectives. The quality and quantity of student thinking can be increased by lengthening the teacher's wait time.

A third way of assessing student thinking is by the quality and quantity of student-to-student interactions. Desirable student interactions include asking each other questions, making statements that link the ideas of other students, and facilitating the talking of their classmates. These behaviors can be interpreted as indications that students are listening, interpreting, synthesizing, and evaluating their classmates' ideas. Teaching students how to facilitate each other's talk can help promote discussions.

The fourth factor teachers need to consider is content knowledge. Content knowledge can be assessed by comparing changes in student responses from the beginning to the end of a teaching unit. Teachers should look for changes in vocabulary and conceptual knowledge.

The rubric described in this chapter can be adapted or enhanced to fit more specific settings and to serve more specific purposes. Approaches to creating rubrics may vary and need not be limited to the recommendations made in this chapter, which are intentionally broad in order to cover a wide variety of discussion contexts.

Application Discussion

A primary purpose of this chapter has been to provide information that you can use to construct your own rubric for assessing student talking. As you read the teacher reflection below, identify the student thinking skills in which this teacher is most interested. Try to determine whether the skills she identifies are related more to elaboration, thinking skills, student-to-student interactions, or content knowledge. Consider which of these four you would find most useful in creating a rubric. After you have finished reading, discuss the following questions.

1. What criteria does this teacher use to assess her students' talking?
2. For what purpose is she assessing their talking?
3. How does she encourage more student-to-student interactions?
4. What data does she collect and how does she collect it?
5. How could you adapt these techniques to your teaching?

Of the classes that I teach daily, I have three eighth grade general math classes. When scheduling is done, the goal is for heterogeneous groupings; however, that usually does not occur because of the need to meet the requirements of special education students.

This trimester I have one class that consists of above average students (I'll call this group A for the purpose of this paper), one class that is a blend of lower ability level special education students and lower math ability regular education students (I'll refer to this group as group B), and one class with special education students having reading disabilities, behavior issues, and mixed math ability levels (I'll call this group C).

I often have students work in partnerships. Usually I allow students to choose their own partners, but occasionally I randomly assign partners. In group A, I allowed students to choose their own group members for the activity that was videotaped. This group was made of three girls: Alyssa, Tiffany, and Cassie. All three girls have received "A" grades in math class this year. In group B, I assigned the members based on one student with regular education reading ability and a special education student having a learning disability for reading. This group was made up of two boys: Jeff and Cody. Both boys have received grades of at least a "B" for this school year in mathematics. In group C, I randomly assigned partners by drawing names. The videotaped group consisted of Jon, an above average student, and Sara, a student who is very capable but has poor attendance and study skills.

The students were told that they were to work together on a "partner quiz." The rules for the activity were:

1. There was a time limit of thirty minutes to accomplish the quiz. (The purpose for this rule was for students to stay on task and not waste time.)
2. They could ask the teacher only one question. (The purpose for this was for the students to use each other as a resource instead of the teacher.)
3. All members of the group would receive the same percent grade on the quiz.
4. All members of the group would complete an evaluation. In the evaluation, they would grade each member of the group for effort and cooperation. An explanation would accompany each grade given as justification for the grade given by them. This evaluation would be an additional part of the grade.

The unit we are presently studying is a transition unit. The concepts and procedures used in the graphing and statistics unit previously studied are used to develop algebra concepts of linear relationships, writing algebraic equations, and solving one- and two-step equations. We have been graphing linear relationships and have recently been writing algebraic equations from these relationships.

When I reviewed the videotape, I used the rubric given to us during our Classroom Discourse class conducted by Professor John Henning. During our class, we had discussed how one session would probably not provide ample opportunity to witness all of the items on the rubric. The areas that I wanted most to observe were:

- makes inferences based on earlier observations or ideas;
- asks questions about the relationship among ideas or observations;
- distinguishes component parts of ideas or observations;

- comments on specific cues that guide thinking;
- gives explanations, justifications, and supporting evidence;
- utilizes conceptual vocabulary from current coursework;
- engagement and participation.

All three groups make inferences based on earlier observations or ideas. Group A tries to interpret the meaning of the expression 5x–3 during the following discourse:

Tiffany:	5x equals five dollars per mile.
Alyssa:	That would be five dollars for one mile.
Tiffany:	You don't minus three each time, right?
Cassie:	Right. So we take five times the amount of dollars.
Tiffany:	No, the amount of miles.
Cassie:	If you make a chart (pause) (makes a table on the paper). Wait I've got them switched around. Let me fix it.
Tiffany:	You add five, then add five, then . . . (voice trails off inaudibly).
Alyssa:	Which would be the same as times five each time.

This discussion also shows them distinguishing component parts of ideas as well as giving explanations, justification, and supporting evidence. They use the table they create to prove their assumptions about the expression. Their dialogue continues until they come to the conclusion that the equation is linear. Linear relationships will be the basis for future algebra study.

Group B uses inferences based on earlier ideas in this discourse while constructing a graph during the activity.

Jeff:	Use a dot for this one. Go by 25 each time.
Cody:	I can't; it's too hard for me. Let me do it my way, like this. (Cody plots the coordinates from the table they had made earlier.) Now I'll use x's for this one.
Jeff:	This ain't Valentine's Day yet, Cody!

This brief conversation shows that the boys know that different symbols are helpful when plotting two different sets of data on the same graph for comparison purposes. Since x's and dots have been used successfully before, they apply the same logic to this situation.

Group C uses inferences based on earlier ideas in this manner.

Jon:	2.5n=d will be our equation, n will equal meters walked. So 2.5 times the number of meters walked would give us (pause). No, n equals seconds. That's better. So 2.5 times the seconds equals meters walked.

(Jon writes on the paper and reads the next part of the problem.) So we'll use the same thing but change to two.

Sara sits quietly smiling alternately at Jon and the person holding the camera. She offers no assistance throughout the activity. Jon continues to explain each step to her (probably for the sake of the videotaping). From his statements, I know that Jon is identifying component parts of the concepts and relating them to Sara. Throughout the activity, Jon talks to Sara in much the same manner so she can follow his reasoning.

Groups A and B both ask questions about the relationship among ideas or observations throughout the activity. Jeff and Cody ask each other to verify the definition of terms used in the activity during the following brief exchange.

Jeff: There is no intersect on here.
Cody: Yeah there is—see?
Jeff: No, intersect is where it crosses.
Cody: Shouldn't it cross? How can we answer this question if it doesn't cross?

The boys instinctively realize that something is wrong. They comment on specific cues that should be guiding their thinking. However, at this stage, neither is strong enough mathematically to make changes.

The girls in group A also ask questions about the relationships in this exchange.

Cassie: $y=-2x$
Tiffany: y is amount of money.
Cassie: x is miles walked.
Alyssa: What could -2 mean?
Cassie: x isn't money; x is number of miles walked. It can't be different things.
Alyssa: If they walked one mile, they'd lose two dollars. That doesn't make sense.
Tiffany: You'd end up paying money.
Cassie: This one is $-x$. How can you walk a negative mile? It doesn't make sense.
Tiffany: This isn't about miles, it's about money.

The girls are identifying what they already know and applying it to a new situation. They realize that the equation $y=-2x$ does not logically work for this situation. They are then able to identify the correct equation from the cues they have been given. Their decision is based on logical explanation and evidence generated through their conversational exchange.

Group C is not able to accomplish this level of thinking because only Jon is engaged in the process. Jon continues to explain step-by-step his thinking process throughout the activity, but Sara remains a passive observer. She offers few comments throughout the videotaped session, none of which can be picked up by the camera microphone.

In all three groups, the students appeared to be enthusiastically engaged in solving the problems presented to them (excluding Sara who was more interested in being seen on camera). Each group had been selected in a different manner, yet each group worked together to accomplish the goal. Of those groups not videotaped, most were on task throughout the activity. In a class with behavior issues, two groups were off task; one group could not work together productively because of personality differences carried over from another class period, and the other group because the work was completed quickly. This last group completed the activity with little conversation. They took turns working the problems independently. The members of groups A and B both encouraged and actively sought the participation of others in the group to accomplish the activity.

I personally am weak in the area of vocabulary. I believe that my vocabulary usage during class time is limited. Therefore, I did not expect to witness much use of vocabulary during the activities. I sometimes use silly words to describe concepts in an effort to catch the attention of students and provide a unique way to remember an idea. I heard several of these slang-type vocabulary items. One time was when Jeff and Cody in group B joked about using x's and o's in the construction of their graph. In groups A and C, references are made to the variables x, y, and d without identifying the letters as variables. The students know that each letter must be identified, yet never is the vocabulary term "variable" used in their discourse. This means that I need to use the terms more often so they also will become comfortable using the appropriate vocabulary.

Overall, I was pleased by what I witnessed during the videotaped activities. Considering the varied ability levels of the students in the classes and the numerous behavior issues that exist in our school, I was pleasantly surprised to hear the mathematical discourse that I did. I truly expected to hear about weekend entertainment, fashion, or popular entertainers. There may be more learning taking place than I thought—wouldn't that be exciting!

Activities

1. Try lengthening your wait time after asking a question to at least two to three seconds. Ask a colleague or a student to record the length of time between when you ask a question and call on a student during one of your discussions. Calculate the average length of your wait time.
2. Create a chart for recording student participation. Then record the student participation during three or four discussions. Analyze your participation patterns, write up a short summary of your findings, and in your summary suggest some strategies for spreading out participation.

3. After a discussion, ask your students some of the reflection questions in this chapter—or create some new ones of your own. Read through their answers, and use them to suggest some strategies for improving your discussions.

4. Use the rubric shown in Table 2.1 as a source for creating another rubric that fits your discussions. Use some of the references suggested in "For Further Reading" to compile a list of desirable thinking skills for your discussions. Weight your rubric according to your goals for your particular class and what you want your students to achieve. You may want to consider creating a rubric that incorporates thinking skills specific to your subject area.

5. Collect several samples of student writing before and after a series of discussions. Determine a specific area of interest that you would like to examine for student growth, e.g., changes in vocabulary, their understanding of relationships, or their ability to justify a position they have taken. Collect evidence related to the change or lack of change in student thinking. Use this evidence to draw some conclusions on the impact or lack of impact of the discussion on your targeted outcome in student writing.

three
Teacher Follow Up Moves

Framing Discussion

Below are two transcript excerpts taken from discussions in a seventh grade mathematics classroom during a unit on surface area and volume. Both excerpts come from the same unit, with the same teacher, and the same group of students. You have seen the first excerpt near the end of the previous chapter. It was taken from a discussion that took place at the very beginning of a unit on surface area and volume. The second excerpt is taken from a discussion that takes place near the midpoint of the same unit. Use what you have learned from the two previous chapters about asking questions and assessing student responses to compare the differences in the two transcript excerpts. Consider how discourse moves may vary at different points during the lesson. After you finish reading the two transcripts, answer the questions below.

1. Which of the two transcripts has a higher ratio of student to teacher talk?
2. What differences do you see in the student responses between the two transcripts?
3. What differences do you see between the teacher's follow up moves between these two transcripts?
4. What advantages do you see in using the teacher follow up moves of transcript #1 over transcript #2?
5. In what situations do you see advantages to using the teacher follow up moves of transcript #2 over transcript #1?

Transcript #1

Ms. Brady: Okay! A lot of you already have some good ideas, so all I want you to do is share your ideas with each other, okay? Share your ideas with each other. Remember that I would like to (inaudible) contributing today. And some of you I've already heard, almost all of you, I didn't talk to each and every one have some idea of why things are shaped . . . are the way they are as far as ice cream containers, so who feels they want to start? Who feels like . . . Barry, go ahead.

Tony: I think they have different containers to fit people's needs because like that one on the end behind, that's like for a person who wants some ice cream on their own and they like have that. And like the gallon, whatever in the box, rectangular prism size is for bigger families or whatever and it's just like . . . yeah . . . different people's needs.

Ms. Brady: So, multiple packages to fit different needs. All right, Bob, go ahead.

Chuck: Well, those, um . . . like the cylinder boxes and those others um . . . those are used a lot by Haagen-Dazs, and Ben & Jerry's, and Blue Bunny and those are really big and well known companies, but like you'll see Hy-Vee ice cream in the square ones and think the little . . . well, those aren't square . . . the rectangular prism boxes are a little cheaper than just the hard ones. But the circular, well some of these, are easier to use because there's no corners for the ice cream to get stuck on.

Ms. Brady: Oh! I've never thought of the corner things.

Chuck: Um . . . we thought the freezer space . . .

Ms. Brady: Wait. Make sure everybody's giving you their attention and respect . . . go ahead.

Chuck: The freezer space because some people have a freezer and some people have a smaller one. We thought that, the gallon one, you would want to bring home a gallon in a box, like a big, big box because gallons take a lot of room. And we thought the small one was made like that was because it's like if you want to buy ice cream like that they make it more expensive because they don't sell it in that one then they'd make more money off this one because if you had five people, you'd probably have to buy two or three of those things. One for each person maybe, or like one for every two persons and then and they're more expensive so that the people make more money than off the other two with discounts.

Transcript #2

Alisha: Um, the surface area for that one is eighty-eight, but on one of the sides you're going to have to multiply twenty-four by two.

Ms. Brady: Um-hum—and that's . . .

Alisha:	Forty-eight.
Ms. Brady:	And then you have to multiply that by two.
Alisha:	Yeah!
Ms. Brady:	Yeah, very good! Anybody else want to say it differently? Larry?
Larry:	Since this is the long one, it's not the longest one, but it's . . .
Ms. Brady:	The longest one would be one by one by forty-eight.
Larry:	Forty-eight. Yeah. This is longer than that and less cubed, cubical or whatever, however . . .
Ms. Brady:	Less cubical?
Larry:	Yeah.
Ms. Brady:	I like that.
Larry:	However you say it. And so it's going to be longer so it's going to . . . it's going to have more surface area.
Ms. Brady:	Everybody okay with that? Is there any one that would be actually . . . yes, this is bigger . . . is there any one that would have a smaller surface than four by two by six? I want you to talk with your partner *only* about that. Is there any one that would be smaller than four by two by six? Remember last time, Larry just hinted at it, it's the one that's closest to a cube if you can get there. Closest to a cube.

Introduction

Interactions between teachers and students usually take place within a three-stage cycle. The first stage consists of an initial teacher question or invitation to speak, the second stage consists of a student response, and the third stage consists of the teacher's follow up to the student response. The first two stages of this cycle, asking questions and student responses, were discussed in the previous two chapters. The primary purpose of this chapter is to examine the third stage of the cycle or the teacher's follow up moves.

Teachers have a wide variety of choices in regards to how they follow up on student comments. They can confirm or reject, silently acknowledge, repeat for emphasis, provide cues, reformulate, elaborate, explain, or probe. To what degree any of these choices is appropriate depends on the larger purposes of the teacher. At times, teachers may be using discourse moves that facilitate the maximum amount of student participation; at other times, they may be using discourse moves that provide more guidance and support for student thinking. Understanding how and when to use these discourse moves can give you greater control over the direction of your discussions.

A second purpose of this chapter is to introduce some larger patterns of discourse moves. Two of them are illustrated by the comparison of the two transcript excerpts at the beginning of the chapter. The first transcript clearly has a much higher ratio of student to teacher talk compared with the second. In addition, Ms. Brady asks very few questions and avoids making evaluative comments (letting the student know their comment was right or wrong). The students elaborate more in the first transcript, but they use very few mathematical concepts. In the second transcript, Ms. Brady provides more guidance to the discussion. She asks more questions, she gives evaluative responses, and she provides additional information and guidance through her follow up responses. The student responses are shorter, but they contain more mathematical concepts and vocabulary.

Both discussions are conducted by the same teacher but for different purposes at different times in her teaching unit on surface area and volume. The first takes place near the beginning of the unit. At this point, the teacher's purpose is to elicit student interest and participation, to assess their prior knowledge, and to create an anticipatory set for the new unit. In contrast, it is much more difficult for students to elaborate in the second excerpt because the concepts are less familiar and therefore more difficult. Therefore, the teacher is providing a more guided discussion. The teacher's approach in both situations is appropriate because each interaction accomplishes a different purpose.

In both of the transcript excerpts above, the cycle of teacher questions, student responses, and the teacher's follow up moves occur in recognizable patterns. By the end of this chapter, you will begin to see how individual discourse moves can be combined into the larger discussion patterns that will be discussed more fully in chapter 4.

Pausing

One of the most important follow up moves for teachers is to pause before responding to a student comment. This pause is referred to as wait time 2, and it carries all the benefits of wait time 1, the pause immediately after a teacher asks a question (Rowe, 1986). As wait time 2 increases, more students participate voluntarily; they tend to make more extended responses; they give better quality answers; and there is increased student-to-student interaction. Despite these benefits, however, the research indicates that most teachers allow even less time for wait time 2 than for wait time 1 (less than a second).

Pausing after a student answers signals the teacher is interested and actively processing what has been said, a message that is further strengthened when teachers incorporate student thinking into their comments or feedback. In contrast, when a teacher hurries on to the next prepared question on their list, it may be interpreted as an indication that student input does not matter or that the teacher is simply not listening to them. If students feel their contributions are not important, they will participate less. Similarly, students are less likely to elaborate when teachers are too evaluative or directive in their follow up comments.

Another way to let your students know you are listening is through your nonverbal cues. These could include looking directly at the speaker, maintaining eye contact, and responding with a variety of appropriate facial expressions, such as smiling, demonstrating surprise or excitement, or projecting thoughtfulness by moving your eyes from side to side. Teachers should avoid folding their arms, standing too far away from students, or adopting any position that communicates lack of interest or resistance (Kindsvatter, Wilen, & Ischler, 1996).

Pausing after a student answers also provides a chance for teachers to consider what direction they might like to take the discussion. For example, should the teacher ask further probing questions, should she add information of her own, or does she say nothing and wait to see if the other students comment? Those decisions are tempered by moment-to-moment judgments concerning what would be most beneficial. If the teacher judges student participation to be the most pressing priority of the moment, she may choose to wait. On the other hand, if time is short or the students appear stymied, she may choose to add key information to scaffold student thinking. In either case, her decision can be informed by a moment's pause.

Evaluative Comments

One of the easiest and most often used teacher follow up moves is simply telling students whether their response was right (confirmation) or wrong (rejection). Affirming the accuracy of student responses through evaluative comments provides feedback to students and can establish a factual foundation for later phases of the discussion.

Confirmations

A confirmation is an indication on the part of the teacher that the student has given a correct answer or, more broadly, that the teacher approves of the student response. During discussions, teachers tend to habitually confirm student responses. Examples of confirmation would include, "Right," "Good job," "I agree," "Okay," and "Good point." Below, Ms. Lowell confirms a fifth grader's interpretation of the actions of a character named Harvey from the novel *Pinballs*.

Sheila:	Harvey liked Kentucky Fried Chicken because every single time his father wasn't there, he went. That is how child neglect and Kentucky Fried Chicken are in Harvey's life.
Ms. Lowell:	Good.

In the exchange above, the teacher is confirming the content of the student's answer. At other times, a confirmation may simply indicate that the student has expressed a valid opinion or made a worthwhile contribution to the discussion. When teachers positively affirm student responses, it promotes participation. Thus, effective teachers ask questions in a way that ensures a high number of confirmations. It should be noted, however, that while confirmations are generally well received by students, they are still a form of teacher guidance. By neither confirming nor rejecting a student response, the teacher shifts more responsibility for learning and thinking to the students. The degree to which teachers should give or withhold confirmations depends on the teacher's purposes, the students, and the specific context of the lesson.

Teachers can also confirm student responses by showing an appreciation for student thinking. One approach is to name ideas after the students who thought of them, e.g., Kerry's idea. Each time the teacher refers to the idea using Kerry's name, she credits her contribution. In the example below, Ms. Lowell makes several appreciative comments (in italics) concerning her students' interpretation of a character named Carly from the novel *Pinballs*.

Sarah:	I think she was mean to them because she thinks they're out to get her.
Ms. Lowell:	*Good way to look at it.* She thinks they're out to get her. Doesn't really know.
Tabitha:	She didn't want to (inaudible).
Michael:	I think Carly (inaudible) because that's how she was raised.
Ms. Lowell:	Maybe how she was raised. *I like the way you started your question.* If I would have just put "She didn't like them" I would say who is she, who is them, and why? *I like how you started out* with "Carly was mean to the boys and Mrs. Mason because" so I took part of my question and put that as part of the answer. What did you have Jenny?
Jenny:	I think Carly was mean to Harvey, Tommy, and Mrs. Mason because she didn't like meeting new people.
Ms. Lowell:	*Good way to think about it.* You were that same way?

Rejections

A rejection occurs when the teacher indicates to a student the answer is not correct. Examples of rejection would include: "No, try again," "Sorry, good guess," and "No, you need to think about that a little more." In the example below, Ms. Lowell rejects Casey's definition of child neglect during a discussion of *Pinballs*.

Ms. Lowell:	So what do you think child neglect is? Casey?
Casey:	Something that you um . . . remember from your childhood?
Ms. Lowell:	No, not really hon. Good guess though.

For the most part, teachers tend to avoid rejections whenever possible because of their inhibiting effect on participation. However, rejecting student answers may be necessary in order to avoid the confusion caused by incorrect information. Even then, many teachers will try to soften the blow, by thanking students for participating or praising their effort. Sometimes a rejection can be avoided by simply ignoring the student response. In that way, the answer may generally pass unnoticed. However, if another student reintroduces or chooses to elaborate on an incorrect answer, then the misinformation may have to be confronted later in the discussion.

The discourse of teachers usually contains a high number of confirmations and rejections. They are part of a cycle that begins with an elicitation (an invitation to speak, usually a question), continues with a student response, and finishes with an evaluative follow up from the teacher. In the transcript excerpt below, Ms. Lowell is teaching a vocabulary lesson. Her elicitations, confirmations, and rejections are italicized, bolded, and labeled in the brackets. The unitalicized statements are examples of other teacher follow up moves that will be discussed in the next section.

Ms. Lowell:	Okay, the last word. *How do I say that last word? [Elicitation]*
Kerry:	Boutique.
Ms. Lowell:	Boutique. *What is a boutique? What do you think a boutique is? [Elicitations]*
Sheena:	Well, I asked my grandma last night and she said it was a store for decorations at home.
Ms. Lowell:	*Okay, that could be one type of a boutique. [Confirmation]*
Cameron:	A place where you sell antiques.
Ms. Lowell:	*No, not antiques. [Rejection]* A boutique is just like a little shop. You can buy clothes at boutiques, or things for your home. It's more like a . . .
Monica:	It's kind of like Goodwill.
Ms. Lowell:	*Not necessarily hon. [Rejection]* I'm trying to think of maybe a boutique that would be downtown Cedar Falls. There's a place called the Chalet. Have you ever seen it? It's on the Parkade, that winding little street.

When a teacher's follow up moves contain a high proportion of evaluative comments, the interaction between teacher and student is usually a high ratio of teacher to student talk. In the following sections, other follow up moves that encourage more student elaboration will be introduced.

Follow Up or Probing Questions

When teachers begin a discussion, they pose an initial question to set the topic. These questions are referred to as *focus questions*, and they were the main subject of chapter 2. This section introduces *follow up or probing questions*. Probing questions are those that follow the initial question posed by the teacher or discussion leader. Examples would include "What do you mean by that?" or "Can you support your answer with examples?" Follow up or probing questions can help students reflect on their initial response, to extend and improve the quality of their initial response, and to elicit higher order thinking skills by developing larger themes in the discussion (Dantonio & Beisenherz, 2001). Ornstein (1988) has shown that asking probing questions is positively correlated with student achievement (see Table 3.1 for a summary of teacher follow up moves).

TABLE 3.1 Summary of Teacher Follow Up Moves

Category	Definition	Example
Probing question	The teacher asks a question that follows up on an initial focus question	T: What were some some clue words to our history mystery today? S: Virginia. T: How come Virginia was a good clue word for you?
Confirmation	The teacher validates a student response	T: Good. I like the way you are thinking about it.
Rejection	The teacher rejects a student response	T: Not quite, Hon. Good try.
Elaboration	The teacher adds information to student responses. Unlike a reformulation, the student response is not incorporated into an elaboration. In contrast to an explanation, an elaboration provides unsolicited information	S: The package is really expensive. T: So my follow up to that would be . . . I will let you know that our costs for these packages were a little bit higher because the actual cost per centimeter was a fractional cent . . .
Cue	The teacher provides a clue or directs student attention toward a particular aspect of a question or problem for the purpose of guiding student responses	T: Sally, you know what you need to remember? Maybe I gave you this hint before. When you're doing the volume, the radius affects it much greater than the height because it's the radius times the radius
Reformulation	The teacher restates a student response to make it clearer, to introduce more formal language, or to make it more accessible to the class	S: Like she's nice, and she doesn't care who she hangs out with or anything. T: Oh. So she's nice to everybody, not just to some.
Recapitulation	The teacher summarizes a series of previous discussion points for the purpose of creating a common understanding and refocusing the discussion	T: Yesterday in our groups we were talking about . . . there was the question that said Carly was the queen of the put downs. She was always putting people down. You had to come up with examples of how she put people down. But why do you think other people put people down?
Explanations	The teacher introduces a new idea in response to a question or a student request of a student	S: Surface area is . . .? T: 4 times pi times the radius.

T indicates Teacher; S, Student (adapted from Henning, Nielsen, and Hauschildt, 2006).

A follow up question can be as simple as following a student comment with the question "Why?" Probing students to justify their answers can challenge them to explore their thinking and clarify their reasoning. In the example below, Ms. Lowell is leading her fifth grade history students in an activity called "History Mystery." During this activity, the students are trying to estimate the date of Thomas Jefferson's birth from a short statement containing a variety of clue words. Ms. Lowell asks her students to identify the clue words, then follows up by asking them probing questions that require students to justify their answers.

Ms. Lowell:	I do. I have it. Okay. Books down, pencils down. Give me what you think were some clue words to our history mystery for today. Clue words. Samantha?
Samantha:	Virginia.
Ms. Lowell:	How come Virginia was a good clue word for you? [*Probing question*]
Samantha:	Because then they would know that it's already become a state.
Ms. Lowell:	Okay. Alex.
Alex:	President of the United States.
Ms. Lowell:	Was he the president then? [*Probing question*]
Alex:	No.
Ms. Lowell:	Oh, okay, that he later became president. Okay. What else. Alice?

Follow up questions can also be used to move the discussion forward after a student has given an incorrect answer (Walsh & Sattes, 2005). One of several approaches would be to probe the reasoning behind an incorrect response or ask for clarity when the response is complete. A second possibility is to rephrase or to pose the same question in different words. A third alternative would be to provide a cue such as "starts with . . .." Fourth and finally, the teacher could redirect a question or pose the same question to a different student, e.g., "Do you agree with what Dan is saying, Sally?" Redirecting questions can enhance student-to-student communication by encouraging students to respond to each other's ideas.

Guiding Responses

Guiding responses are teacher follow up moves that encourage student thinking, yet still permit some teacher control over the direction of the discussion. They often follow and are associated with student responses to divergent questions. Guiding responses can help students discover new perspectives, deepen their understanding by discovering new relationships, or acquire new factual information. In the following sections, a variety of guiding responses and their applications will be discussed. These discourse moves are common across many different types of classrooms, and becoming aware of them will increase the number of choices you have during a discussion. Most of the following were identified by the research of Neil Mercer (1995, 2000).

Repetitions

Repeating all or part of what a student says is one of the simplest teacher follow up moves, yet it can perform several important functions. One purpose is to repeat what was said to make sure the other students could hear it. Another purpose is to confirm and emphasize the comment so that other students will pay attention to it, e.g., a student may have made a thoughtful comment to which the teacher wants the rest of the class to pay particular attention. However, if the teacher repeats the comment in a questioning tone, it may be to suggest the student should reconsider his answer, or it may be an invitation for the student to develop his comment further. In the statement below, Ms. Lowell repeats the word "Harvey's father" to confirm a student's answer during a discussion of *Pinballs*.

Shelly: Harvey's father.

Ms. Lowell: Yeah, [*Confirmation*] *Harvey's father.* [*Repetition*] What does it mean if somebody is an alcoholic? What does that mean?

Depending on the tone the teacher takes, repetitions can serve a number of useful purposes, including confirming, emphasizing, or questioning student responses. However, like other teacher follow up moves, repetitions can be overused. In that case, repetitions can become a purposeless mimicry of student responses that can reduce wait time and lower the quality of the discussion. Mimicry can also condition students to become dependent on the teacher's repetition of student responses, thus conditioning them not to listen to their classmates and perhaps lessening the amount of student-to-student interaction during the discussion.

Elaborations

The teacher may also elaborate on a student response in order to introduce more information into the discussion. By adding related information, the teacher can introduce points that students may not have considered, provide information that helps integrate diverse student comments, or add another layer of depth to the current level of understanding. In the example below, Ms. Lowell elaborates (in italics) on a students' comment made while discussing *Pinballs*.

Shelly: Kentucky Fried Chicken was the light of Harvey's life because whenever his dad was late from work Harvey would go get some Kentucky Fried Chicken and child neglect was related to Harvey's life because his father neglected him.

Ms. Lowell: Yeah, his father really didn't take good care of him. *So when his father was late, it was easy for Harvey to go on over across the street to Kentucky Fried Chicken.* So that's the way that they're connected. Very good. What did you have?

Elaborations provide teachers with an opportunity to build on existing student understanding. This additional information is often important for giving direction to the discussion and helping students achieve the learning goals. However, overuse of elaboration may shift the focus of the discussion to the teacher, thus precluding student participation or causing students to become more passive and less participatory.

Reformulations

A reformulation is a restatement or a paraphrase or "revoicing" of the student's response. The teacher may reformulate to clarify for other students, to make the ideas expressed more accessible for other students, to provide another perspective, to bring the answer closer to the learning goals, or to introduce more technical vocabulary words. Reformulations give teachers the opportunity to scaffold student thinking. In the example of a reformulation below, the student is commenting on the behavior of a character in *Pinballs*.

Tammy:	Like she's nice, and she doesn't care who she hangs out with or anything.
Ms. Lowell:	Oh. So she's nice to everybody, not just to some.

In this case, the teacher reformulates the student response into a generalization about the personality of the character. The teacher may have introduced this idea because she intends to build on it further, perhaps at a later point in the discussion or in a future discussion.

Sometimes it is difficult to distinguish a reformulation from a repetition coupled with an elaboration. When reformulating, a teacher paraphrases what the student has said, as in the example above. When repeating and elaborating, the teacher repeats the student's comment verbatim and then adds new information as shown in the example below. The example below is taken from Ms. Brady's seventh grade math class.

Samuel:	The diameters are supposedly the same?
Ms. Brady:	The diameters are supposedly the same. [*Repetition*] Which means the radius is the same and do you notice that the heights are nearly equivalent? Again, these didn't come from the same set of solids, but they're nearly equivalent as well. So the heights are the same, the radius is the same approximately, so that is good. [*Elaboration*]

Recapitulations (Recaps)

Recapitulations are short summaries that focus the class on discussion points the teacher wants to emphasize. The teacher summarizes previous statements in order to draw students into a common understanding. There are three kinds of recaps—summary, reconstructive, and "we" statements. A summary recap simply reiterates previous comments. A reconstructive recap reinterprets and re-represents what has been done previously as a way of guiding student thinking. A "we" statement reminds students of past activities to make clear how new activities are relevant to the past. The example below is an example of a "we" statement recap taken from a discussion of *Pinballs*.

Ms. Lowell:	Yesterday in our groups *we* were talking about . . . there was the question that said Carly was the queen of putdowns. She was always putting people down. You had to come up with examples of how she had put people down. But why do you think other people put people down?

Explanations

An explanation introduces a new idea or a new concept the teacher believes is relevant to the discussion. It is different from an elaboration because an elaboration builds on information introduced by students. In contrast, an explanation often occurs in response to an explicit request or question asked by students, and it does not build on information introduced by students. An explanation introduces a wholly new idea, often for the purpose of bridging gaps in the discussion. In the example below, the teacher responds to a student request for information with an explanation needed to solve a problem related to surface area.

Justin:	Surface area is . . .?
Ms. Brady:	4 times pi times the radius. Just go ahead. Four times pi times r squared. So pi r squared is like the area of a circle. So it's four circles. So it's the area of four circles. So think about this. Think about this with me for a second, okay? Picture a basketball. All right? Picture a basketball. Picture like cutting that basketball in half.
Justin:	Yep.
Ms. Brady:	Okay the circle that you would see, it's like four of those laid out on top of a sphere, okay?

Cues

A cue highlights certain information as a way of guiding student thinking. By giving a cue, the teacher is trying to focus student attention on a particular aspect of a question or a problem. Example phrases might include "take a look at this" or "consider this as you are thinking." In the example excerpt below, the cue directs the student's attention to a key piece of information for calculating volume.

Shelly:	This is the one I tried but I can't.
Ms. Brady:	You know how to do it?
Shelly:	I couldn't figure out . . .
Ms. Brady:	Yes. Hmmm. Sally, you know what you need to remember? Maybe I gave you this hint before. When you're doing the volume, the radius affects it much greater than the height because it's the radius times the radius. Okay? The radius is going to affect it much greater than the height because it's the radius.

Cues may be embedded within a question or attached to the question as some form of addendum that refers to only part of the question. Mercer (2000) refers to these types of questions as cued elicitations. In the excerpt below, Ms. Lowell cues her students to Henry's feelings (from *Pinballs*) by asking if something similar ever happened to them.

Ms. Lowell:	How's Harvey feeling? Has it ever happened to you where you think that somebody has promised that they're going to do something with you or for you, and then they come back and say they never promised that. Has that ever happened to you? Can you think of a situation where that has happened?
Larry:	Many times.

Participant Frameworks

Chapters 1, 2, and 3 have each described a separate phase of a cycle that is commonly observed in classroom interactions. The cycle begins when the teacher asks a question or provides some other invitation for the student to speak, is followed by a student response, and concludes with a teacher follow up move. This cycle of teacher questions, student responses, and teacher follow up moves has been referred to as a "participant framework" (O'Connor & Michaels, 1996). That term emphasizes the role of the teacher's talk for creating a "framework" that invites student participation.

For example, the participant framework that allows the least amount of student talk is referred to as the Inquiry–Response–Evaluation (IRE) cycle. The IRE cycle begins with a recall question, which is followed by a brief, convergent student response and an evaluative follow up by the teacher. The IRE cycle, which occurs primarily on the knowledge level or the lowest level of Bloom's taxonomy, is often referred to as a form of recitation rather than discussion, and has been criticized repeatedly for limiting student interaction. However, an IRE pattern can serve the important purpose of establishing a solid base of factual information very quickly, often an important preliminary step leading to high level follow up questions and a more open phase of discussion (Stodolsky, Ferguson, & Wimpelberg, 1981; Wilen 1990; Wells, 1993). Thus, the IRE participant framework can be used effectively in conjunction with other participant frameworks that do enable a higher ratio of student to teacher talk.

A participant framework that would enable more student participation would include divergent questions from the higher levels of Bloom's taxonomy, divergent student responses, and guiding teacher responses. To create a more open participant framework, ask clearly phrased, high level questions, i.e., questions from the comprehension, application, analysis, synthesis, and evaluation levels of Bloom's taxonomy. After posing a question to the class, three to five seconds of wait time should be allowed before requesting a student's response, particularly when high cognitive level questions are asked. Teachers should try to encourage students to respond in some way to each question asked and balance responses from volunteering and nonvolunteering students. They should also try to elicit a high percentage of correct answers from students, acknowledge correct responses from students, use praise specifically and discriminately, and assist with incorrect responses. Call outs should be permitted in low socioeconomic status classes and suppressed in high socioeconomic classes, especially in elementary settings (Wilen & Clegg, 1987).

After the students respond, teacher follow up moves should include (a) probing questions that help them clarify ideas, support a point of view, or extend their thinking, and (b) guiding responses that let students voice their ideas while simultaneously giving the teacher opportunities to guide student thinking. See the middle section of Table 3.2 for a summary of the discourse moves that characterize this participant framework (Henning & Lockhart, 2003; Henning, 2005).

As illustrated in the right hand column of Table 3.2 and described previously in chapter 1, teachers can create even more open participant frameworks by asking fewer questions or by not asking any questions. In place of asking a focus question to begin the discussion, the teacher can simply invite students to participate by saying "Let's discuss . . ." Within this participant framework, the teacher makes very few comments, the level of student-to-student interaction is very high, and student comments provide the direction for the discussion. The teacher's follow up moves offer only minimal guidance to the discussion: the teacher may make a statement, provide for a student question, give a signal that acknowledges the student comment, or maintain a respectful silence.

The degree to which a teacher provides guidance for a discussion depends on her purpose. If a higher level of student participation and engagement is desired, then less direction should be provided. Rushing to achieve the curricular goals too quickly may

TABLE 3.2 A Comparison of Participant Frameworks

	Convergent (Closed) ◄———————►		Divergent (Open)
Teacher to student interaction	Increased teacher talk		Increased student talk
	Primarily teacher to individual student interaction		Increased student-to-student interaction
Teacher initiations	Recall/remember questions	Divergent questions	Questions replaced by broad invitations
Student responses	Convergent student responses	Divergent student responses	Highly divergent student responses
Teacher follow up moves	Confirm/reject	Repeat	Make a statement
		Reformulate	Provide for a student
		Elaborate	Give a signal
		Explain	Maintain a silence
		Cue	Paraphrase
		Recapitulate	Describe state of mind
		Ask probing questions	

Adapted from Henning (2005).

cost some insight into student thinking and perhaps some truly original thinking. On the other hand, if a critical content objective must be achieved, then the teacher may guide the discussion in that direction and provide more support as students engage with unfamiliar ideas. Both teachers and their students want to feel as if the discussion led somewhere, as if they accomplished something.

Analyzing Participant Frameworks

Teachers can analyze their participant frameworks by listening to audiotapes of their teaching, watching videotapes of their teaching, or by examining transcriptions of audio or videotape recordings of their teaching. Analyzing participant frameworks involves applying the information presented in chapters 1–3. Through this analysis, teachers can become more aware of their current interaction patterns and then use that information to improve instruction.

When conducting an analysis, it is important to know that identifying specific discourse moves can be messy. Although the categories described in this chapter are useful, at times it can be difficult to discern the difference between comments, e.g., distinguishing a reformulation from a repetition followed by an elaboration. In part, this occurs because teachers often try to accomplish many different purposes simultaneously. Thus, it is not hard to imagine a teacher confirming, reformulating, and elaborating within the space of a single follow up comment. Fortunately, it is not critically important that teachers are able to sort out every type of comment at the same level of precision as an educational researcher. Teachers can choose the degree of precision at which they would like to conduct their analysis. But at whatever level it is conducted, the analysis can reveal patterns of interaction based on the discourse moves of teachers and students.

What Teachers Need to Know

Knowing which discourse moves lead to increased student talking is an essential first step for improving your discussions. A wide variety of choices is available to teachers, as illustrated in chapters 1–3. An accomplished discussion leader has the ability to use the right discourse move in the right context. While is it difficult to pinpoint an ideal pattern of teacher discourse, in general, a richer and more varied teacher dialogue allows the students more opportunities to participate and greater control over the discussion. Repeatedly employing a limited range of discourse moves is a likely indication that further improvement is possible. When examining your practice, it is not necessary that you precisely determine each and every type of discourse move you employ. But it is important that you can recognize the broader patterns described in this chapter. Becoming more aware of your discourse patterns gives you a greater capacity to change them.

Application Discussion

Below is a transcript excerpt from Ms. Lowell's classroom discussion of *Pinballs*. Each discourse move in the transcript has been numbered. As you read through the transcript, use the list of terms given below, Table 3.1, and/or any other information presented in this chapter to identify each of these discourse moves. Write your response in the numbered blanks below. After you have finished, discuss the following questions.

1. Which of the three participant frameworks in Table 3.1 would best describe the transcript excerpt below?
2. What changes in the discourse moves of the teacher could be made to increase student participation?
3. What discourse moves would make the discussion more teacher directed and could cause participation to decrease?

| focus question | confirmation | reformulation | cue |
| probing question | rejection | repetition | elaboration |

Ms. Lowell:	1. What is the relationship between Kentucky Fried Chicken and child neglect in Harvey's life? 2. What does it mean if you neglect something? 3. If you have a pet and you are neglecting it, it means that you are not doing what?
S:	Taking good care of it.
Ms. Lowell:	4. You're not taking good care of it. 5. So what do you think child neglect is? 6. Casey?
S:	Something that you um . . . remember from your childhood?
Ms. Lowell:	7. No, not really hon. Good guess though.
S:	Not taking good care of it.
Ms. Lowell:	8. Yeah, 9. not taking good care of a child. 10. That's what child neglect is. 11. So what is the connection between Kentucky Fried Chicken, child neglect, and Harvey? 12. Those 3 things kinda fit together in a triangle and what is it that makes those things fit together? 13. Why are they all related? 14. Elana, what did you say?
S:	Kentucky Fried Chicken was the light of Harvey's life because whenever his dad was late from work Harvey would go get some Kentucky Fried Chicken and child neglect was related to Harvey's life because his father neglected him.
Ms. Lowell:	15. Yeah, 16. his father really didn't take good care of him. So when his father was late, it was easy for Harvey to go on over across the street to Kentucky Fried Chicken. So that's the way that they're connected. 17. Very good. 18. What did you have?

| S: | Harvey liked Kentucky Fried Chicken because every single time his father wasn't there he went. That is how child neglect and Kentucky Fried Chicken are in Harvey's life. |
| *Ms. Lowell:* | 19. Good. 20. And you. |

1. _____

2. _____

3. _____

4. _____

5. _____

6. _____

7. _____

8. _____

9. _____

10. _____

11. _____

12. _____

13. _____

14. _____

15. _____

16. _____

17. _____

18. _____

19. _____

20. _____

Activities

1. Analyze an audio or videotape of one of your classroom discussions. Determine the level of student participation and the types of discourse moves you currently use. Then determine what discourse moves you could add to your repertoire. Write a reflection paper that shares your findings.

2. Develop a plan for a discussion that incorporates some of the discourse moves that you are not currently using.

Study Group Activities

3. Bring a videotape to share with your study group. Target a specific portion of the discussion (about five to ten minutes in length) for the group to analyze. If you have analyzed this videotape previously, see if your interpretation matches the other members of the group.

4. If you are unable or prefer not to share a videotape of your teaching with your study group, then write a reflection paper based on an audio or videotape of one of your class discussions. Share the paper with the study group. Ask for new interpretations of your data and some suggestions for new strategies.

part two
Guiding and Creating Discussions

The second section of the book will address guiding and creating discussions. Chapter 4 will show you how the individual discourse moves you learned in the first three chapters can be combined into larger patterns of discussion. These patterns provide templates for either leading students to new concepts or discussing applications of newly learned concepts in real world settings. Being aware of these larger discussion patterns will make it easier for you to anticipate student responses, to maximize student participation, and to meet your curricular objectives. Chapter 5 will show you how to create a favorable environment for discussions using four specific approaches: responding to a problem, responding to an observation, responding to a reading, and reflecting on an activity. These four approaches will enable you to generate new discussions in diverse contexts with widely varying subject matter. Students of any grade level or subject area will respond enthusiastically to a discussion that has been well framed and for which they have been well prepared.

four

Guiding Discussions

Framing Discussion

The teacher reflection below is taken from a seventh grade geography discussion. In this reflection, Mr. Stolzman has italicized his students' comments and underlined his own thoughts. As you read through this reflection, notice how Mr. Stolzman's intentions and discourse moves change. Compare the difference between the discourse moves he makes at the beginning and the end of the transcript excerpt. Can you identify a pattern to his discourse moves? After you finish reading, answer the following questions.

1. How did Mr. Stolzman prepare his students for this discussion?
2. What kind of teacher discourse moves do you notice in this excerpt?
3. Does Mr. Stolzman ask questions? Where in the discussion does he ask questions, near the beginning or the end?
4. What do you notice about the students' participation and their ability to elaborate? Is there a high student to teacher ratio of talking?
5. What kind of follow up moves does Mr. Stolzman use?
6. Consider the participant frameworks (teacher invitation to speak, student response, and teacher follow up) in this discussion. Is the discussion more open (encouraging more student participation) or more closed (teacher directed)?
7. Is the discussion more open at the beginning or the end of the transcript?

Purpose and Desired Outcomes

This purpose of this discussion was to compare Bangladesh and the United States in terms of disaster preparedness. It was the final activity in a lesson that focused on the affect of preparedness on the consequences of natural hazards from place to place. We started with the Weather I.Q. Fun Quiz to get the learners thinking about weather hazards such as thunderstorms, hurricanes, and tornadoes. Next, we studied a graph that recorded where people died as a result of natural hazards. Then we discussed a table that recorded the death toll of selected storms from the twentieth century. The students worked in groups to read articles about deadly storms in Bangladesh, and we recorded the reasons mentioned on the board. This part of the lesson concluded with the students ranking the causes in terms of their contribution to loss of life in Bangladesh.

The discussion I videotaped took place after the students read an article describing the steps Bangladesh and the United States took to prepare for typhoons or hurricanes. The students received a graph that identified five categories and were asked to analyze each country's effectiveness in each category. They were asked to think about wealth, technology, government action, public education, cultural beliefs, and economic development. A one meant the student felt the country was not very prepared or effective in that area, and a five meant they were very prepared. They completed the graph outside of class. We had this discussion at the beginning of class. The students shared their rankings and explained why they made the decisions they did. The desired outcome was for the students to see that the different countries approach a similar natural hazard in very different ways. The students need to understand that both countries have problems but that Bangladesh is mainly concerned with saving lives and the United States can usually avoid major loss of life but property damage remains high.

Participants

I teach 100 seventh grade geography students at West Middle School in Anamosa, Iowa. This group of twenty-one students meets from 12:50 until 1:36 five days a week after lunch.

Setting

Geography is one of the five core classes that seventh graders take every day for fifty minutes. We are in our eighth unit out of nine called South and East Asia: Natural Hazards and Populations. These units are designed around the geographic inquiry method. Each lesson centers on a question, and this lesson is the last lesson in the unit. The students are given more evidence as the lesson develops to develop answers to the questions.

Assessment of Student and Teacher Discourse

This interaction could be best described as whole class interaction. These students had completed an assignment and were asked to share the decisions they made and their reasons for making them. I have put my commentary on the student discourse in italics and underlined my comments on myself.

Dialogue

Mr. Stolzman:	(1) Let's discuss how you think the United States compares to Bangladesh in terms of control works. <u>With this sentence I set the stage for our discussion.</u>
Sally:	What are control works?
Mr. Stolzman:	(2) Bridges, dams, flood walls . . . things that control floodwater. <u>I had taught this concept the day before when we started to fill out the chart so I gave a clear but quick explanation.</u>
Sarah:	I put the U.S. up high. Because we are prepared for everything because we have to have it in order to build places even if there aren't floods but because we have it we are prepared for floods. *The nature of this assignment asked the students to make a decision based on evidence. This discussion allowed them to elaborate on their ideas. I thought this first student gave a thoughtful answer with appropriate justifications.*
Mr. Stolzman:	(3) Okay. <u>At this point I wanted to affirm the student's comment but not judge it.</u>
Steve:	We have a lot to build.
Mr. Stolzman:	(4) So you are saying just sheer quantity we have a lot. Okay. <u>I saw this as a new idea and I restated it to make sure I understood correctly. These three comments reflect that I was trying to make sure that everyone heard the ideas and affirm the students, but I was trying to refrain from building on the comments to encourage student participation.</u>
Sarah:	And we have the money to do it. *Here is an example of co-construction of knowledge. Sarah agreed with Steve and added a new piece of evidence to support the original idea.*
Mr. Stolzman:	And we have the money to do it. Dave.
Dave:	I didn't rank it quite as high because we don't like some of the like we don't have? Sometimes it doesn't work and that's the funny thing so I didn't rank it quite as high as a five. *Dave realized he has a slightly different position and introduced a new idea to defend it.*

Mr. Stolzman:	(5) All right, so you kept it down from a five because sometimes it doesn't work, that's basically what you are saying. We have some ideas that build on that.
Ron:	Um I didn't get mine done but I wouldn't have put it that high because a lot of things they built nowadays aren't perfectly put together because they are built so fast that it doesn't always stay together. *Ron seemed to be building on the comments of Dave but did not verbally express that connection.*
Mr. Stolzman:	(6) More than Dave you are kind of talking about the quality of what they build. <u>With this comment, I am trying to help the student connect her idea to another student.</u>
Mandy:	I had a four because we have it but the quality isn't the best.
Mr. Stolzman:	(7) One thing that you guys have made me think of is sometimes the stuff it just gets old, we had it and it worked for a while but it's older and maybe it won't work anymore. <u>This is an example of co-construction in that it builds on the students' ideas and is intended to take them to a new place. It also models the thinking process.</u>
Sarah:	But there are a lot of sturdy materials like concrete and stuff. *Sarah continued to defend her position by adding new evidence to the discussion.*
Mr. Stolzman:	(8) So you're going back to the idea of the quality of the material to start with. Okay.
Steve:	When it comes to age though . . . the Hoover Dam is really old and it like it still holds. *Steve is integrating previous knowledge with the current topic.*
Mr. Stolzman:	(9) It still works really well because they have maintained it put a lot of money into it . . .
Craig:	. . . it just depends on what materials it's made of . . .
Alison:	. . . and how old they are getting . . . *On the tape, these students were making good eye contact and commenting directly on each other's ideas.* <u>My words helped link the students' thoughts together.</u>
Mr. Stolzman:	(10) Okay. Bangladesh. Anyone want to say anything about the control works in Bangladesh? <u>This question reframes the dialogue and moves the class to the next section on the work sheet.</u>
Dave:	I ranked mine a little bit above low. They do have some things and they work sometimes. *This is a very vague comment but it got the discussion started.*
Mandy:	I have mine ranked at a two because they are trying but ??

Mr. Stolzman:	(11) There's some good evidence there.
	<u>This is an expression of appreciation for the student's thought process.</u>
Bridget:	I have mine at a three because they are trying but they don't have the money to spare.
	Bridget hinted at some of the information we had learned in a previous lesson on poverty in Bangladesh.
Mr. Stolzman:	(12) So their limitation it's not about desire but it's about ability about being to afford it. Okay, the next one was about building design and construction. This would be the same idea this would be homes and public buildings. Building design and construction.
	<u>The purpose of this comment is to connect Bridget's ideas to the content and to move the dialogue to the next category.</u>
Sarah:	I ranked mine at a four because we have pretty sturdy homes. Houses can last a long time but sometimes it's crumbly, cheap on the inside.
Mr. Stolzman:	(13) What else?
	<u>This question was intended to explore the group's thinking.</u>
Larry:	I put mine between four and five. We have been trying to advance the technology to keep everybody safe but we're still not there yet.
	Larry synthesized this lesson with a lesson on precautions developed countries like Japan were taking to increase safety through the use of technology.
Mr. Stolzman:	(14) So you're saying there is more that can be done. What about Bangladesh?
Mandy:	I have mine really low. Their house quality are made of straw and bamboo. They don't have a lot of money.
	Here is another argument with a justification.
Mr. Stolzman:	(15) They are very temporary aren't they?
	<u>This question asks the students to make inferences about the comment that was just said.</u>
Craig:	I think the reason they are temporary is because they don't want them to get knocked down during the typhoon so they have to spend a lot of money to rebuild them.
	Craig introduced a new perspective into the discussion. The idea that this type of home was easy to replace was not in the source material.
Mr. Stolzman:	(16) If their temporary shelters get knocked down it's not that big a deal.
Steve:	I didn't even have that one down because I don't think they (qualify as) houses.
Sarah:	For Craig it would be better to lose something you didn't put much work into rather than to be iffy about something they spent a lot of money on.

This is the first time a student directly identified whose idea she is responding to.

Mr. Stolzman: (17) Right. Right. Yeah. I think that's the point he was making.
                <u>These comments affirm what the student said and help make the connection between the two students' ideas.</u>

Ron: I don't think that is right. I think they try to make their houses nice but look at what they have to work with. They don't have a lot of money so they can't make their houses as nice as ours.

Craig: They have a lot of people.

Ron: Most of the time they make their own houses. They don't have other people constructing them, as perfect, as well constructed, as they should be so you have to give them credit.

Annie: They are trying to make them level.
                This is in reference to the reading, but the student took the information out of context.

Mr. Stolzman: (18) They have thought about that. Now remember that was more for just the regular storms. It doesn't necessarily do much when you get a major typhoon. What about, no one really has talked about building codes. In the United States . . .
                <u>At this point, Annie has used a piece of evidence to suggest they are doing what they can to protect their houses. I wanted to remind the students that this measure may be helpful in a typical storm but would have little impact on the floodwaters associated with a hurricane. The second part of my comment was designed to introduce the idea of government policy into our discussion.</u>

Stephanie: 52205

Mr. Stolzman: (19) What's that?

Stephanie: 52205

Mr. Stolzman: (20) What's that?

Stephanie: A building code, I don't know.

Mr. Stolzman: (21) That's a zip code. Where they tell you how to build a building.
                <u>Here I used an explanation to clear up a misconception.</u>

Dave: They have that so (inaudible) have like certain people (inaudible).

Mr. Stolzman: (22) That would be for earthquakes. They don't have that standard here do they?
                <u>I restated Dave's response and reformulated it into a question.</u>

Craig: Like the Sears Tower in Chicago that's built to sway because of the high winds.
                Here Craig showed flexibility in his thinking and making a comparison to a situation he has first hand experience with.

Mr. Stolzman: (23) That's built for that reason not for earthquakes. On the coast especially the West Coast where that's more likely it's worth spending the extra money to do that. So that's in the code there . . . you have to do that. We attach our rafters to our homes a certain way. In Florida they attach them a different way so they can withstand all the winds from a hurricane. It's not because they think "Oh, that's a good idea." It's because the government says you have to do this or you're going to pay big fines. My question for Anamosa. Is there a building code now for new buildings in Anamosa?

Again, I start by clarifying Craig's comment and then I start to add information to our discussion. I end my comments with a question that gives the students an opportunity to compare my comments to their own experience.

Assessment of Student Discourse

I did not include the entire dialogue but, in the end, fourteen of my twenty-one students willingly participated and two others commented after I called on them. Those that did not participate were enthusiastic and many actively listened. I have identified several examples of elaboration. The students were able to defend their rankings. The discussion also shows evidence of synthesis as students tied their ideas about the United States and their personal observations to the information they read about Bangladesh. They also brought up ideas mentioned in others parts of the unit. I also found evidence that they were analyzing the information to make their decisions and building on each other's ideas. I would like to see more evidence of conceptual knowledge. The question at the beginning about what are control works suggested a lack of understanding related to different categories. More widespread was the lack of discussion of government policies, education, beliefs, and economic development. Instead, the responses seemed to be limited to wealth and technology.

Assessment of Teacher Discourse

After analyzing the dialogue, I feel that I successfully encouraged dialogue with affirmation, but not confirmation. As a result, the dialogue flowed with very few questions. I would use this tool to reframe the dialogue or to push deeper into topic. The students were able to build off my ideas as well as each other's. Beside some vocabulary, I did not use this opportunity to model discourse. I think my explanations were clear and clearly connected to course content.

Reflections

This discussion went very well. Having the students decide how to rank the countries gave them a position so they came to the discussion with an argument for their position.

I think using small groups before this discussion that are focused on the different conceptual areas might help make the arguments stronger. Also, as I think more about the student discourse skills, I will be more deliberate about identifying them as I see them. For example, if I noticed a student had an effective response, I might say, "You did a nice job of elaborating on your answer because you gave supporting evidence." I am working on making this a part of my day-to-day discourse with students not just for this particular activity.

Introduction

You may recall that two transcript excerpts with distinctly different patterns of discourse were compared at the beginning of the previous chapter. The first one was characterized by fewer teacher questions, fewer evaluative teacher follow up moves, and a higher ratio of student to teacher talk. The second one was characterized by more teacher questions, more evaluative teacher follow up moves, more teacher elaboration, and a greater quantity of mathematical concepts and vocabulary in the student responses. Both of these discourse patterns are combined above in Mr. Stolzman's teacher reflection.

Toward the beginning of the discussion, Mr. Stolzman deliberately tries to avoid asking questions and making evaluative follow up moves, as part of his goal to maximize student participation. Later in the discussion, he asks more questions and provides more guidance in order to introduce information overlooked by the students. His discourse moves have changed from the beginning to the end of the discussion in order to accomplish two competing goals: maximize student involvement and introduce new learning.

All teachers generally try to accomplish these two goals during a discussion, regardless of the subject area or grade level. When only one of these goals is met, the discussion fails, either due to the lack of student participation or because the learning goals are not achieved. Roby (1988) has described these two types of discussion failures as "bull sessions" and "quiz shows." A bull session is a discussion in which teachers ask divergent questions that engage students, but the discussion does little to extend existing student knowledge. Both teacher and students share answers that can't be wrong because they are rooted in the personal experience of the discussants. During a quiz show, the teacher asks convergent questions that initiate the IRE participant framework, i.e., a recall question, a short answer by the student, and an evaluative follow up by the teacher. The students give short answers based on their recall knowledge; they don't elaborate or engage at the higher levels of Bloom's taxonomy, and there is very little student-to-student interaction during the discussion.

Simultaneously accomplishing the two competing goals of eliciting student participation and reaching the curricular objectives requires moving through different phases of the discussion. These phases follow predictable patterns and, if you understand them, then you can better anticipate and follow up on student responses. An awareness of discussion patterns can also help you avoid bull sessions and quiz shows, as well as facilitate your ability to create and design new discussions, a topic that will be addressed in chapter 5.

Convergent and Divergent Discussion Patterns

Divergent to Convergent Pattern of Discourse Moves

The teacher reflection at the beginning of the chapter is a good example of a divergent to convergent pattern of discourse moves. The discussion moves from very open, student centered, divergent discourse moves to relatively more leading, teacher directed, convergent discourse moves. This approach encourages maximal student participation and involvement at the beginning of the discussion. For example, you might begin by asking a divergent question, or perhaps by offering an even broader invitation to speak, such as "Let's discuss . . ..."

The initial question or invitation should elicit multiple student responses, which will provide the teacher with several alternatives. For instance, you can choose to follow up on one of these student answers in more depth, or recap two or three student responses as a way of setting a direction for the discussion, or simply let the student comments continue to set the direction for the discussion. If you choose to follow one of the student answers, you may use probing questions to more deeply explore that direction. If you select two or three student answers, you may revoice those answers through a reformulation or a recap in order to set the new direction. If you decide to let students set the direction of the discussion, you may use one of Dillon's alternatives to asking questions, such as maintaining silence, giving a signal, or making a statement.

During this early phase of the discussion, the teacher might choose to ask very few questions and provide only minimal guidance through follow up comments, e.g., make a statement or provide for a question. Then, as student input begins to decline or time becomes short, the teacher may decide to offer more guidance by asking more probing questions, providing more cues, and making guiding responses, such as repetitions, reformulations, and elaborations. The first part of the discussion enables a high level of student participation: in the latter part of the discussion, the learning goals can be achieved

Convergent to Divergent Discourse Moves

Discussions can also move in the opposite direction, from convergent to divergent discourse moves. In other words, they can begin with more closed, teacher directed, convergent discourse moves and then move to more open, student centered, divergent responses. This pattern would begin with questions on the knowledge level of Bloom's taxonomy, then move to more questions on the synthesis, analysis, or evaluation levels (Wilen, 1990). For example, the direction of the discussion at the beginning of the chapter could be reversed to fit a convergent to divergent discussion. In that case, Mr. Stolzman might begin the discussion by asking the class some factual questions regarding disasters in Bangladesh and the United States, such as which country experienced the most disasters, which country spent the most money on disasters, and can you summarize the differences in disaster preparation between the two countries. After establishing a firm foundation of facts, the teacher could then begin to ask more divergent, interpretive questions, such as asking the students to evaluate the strengths and weaknesses of each country's disaster policy or to create a new disaster policy for each country.

Summary

To accomplish the dual goals of maximizing student engagement and introducing new learning, the teacher can move the discussion between more convergent and more divergent discourse moves. Discussions can either move from more divergent (open) to more convergent (closed) discourse moves or from more convergent to more divergent discourse moves. When moving from more convergent to more divergent discourse moves, the discussion moves from more to less teacher guidance. When moving in the opposite direction, from more divergent to more convergent discourse moves, the discussion moves from less to more teacher guidance.

Inductive and Deductive Discussions

Inductive Discussions

A second discussion pattern is based on the relationship between the direction of the discussion and student knowledge. For example, in an inductive discussion, students move intellectually from their everyday experience to more formal concepts (such as formulas, scientific laws, constitutional principles). Student participation is maximized near the beginning of the discussion, where student knowledge is high. As an inductive discussion proceeds toward new learning or new concepts, teacher guidance will increase in most circumstances. An inductive discussion can begin with any kind of medium that will serve as a vehicle for eliciting previous student experience, e.g., a controversial issue, an observation, or a story.

For example, in social studies, listening to a controversial Eminem song could lead to a discussion about the importance of civil liberties, such as the protections and limitations of the First Amendment. Including Eminem within the discussion has placed at least part of the discussion in more familiar terms for the students. Thus, students may be more willing to participate and will probably be able to make more extended comments in response to the teacher's questions. In addition, the subject matter lends itself to multiple points of view and therefore enables diverse student responses. Finally, the topic has been carefully selected because of its relevance to the First Amendment, thus creating an appropriate context for deepening students' understanding of their First Amendment Rights.

In English, the teacher could begin by eliciting divergent student responses to a short story, then gently guide the discussion toward the story's theme. In math, the teacher could ask the students to solve a problem using estimation, rules of thumb, or counting strategies, then gradually move them toward a formula. In science, the teacher could base a discussion on a series of experimental observations. The discussion might begin by asking students what they observed, followed by a series of probing questions intended to move students to a deeper understanding of what they have seen.

Deductive Discussions

The purpose of a deductive discussion is to apply new learning to a real world application. For example, the teacher reflection at the beginning of the chapter describes a discussion in which students were asked to apply their newly learned concepts on disaster preparedness. New learning could include a new concept: a skill, a definition, a formula, a maxim, or a principle. Applying new learning in a practical setting can enrich and extend student understanding by helping students make connections between formal concepts and their applications in real world settings.

In social studies, a deductive discussion could begin with a reading from a text on the First Amendment, which is then applied to a discussion on censorship in schools or other First Amendment issues. In English, a deductive discussion could apply the formal definition of flat and round character to better interpret a character's role in a short story. In math, a deductive discussion could be constructed around how to use a formula for surface area to construct the least expensive deck patio. In science, a deductive discussion could use Boyle's Law to interpret the results of an experiment involving heat and pressure.

Summary

Discussions that move from student experience to new learning are called inductive discussions; discussions that move from new learning to real world applications are called deductive discussions. When planning inductive discussion patterns, teachers anticipate guiding their students from their previous experience to some form of new learning such as a concept or idea. When planning deductive discussions, teachers anticipate guiding their students from a newly learned concept to an application of the concept in a real world setting.

Understanding the directions in which discussions move can make it easier for teachers to invent new discussions or redesign existing ones, such as converting a deductive discussion into an inductive discussion and vice versa. By analyzing or reflecting on your current discussion patterns, you may find that you have a tendency to favor one particular kind of pattern. If so, you could open up the conversation in your classroom by experimenting with a different pattern, by either designing new discussions or redesigning existing ones. For example, the deductive discussion described in the teacher reflection at the beginning of the chapter could be converted to an inductive discussion by introducing the discussion earlier in the unit. In this case, the teacher would introduce the students to a situation or a set of facts related to disaster preparedness in Bangladesh and the United States, then use a discussion to guide their discovery of key elements of disaster preparation such as wealth, technology, government policies, education, beliefs, and economic development. With two approaches to accomplishing the same outcomes, you can choose to use one or the other, or use them both so that each complements the other.

Combining Discussion Patterns

The purpose of introducing discussion patterns has been to provide teachers with some general guidance for planning purposes. However, these descriptions are not intended to impose rigid guidelines. They are intended only as a rough template to be supplemented by your creative impulses as you improvise your way through a maze of unpredictable student responses. At any given point during a discussion, a teacher may try to elicit more student participation by asking divergent questions or, conversely, to establish a knowledge base by asking a string of factual questions. For example, a science teacher could move from divergent to convergent to divergent teacher discourse moves by asking divergent questions to elicit student participation about their observations of an experiment, followed by convergent probing questions designed to ascertain the relevant factual information, and concluding with more divergent questions that invite students to analyze and synthesize those facts into a hypothesis or an explanation. In the four sections below, the convergent/divergent and inductive/deductive discussion patterns described previously are combined in multiple ways. These combinations are intended to illustrate the potential complexity of classroom discussion patterns.

Inductive Discussion: Divergent to Convergent Discourse Moves

Inductive discussions often begin with divergent teacher elicitations and then move to more convergent ones. This is because it is common for inductive discussions to begin within the personal experience of the student, where student knowledge is high, thus requiring less teacher guidance. As new learning is introduced, more teacher guidance is needed. A previous example of an inductive discussion that moves from divergent to convergent responses is the industrial technology teacher's reflection at the beginning of chapter 2. In this reflection, the teacher begins with very open-ended questions about the safety features on cars before moving to more focused, probing questions concerning specific features. The open-ended questions are intended to elicit the students' current knowledge, and the more focused questions are intended to lead students to new knowledge.

Inductive Discussion: Convergent to Divergent Discourse Moves

Inductive discussions could also move in a convergent to divergent direction. In a science or math class, the students could make a series of observations about an experiment or a graph. In a social studies or English class, the students could respond to reading a narrative. The teacher could begin the discussion by asking recall questions to check the students' factual knowledge. After a factual basis has been established, the teacher gradually begins to move up Bloom's taxonomy by asking more divergent, higher level questions. These questions require students to apply, synthesize, and evaluate the facts previously established during the initial phase of the discussion.

Deductive Discussion: Divergent to Convergent Discourse Moves

Deductive discussions can also move from more divergent to convergent discourse moves. An example would be the teacher reflection at the beginning of this chapter. The teacher began with a very broad invitation for students to speak (see Mr. Stolzman (1) above), "Let's discuss how you think the United States compares to Bangladesh in terms of control works." In response to this initial elicitation, student participation was widespread, and the teacher limited his follow up moves to brief acknowledgments and restatements of student comments. As the discussion progressed, the teacher gradually began to ask some probing questions and add information through elaborations (see Mr. Stolzman (10)–(23) above). Thus, the students were informed by their classmates in the initial phase of the discussion and then by the teacher's contributions during the second phase of the discussion.

Deductive Discussion: Convergent to Divergent Discourse Moves

In a deductive discussion that moves from convergent to divergent discourse moves, the teacher could begin by reviewing the students' understanding of a recently learned concept. The concept could have been learned through reading a text, a lecture, or an inductive discussion based on an activity. The initial questions would be based on recall knowledge of the concept or principle. After reviewing the concept, the teacher would ask students more divergent, higher level questions on Bloom's taxonomy. These questions would require students to apply, synthesize, and evaluate the facts previously established during the initial phase of the discussion.

What Teachers Need to Know

Teachers need to know that discussions must move through different phases to satisfy the twin goals of maximizing student participation and introducing new learning. This movement can be broadly described in two ways. The first is according to a gradual change in discourse moves. Discussions can move from divergent (higher student participation) to convergent discourse moves (more teacher guidance), or they can move in the opposite direction, from convergent to divergent discourse moves. The second is in relation to student knowledge. Teachers can either plan to start discussions with the previous experience of students and move to new learning, or ask students to apply new learning in a real world setting. These two larger patterns of discussion can serve as helpful templates for guiding and planning discussions. However, it is also true that, in practice, teachers mix, expand, contract, or combine discourse into different patterns to achieve their learning objectives.

Guiding students from their personal experience to new learning is challenging both pedagogically and in regards to content knowledge. In regards to pedagogy, teachers must be able to anticipate the parts of the discussion in which students will require more and less guidance. In regards to content knowledge, teachers need to know how to locate their subject matter within the students' preexisting knowledge base and then to understand the content well enough to provide step-by-step guidance as students discover it through discussion. The effectiveness of any discussion depends in good part on the teacher's ability to incorporate the curriculum into the everyday world of students. Teachers who can effectively address both the pedagogy and the content are well positioned to balance the competing goals of maximizing student participation while simultaneously fostering new learning.

Application Discussion

Below is a teacher's reflection on a discussion from her fourth grade science classroom. As you read, try to identify whether this is an inductive or a deductive discussion. To answer this question, you must determine whether the discussion is moving from student experience to a new concept (inductive discussion) or whether students are applying a newly learned concept in a real world setting (deductive discussion). Also try to ascertain whether the discussion moves in a divergent (more open) to convergent direction (more closed), or in the opposite direction, from convergent to divergent discourse moves. After you have finished reading, discuss the following questions.

1. What is the teacher's purpose for this discussion, to lead students to a new concept or to apply an already learned concept? Does she intend this to be an inductive or a deductive discussion?
2. What kind of discourse moves does the teacher employ?
3. In one place, the teacher feels she was rejecting too many student answers. How could she have taken a different approach?
4. If you were leading the discussion, what would you want your students to know at the end of the lesson and how would you use that knowledge base in future lessons?
5. Is this pattern of discussion familiar to you? Share your experiences with similar discussion patterns that you have led or in which you have participated.

Purpose and Setting

The lesson that will be discussed in this paper is an introductory lesson to the Foss Science Kit, *Magnetism and Electricity*. There were two main purposes to this lesson. The first was to get all students involved in the discussion. To accomplish this task, a game would be introduced that is similar to the twenty questions game the class has already played. One student would be in charge of describing a magnet that is in a bag, and the rest of the class was to try to figure out what it was. Since this was introduced as a game, it is expected that the students who are least likely to participate in science discussions will find this a safer environment in which to participate. The second purpose was to draw on previous knowledge and create a new knowledge base that we could draw from in future lessons. This would be accomplished by guiding the end of the discussion with cued elicitations toward the student knowledge about magnets and what magnets are attracted to.

Participants

This activity was completed by all students in one fourth grade classroom. There were twenty-four students total. This class is a fully integrated science class with nineteen general education students, one resource student, and four mainstreamed students. Their ability levels range from mid-first grade to sixth grade. Of the twenty-four students, seventeen participated in the verbal discussion. All of the students participated in the drawing piece and the experimentation portion of the lesson.

Assessment of Discourse

When planning this lesson, I was hoping for an open discussion between the students in the class. In analyzing the discussion, I found that the students were making attempts at an open discussion, yet the teacher continued to make confirmations or rejections at the beginning.

S1:	It is hard, smooth; uh . . . I don't know.
T:	Stay here . . . Bria.
S2:	Ball?
T:	No.
S3:	Washer.
T:	No.
S4:	Battery.
T:	No.

After the discussion had been going on for two or three minutes, the students took over and student one took on the role the teacher had played at the beginning, making confirmations and rejections.

S5:	A candle?
S6:	Light bulb?
S7:	Uh . . . is it about that big? Robby.
S8:	Is it bumpy?
S1:	No, Dennis.
S7:	Is it kinda scratchy?

S1:	Can't really tell. Jamie.
S9:	Is it little or big?
S1:	Medium. Dennis.
S7:	What is the shape of it?
T:	Good question.
S1:	Circle. Sabrina.
S10:	A rock?
S11:	A bolt?

This is the point when the lesson needed to begin to close so that all the students could end the lesson with the same knowledge base. To begin this process, the teacher had the students recap what they knew so far; then, to make sure everyone was participating had everyone draw a picture of what they thought was in the bag. After the pictures were drawn, the discourse became a series of elicitations and elaborations.

S3:	It has 2 circles. Ummm . . .
T:	Describe its size.
S3:	It is like maybe an inch.
T:	How thick is it? Think of something to compare it to.
S3:	Um . . .it is about as thick as an eraser.
S15:	It is a magnet.
T:	How do you know?
S15:	Because I have seen them.
T:	But from just looking at it can you tell it's a magnet? I'm going to give each one of you one of these and I want you to observe it. Look, play, and touch.
S3:	It's a magnet. Everyone is sticking it to their desks.
S9:	I though it was a wheel.

Some students began to analyze and synthesize what they were hearing and seeing in the classroom.

T:	But from just looking at it can you tell it's a magnet? I'm going to give each one of you one of these and I want you to observe it. Look, play, and touch.
S3:	It's a magnet. Everyone is sticking it to their desks.
S8:	It is a magnet.
T:	How do you know?
S8:	Because it sticks to my desk.

At the end of the lesson, students were elaborating on what objects the magnet would stick to. One student used synthesis to predict what other objects the magnet would stick to and why.

T:	Was there anything else Daniel gave us . . .. Okay, I'm going to hand out the green notebooks. On the back page draw a picture of what you think it is. You have 2 minutes.
S14:	Does everybody get to feel it?
T:	No. Be thinking what could be round and smooth as well as hard.
S8:	Where do we draw it?
T:	On the back . . . I see some people getting a picture drawn. Connor can you come up and give them another description.
S3:	It has 2 circles. Ummm . . .
T:	Describe its size.
S3:	It is like maybe an inch.
T:	How thick is it? Think of something to compare it to.
S3:	Um . . . it is about as thick as an eraser.
T:	Okay, turn off voices. Did everyone get something drawn? . . . It fits my hand, Connor was close when he guessed washer. It is the shape of a washer.
S15:	It is a magnet.
T:	How do you know?
S15:	Because I have seen them.
T:	But from just looking at it can you tell it's a magnet? I'm going to give each one of you one of these and I want you to observe it. Look, play, and touch.
S3:	It's a magnet. Everyone is sticking it to their desks.
S9:	I thought it was a wheel.
T:	Besides just tossing it on your desk what other things can you do to observe it?
S3:	How do you do that Trevor?
T:	Some people are making very good observations . . . Okay, now take this item and place it at the center of your desk on your name tag. So I can see it. What can you tell me about the item I gave you? Jamie.
S9:	It looks like wheel.
S8:	It is a magnet.
T:	How do you know?
S8:	Because it sticks to my desk?
T:	All parts of your desk?
S3:	Just to the metal.
T:	Jordan.
S16:	It rolls down your desk.

T:	Kristi.
S12:	It is black.
S6:	It will go on my pencil top.
T:	What do you mean by go on?
S6:	I don't know? Umm . . .
S7:	It is sticking to the pencil.
T:	Dennis has it. Were there other things that we could say it sticks to?
S3:	Rings on binder.
S2:	Chair.
S7:	The lid of my chap stick.
S17:	A paperclip I think.
T:	Why do you think it would stick to a paperclip?
S17:	Because it is metal?
T:	So what is an important thing about all of the items that your object stuck to? Jamie.
S9:	Metal is what it sticks to.
T:	They are all made of some kind of metal. Have you ever seen magnets before?

Activities

1. Think of five discussions you have led. Take a moment to visualize where your discussions began and what you wanted your students to understand by the end of the discussion. Write a short description of each discussion and, based on that description, decide whether the discussion was inductive or deductive. Support your answer by identifying key elements of the discussion associated with either inductive or deductive discussions.

2. If you have not led any discussions, try Activity #1 using discussions in which you have participated.

3. Create two new lesson plans, one for an inductive lesson and one for a deductive lesson.

4. Examine the description you created in the first or second activity. Do you find that you are more familiar with either the inductive or the deductive discussion? If so, how could you use the less familiar discussion pattern to create new discussions that you are currently not utilizing? Under what circumstances do you tend to use one instead of the other?

5. Pick one of the discussions which you described in Activity #1 or #2 and, using the information learned in this chapter, try to change it from a either a deductive to an inductive discussion or from an inductive to a deductive discussion.

Study Group Activity

6. Write a reflection paper for one of your discussions. Share your reflection papers in your study group. Explain whether your discussion was inductive or deductive and in what way your discussion pattern served your learning goals. Then discuss whether you have any tendencies for favoring one discussion pattern over the other, and then share some strategies for using your understanding of discussion patterns to create new discussions.

five
Creating Discussions

Framing Discussion

In the reflection paper below, a second grade teacher describes how she plans to start her discussion with an activity. As you read, try to identify the elements of the activity that are likely to encourage participation. After you finish reading, discuss the following questions.

1. How and why does the introduction of an activity change the nature of the lesson?
2. How does the teacher prepare her students for the discussion and what impact do her strategies have on student participation?
3. What kind of student responses does the teacher anticipate?
4. How does the teacher plan to encourage higher level thinking?
5. Will this be an inductive or a deductive discussion?
6. What does this teacher's reflection indicate about the relationship between activity and discussion? How can activities be used to increase student participation?

Background

From the first day I began working with my second grade students, I knew that I would need to develop and continually practice how to communicate appropriately within the classroom. My group of children came to school with a wide variety of backgrounds. They began demonstrating a habit of shouting to each other across the room and interrupting others. I have worked hard for two years on improving this constant interruption. Working through several management strategies, I finally found a simple one that works. Every time a child interrupts another person, I add a dot to my tally sheet by their name. At the end of the day, children graph their interruptions for the day. This is a way to monitor the behavior. By doing this management strategy, I am able to teach without a large number of interruptions. Others are allowed to learn without a classmate taking time away from them. When it is time for a discussion, I find that it takes a lot of modeling and directing for my students to understand what a discussion should look and sound like.

Lesson Description

In second grade, students are learning how to become more experienced readers and writers. The students are asked to no longer rely on "I like _____." sentences. In second grade, we "retire" these easy to use sentence starters. We begin talking about the parts of speech and what makes a good sentence and story. For example, what is a noun? Where does it belong in a sentence? Why do we need nouns? This can be a dry type of lesson and children are often overwhelmed. Students often confuse the various parts of speech. This causes them to shut down and become silent in later lessons/reviews about the parts of speech. Little conversation by students is made throughout these lessons. I would like to change this by adding a bit of a twist to the whole presentation on this topic.

In the lesson I propose, I am going to be teaching my students about adjectives, using Bubble-Yum bubble gum as a manipulative. In general, everyone enjoys eating. It is a good conversational piece for most people. My goal is that the students will be able to describe what an adjective is by the end of the lesson. I am hoping that they will all be able to relate to gum chewing, maybe having chewed it prior to this lesson, making the connection to something already in their background.

Restructuring the Lesson

To grab my students' attention, I will begin the lesson by chewing a piece of gum myself. Children are quick to point out anyone not following rules—I would be breaking a school rule by chewing gum. "How did you know I was chewing gum?" I would ask them. As they answer, I would begin jotting down their descriptive words. Next, I would hand them a piece of paper and ask that they begin writing down anything they know about gum. "I want you to write down any words that you can think of that describe gum." By giving clear explanations, the idea is stated clearly and students are able to begin working without confusion.

After a few minutes of independent work, I would like the students to break off into small groups to share their thoughts and ideas. I would wander the room asking questions to get the group discussing, not just reading the list of words they have written down. I would try to think of good questions that draw inferences and encourage thinking processes. "Why did you write that word down?" "If you were an elderly person do you think your list would be the same? How about a very young child chewing gum for his/her first time? Would your descriptive words change? What other words could you add?"

In these small groups, I would hope that the students would begin questioning each other. "Why did you write that gum smells fruity? Mine smells like mint." Hopefully, the listeners would relate someone else's descriptive words to their own. "You chose the word chewy. I said gum was tough, it makes my jaws hurt after a while. Would that be the same as your word chewy?" The type of gum each child was thinking of while writing would be an interesting comparison between the word choices on their lists. Would the adjectives be really different? Would two people who chose the same brand of gum have a comparative list of descriptive words? In these small groups, I would think that the participation would be pretty high. Each child would have an opportunity to brainstorm alone and then join a group with ideas already written down.

Upon completion of the small group work, I would invite all students to join in a whole class discussion. For some of my low esteem children, all the preparation (independent and small group work) for whole group talk would be important. As a large group, I would ask students to share their thoughts and ideas with everyone. "What words did you write down or think of while working independently or with a small group? What words describe gum for you?" To encourage students to participate appropriately, I might even offer a piece of bubble gum for their first time sharing with the group, but telling them to continue participating as much as they'd like.

After sharing a list of words that describe gum, I would make sure all children enjoyed their own piece of gum. At this point, I would begin the conceptual portion of the discussion. As the children touch and smell their gum, we would go through the list of words, checking for evaluation of the adjectives. I would continue the lesson, describing and explaining that they created a list of words that are called adjectives. Perhaps I would read from the dictionary the definition of an adjective. I am hoping that co-construction of knowledge will occur for my students by using gum as the familiarity to connect with the unfamiliar—adjectives.

At the conclusion of this lesson, I would ask that each child use their list of words to write a story about gum, using as many adjectives as possible. This would be a good assessment to evaluate students as they begin to use the words appropriately in each sentence. The gum chewing could be done at this time. Perhaps it would develop a few more adjectives for students to add to their lists. At the end of the writing process, I would ask students to share the adjective stories. This would allow for classmates to give feedback.

Expected Discourse

Chewing bubble gum is a fun activity that young children enjoy doing. I think that, by choosing an activity such as this, I would hear lots of on-task discussion. In this lesson, children would be able to see, feel, smell, and taste the gum. This would cause excitement for most students, and they would be very eager to get started. I think they would develop a great list of descriptive words. Gum is a topic about which I think my students would enjoy sharing adjective ideas/words with their friends.

Throughout the lesson, some students may need more prompting than others. "I see you have used many words to describe how the gum tastes. Can you think of words that use another one of your five senses?" Prompting and asking reflective questions may help everyone to be successful throughout the lesson.

Introduction

The teacher reflection above shows how introducing an activity can create a discussion-based lesson. As this reflection illustrates, the quality and quantity of student participation is often determined by what the teacher does before the discussion. The above plan for discussion will both engage students and meet the learning goals of the lesson, primarily because two conditions have been satisfied. First, the teacher has created an activity that enables multiple student answers to a single elicitation, i.e., there is more than one possible answer to the question. Second, the topic is positioned so that the students can elaborate by drawing on their previous knowledge. The first half of the chapter will explain how meeting these two requirements will enable more student participation.

The second half of the chapter will show how these two requirements can be met in classroom settings. Four specific approaches will be discussed, including responding to a problem, responding to an observation, responding to a text, and reflecting on an activity or a series of activities. These approaches are easily adaptable across many different subject areas and grade levels. Specific examples in this chapter will be given for social studies, English, math, and science.

Eliciting Multiple Student Responses

At the core of every argument is the element of uncertainty. Uncertainty or ambiguity allows for the expression of differing viewpoints of equal or comparable merit (in other words, there is no single "right" answer or at least not one that is immediately apparent). Some discussion topics seem inherently or naturally ambiguous, such as topics that address individual or social values. With other topics, the teacher might have to make a greater effort to incorporate ambiguity. This is often the case in discussions that introduce ideas that are widely accepted as factual.

Exploring Values

Any discussion that is based on values, whether they are social values or the individual values of the participants, will enable divergent responses and potentially a high level of student participation. For example, in social studies or English, a discussion could begin by simply asking students for their opinions about a controversial issue such as stem cell research. Values oriented discussions are familiar to most teachers and can be easily applied to many topics in social studies and English. They are well suited to courses in which judgment and expression concerning contemporary political and social matters is most relevant, e.g., animal rights, gun control, or racial discrimination (Greene, 1954). At the elementary level, the topics need to be located at a more personal level so they fall within the scope of the students' experience. For example, a discussion on prejudice might begin with the question: "Has there ever been a time when you feel you have been treated unfairly?" The purpose of such discussions is to inform students about other points of view and to deepen their understanding of the issue.

Values-based discussions are also possible in science and mathematics. For example, a science class could argue the desirability of constructing nuclear plants in populated areas or cloning animals to increase food production. In both of these cases, the discussion would hinge on how the participants employed their personal values to resolve the tension between the benefits of technology and the risk to the environment. Similarly in math, students could read a biographical narrative of mathematical discovery, such as the discovery of the Pythagorean theorem. The purpose of the discussion that followed would be to explore the experience of mathematical discovery and the personal qualities associated with it. Like values-based discussions in social studies and English, these discussions enable highly divergent responses and a high level of student participation.

Seeking Facts or Relationships

Not all discussions in English and social studies are based on expressing opinions, and there are even fewer in math and science. The purpose of many math and science discussions is to discover new relationships among a set of objective facts, e.g., a scientific proposition or a mathematical formula. These types of classroom discussions are often based on observations of natural phenomenon, laboratory experiments, problem solving, or the interpretation of data. Their purpose is to help students internalize the thinking processes that mathematicians and scientists employ during the discovery process.

Traditionally, many formal concepts in math and science have been taught through direct instruction. In part, that may be because concepts like Boyle's Law or the distributive property do not appear to leave much room for argument. However, all scientific propositions and mathematical formulas can be made arguable by relocating them in a real world setting. It is much easier to discuss applying the formula for surface area to the construction of a deck patio than to discuss the formula itself. Similarly, discussing whether someone's freedom of speech rights have been violated is easier than trying to discus the merits of the Bill of Rights. In both cases, the topic is made less arguable when treated as a decontextualized generalization (e.g., a formula or law) and more arguable when it is contextualized in a specific real world setting.

The difference in the thinking processes associated with reasoning about general principles and real world applications is encapsulated by Aristotle's distinction between the syllogism and the enthymeme. The syllogism or complete argument is a highly formal and tightly constructed argument, proceeding inevitably from premise to conclusion. For example, "All men are mortal; Socrates is a man; therefore, Socrates is mortal."

Given the first two statements, the third statement inevitably follows, leaving little room for further discussion. Any formula, law, or basic principle that can be applied reliably across many different contexts works like a syllogism.

In contrast to the syllogism is the enthymeme. The logic of enthymemes is not as predetermined or fixed as that of syllogisms because they are located in real world settings, which often contain unknown or partially understood dimensions. Thus, the premises may be hidden within the complexity of a real world setting. The resulting uncertainty requires a discussion to uncover the relevant facts, to clarify the premises, and to reason through the problem (Corbett & Connors, 1999; Slob, 2002).

Student Knowledge

The second condition for creating a discussion is sufficient student knowledge. The more students know about a topic, the more likely they are to see it from multiple perspectives. For example, a study on reading historical texts found that college students read the text as an immutable, objective, and therefore inarguable source of information. They did not question the author's statements, which they took to be factual. In contrast, professors in the same study read the same text as tentative, subjective, and debatable. They qualified or disagreed with a number of the statements the author made (Wineberg, 1991). The apparent difference between professors and students was the professors' extensive knowledge of the subject. Therefore, whether or not a discussion topic is debatable depends on how much students know about it. For example, while students would have a great deal of difficulty arguing about scientific formulas, the Bill of Rights, or other advanced concepts, scholars and scientists are constantly engaged in such debates.

There are two approaches to ensuring sufficient student knowledge to allow a discussion. The first is to position the topic within the students' previous experience. The teacher reflection at the beginning of the chapter is a good example: the teacher began a discussion on descriptive adjectives by asking for her students' observations on chewing bubble gum, a familiar experience for most students. By positioning the topic within the students' previous experience, the teacher can create a discussion at any point during the unit, including the very beginning of a unit before any new information has been taught.

A second approach is to increase the students' knowledge before the discussion. The more they know, the easier it is for them to contribute, and the less necessary it is for the teacher to provide elaborations and explanations. One approach is to "prime the pump," which simply means letting them share ideas with each other in small groups before beginning the whole class discussion (Hyman & Whitford, 1990). Sharing information allows students time to multiply what they already know, whether that is from their previous personal experience, previous schooling, or the previous night's assignment. It also provides them with an opportunity to try out their ideas by articulating them in front of a smaller audience, thus increasing their comfort level when contributing to the large group discussion. More extended preparation would include engaging students in an extended inquiry, conducting experiments, doing research in the library, working on group projects, and participating in group activities. The discussion that follows would serve as a way of affirming, multiplying, and integrating student knowledge.

Discussion Designs

The remainder of the chapter is devoted to describing four approaches to creating ambiguity and locating the topic within the students' knowledge base. They include responding to a problem, responding to an observation, responding to a reading, and reflecting on an activity. Understanding how to use these approaches can benefit you in two important respects: first, by helping you create and plan a wider variety of discussions and, second, by helping you guide them more capably.

Responding to a Problem

A discussion can be launched by simply asking students to respond to a problem. If the problem is situated within the students' previous knowledge base and asks them to express or evaluate their values, the discussion can be launched with very few preliminaries. For example, problem posing in social studies or English is often rooted in values-based issues with which students have some familiarity. To quickly start a discussion at the secondary level, the teacher could ask a controversial question such as "Should evolution be taught in schools?" The topic allows for multiple responses, and most students are familiar enough with the issue to elaborate.

Other examples could include the death penalty, abortion, gun control, and prayer in schools (Hess & Posselt, 2002). Even closer to student experience would be topics like locker or car searches on school grounds, or the degree to which school administrators can limit free expression in the yearbook and school newspaper, or wearing school uniforms (Hoge, Stuart, Foster, Nickell, & Field, 2002). Historical dilemmas could include questions like "How can slavery be legal in a free country?" (Mizell, 1998) or "Was dropping an atomic bomb on Japan the right decision?" (Holmes, 2005). At the secondary level, a discussion on special interest groups could begin with the question "How can the same government that puts a health warning label on cigarettes subsidize tobacco farmers?" Similarly, a discussion on individual rights could begin with "How can 18-year-olds be denied the right to consume alcohol when they are treated as legal adults in all other matters?"

In math or science, a discussion might begin with a problem that allows the possibility of multiple responses, such as problems with multiple solutions (Kalman, 2004). For instance, creating problems that incorporate pictorial, graphic, tabular, and algebraic solutions can enable a discussion that moves from manipulative to iconic to abstract solutions. One of the most common examples would be the classic handshake problem, one version of which asks students to determine how many handshakes would be exchanged if ten people attending a party shake hands once. This problem can be solved by acting it out, by discovering a pattern that leads to the solution, or by using an algorithm. Other types of problems are located in the everyday world by their very nature—like estimation problems. Creating a discussion for an estimation problem could be as simple as asking students to estimate the weight of a backpack before engaging in a more mathematical solution (Lawrence & Hennessy 2002). Estimation leaves enough uncertainty to provide for multiple responses, while opening the door to a more mathematical dialogue.

A responding to the problem discussion could be constructed either inductively or deductively. It would be an inductive discussion if the objective of the lesson has not been taught previously, and if key points regarding a scientific proposition, social principle, or formula are intended to be discovered or constructed through the discussion. For example, an inductive discussion on prejudice could begin by discussing how it feels to be excluded; a lesson on the democratic process could begin by asking what it's like to compromise with siblings; or a lesson on individual rights could begin by asking whether it is ethical to torture a terrorist in order to find a hidden bomb. As the discussion moved toward less familiar ideas, more teacher support and guidance would be needed to scaffold student understanding. Gradually, the discussion would foster an increase in the number of convergent student responses through leading questions and guiding or evaluative follow up teacher comments.

Responding to an Observation

A second way to start a discussion would be by asking students to respond to an observation by describing or reporting on what they see, and then drawing conclusions. The sources of these observations could include experiments, naturally occurring events, video or audiotape recordings, graphs, charts, figures, diagrams, calculator displays, works of art, period photographs, posters, or political cartoons (Vogler, 2004). Observations need not be limited to visual media; discussion could also be started with historical artifacts, music, and recordings. Similarly to posing a problem, responding to an observation requires little student preparation and therefore provides an opportunity for a quick starting discussion.

The observations above would permit multiple interpretations and thus divergent student responses. The observation will also serve as a stimulus to the students' knowledge base, by providing visual information that informs the student and enables more elaboration on the topic. For example, to begin a discussion on the growth of presidential powers (e.g., chief executive, chief diplomat, chief of state, and commander-in-chief), show a picture or series of pictures of the president carrying out the functions of his or her office. Similarly, in a history class at the elementary level, students could be shown a period painting such as "American Gothic" in order to begin a discussion on life at the turn of the century. Begin the discussion by simply asking students what they see or ask them about primary features of the picture, such as the people, objects, or activities in them (Stuart, Hoge, & Rosch, 1999). Such broad questions pose very little risk and should result in a wide range of responses from students of all ability levels. Their responses will reveal much about what interests them, what is most important to them, and the level of detail to which they are attending. Teachers should try not to cut off responses too quickly by asking leading questions. Exerting too much control may preclude important insights that could lead to effective teaching strategies. Instead, ask follow up questions that encourage students to clarify, reflect on, or extend their previous answers. As the discussion unfolds, reformulate and elaborate on student comments to suggest even further possibilities.

Another approach is to present two examples of a phenomenon, whether it be a picture, graph, or another type of example. Then ask students to compare the examples for differences and similarities. To maximize student participation, the visual should illustrate highly salient relationships that can lead to a discussion of more abstract mathematical concepts. Sometimes providing a very sharp contrast can be effective. For example, Table 5.1 compares the offensive performance of two basketball players. Each box represents the points scored per game.

To begin the discussion, the students can be asked which player they would rather have on their team. During the discussion, they may justify their choice based on either Brian's single game performance or Rafael's more consistent performance over several games. As the discussion gradually becomes more mathematical, students would discover that, although Brian had the highest single game score, Rafael had the higher mean and mode scores, and both had the same median score. However, even after calculating the mean, mode, and median, personal judgment will continue to play a role in the discussion because of the different strengths each player offers to the team.

This approach both allows for differing perspectives and enables students to speak at their current level of knowledge and insight. Therefore, it provides a wonderful opportunity for teachers to assess their students' initial understanding of the concept. It also simultaneously provides an opportunity for the teacher to scaffold student thinking by pointing out elements of the phenomenon that the students are not seeing. Eventually, the teacher can combine student input with teacher scaffolding to fashion the concept or idea embodied in the picture.

Responding to a Reading

A third approach to starting a discussion is by responding to a reading. A narrative reading or, more simply, a story lends itself especially well to discussions because they enable multiple interpretations and because they are rooted in the everyday experience of students. In addition, the text provides students with information they can use to elaborate on their responses to the questions. For example, students at the secondary level can read a narrative account of a court case (e.g., Gideon v. Wainwright), discuss and interpret the underlying facts, and then compare their decision with the Supreme Court ruling (Hess & Marri, 2002) At the elementary level, a pioneer's description of

TABLE 5.1 Offensive Performance of Two Basketball Players

Players	Points Scored Per Game				
Rafael	18	20	16	18	18
Brian	26	20	18	10	10

a prairie fire can be used to start a discussion comparing contemporary and frontier living.

Other narratives in social studies would include current events as described in news magazines or newspaper accounts, historical fiction (Mathis, 2001; Palmer & Burroughs, 2002), case law (McDonnell, 2002), and even movies or television shows. Narratives in English would include works of fiction, nonfiction, plays, and films. In science, examples could include case studies (Irwin, 2000), bioethics (Guyer, Dillon, Anderson, & Szobota, 2002), or stories of scientific discovery. Examples in math would include stories of discovery (Laubenbacher & Pengelley, 1998), word problems (Amit & Klass-Tsirulnikov, 2005), or stories or movies that illustrate math concepts (e.g., Chappell & Thompson, 2000; Thiessen, 2004).

Literature in mathematics has been used to teach linear functions (Billings & Beckman, 2005), factorials (Bintz & Moore, 2003), permutations, combinations, and probability (Lawrence, 1999; Thompson & Austin, 1999), graphing (Maus, 2005), algebraic patterns (Austin & Thompson, 1997), and geometry (Little, 1999). For instance, a tale like *One Grain of Rice: A Mathematical Folklore* (Demi, 1997) can illustrate a lesson on exponential growth (see also Zambo, 2005). The story is about a village girl who asks to be rewarded for doing a good deed with a single grain of rice—to be doubled each day for thirty days. The discussion can begin with student predictions about the size of the reward. As the story unfolds and the students begin to grasp the power of exponential growth, they can revise their predictions, thus creating openings for a more mathematical discussion.

A narrative can be used for starting a relatively brief or a more extended discussion or series of discussions, depending in part on whether the reading is a short current events piece or a historical novel or movie. The discussion can begin with a very broad question such as "What is your reaction to the reading?", or a broad statement like "Tell me about the reading", or a more focused question such as "What are the key facts in this case?" Broader opening questions are more inviting to students, but they also increase the time needed to reach the lesson objectives. Selecting narratives for discussion should be based on interest and content. The more factual information in the narrative account, the more potential it provides for extending student thinking.

Another type of reading that lends itself to discussion is one that argues a particular point of view by introducing a thesis or main idea, supported by subordinate ideas and facts and examples. To start a discussion with this type of reading, simply ask students whether they agreed or disagreed with the author's point, then require them to support their position with evidence. Examples of these types of readings would include editorials, issue papers, and even research studies. Research studies are arguable because they always include an observational, descriptive, or narrative element, which can be interpreted differently by different readers (Henning, 2005).

The least accessible readings for discussion are textbooks, which are organized in a conceptual hierarchy and are lacking in narrative exposition or arguments defended by evidence. Thus, it is usually more difficult for students to respond to a textbook from multiple points of view. However, even textbooks can be used effectively as part of a discussion by applying an additional strategy or activity to make them more interpretable and, therefore, more discussable. The discussion can begin by ascertaining the facts as they were presented in the text. This part of the discussion would consist primarily of recall and comprehension questions. Gradually, the teacher could move the discussion to a second phase by asking students to apply, analyze, synthesize, or evaluate the facts established earlier. For example, after reading a summary of the causes of the Civil War, students could compare and contrast those causes with other wars, compile a list of universal causes of war, and use that list to evaluate the degree to which the Civil War may have been avoidable. After reading a list of recommendations for structuring a cover letter and resumé in an English class, students could discuss how their organization could change depending on the job for which they were applying.

Reflecting on Classroom Activities

A fourth approach is to use a classroom activity or a series of activities to start the discussions. The activity should be designed to enable multiple interpretations. For example, a science discussion could begin with an experiment or a series of experiments intended to help students think more deeply about what they observed. In math, students could engage in problem solving, then discuss alternative solutions. In social studies and English, this could include debates, skits, plays, service learning projects, role playing (Smith, 2004), mock trials, mock elections, mock Supreme Court sessions (Bell, 2002), or reenacting a historical event, such as the writing of the Declaration of Independence or the pre-Civil War debate on slavery. In each subject area, the discussion is based on an activity located in the real world that enables multiple perspectives and interpretations. Their active participation in the activity gives them experiential knowledge on which they can elaborate during the discussion.

Preceding the discussion with activities is especially useful when the activities are beyond the everyday experience of students, e.g., scientific experiments or courtroom trials. Providing students with specialized experiences not available in their everyday life creates a foundation for building new knowledge. The teacher can begin the discussion by asking students what they observed, discovered, or concluded. Like the previous three discussion approaches, reflecting on activities offers the teacher an opportunity to guide students from a set of initial observations to more carefully reasoned conclusions.

What Teachers Need to Know

To create discussions that can maximize student participation while introducing new learning, teachers need to meet two conditions simultaneously. First, the topic must be ambiguous in order to enable divergent points of view. Second, the topic must be framed in a way that maximizes existing student knowledge. One approach to satisfying these conditions is to design a discussion rooted in individual or social values. Values-based discussions inherently allow for multiple points of view. A second approach is to locate the topic in a real world setting, as either a starting point for initiating the discovery of a new concept or an application point for a previously learned concept. The second approach is particularly useful for discussions that seek to discover new relationships among a set of objective facts.

Four specific approaches for meeting these conditions were presented in this chapter, including responding to a problem, responding to an observation, responding to a reading, and reflecting on an activity. One purpose of this chapter is to encourage you to give careful consideration to all four approaches. If you are not already using all of them, experimenting with the unfamiliar ones may be a way of increasing the level of student talk in your classroom.

Application Discussion

In the reflection paper below, a teacher reflects on a discussion he conducted in his ninth grade science classroom. Read the reflection below and then discuss the impact of his activities on the discussion. What do you notice about the relationship of the activities he describes and his students' responses? What conclusions can you draw about the relationship between activity and discussion? After you have finished reading, answer the following questions.

1. How does the teacher prepare his students for the discussion, and what impact does this preparation have on student participation?
2. Is this an inductive or a deductive discussion?
3. What kind of discourse moves did the teacher make?
4. What impact did the teacher's discourse moves have on student responses and student thinking?
5. What techniques did the teacher use to encourage higher level thinking?

As all teachers know, most of their students are very social beings. They seem to take advantage of every possible opportunity to talk to other students. By our own nature, teachers are quite social as well and can spend a lot of time talking (some more than others). If you can harness these collective urges to talk, class discussion can become an effective instructional tool.

The discourse of this lesson very closely parallels the ideas found in chapter 7 of a book entitled *Teaching and Learning Through Discussion*. In this chapter, Ronald T. Hyman and Ellen V. Whitford identify eight tactics that teachers use to conduct effective class discussions. I actually read this chapter after I had performed this lesson and was amazed at how closely their ideas matched my execution of this lesson in my class. I guess it is a testament to my preservice teacher education that I was instinctively doing almost exactly what this model says to do.

This particular audiotape is of a lesson I did with my freshman environmental science class fifth hour. Environmental science is the required freshman science class and my fifth hour has twenty-seven students in it. We had just finished a unit on waste, and this activity was the first one in our next unit: water. For this activity, I had the students write down everything they knew about water; then we used their ideas to generate a large concept map on the board. I had a few expectations for the purpose of this lesson. First, I wanted to do this activity at the beginning of the unit to gauge my students' understanding of water, its characteristics, and its uses. Second, I intended to show my students the interconnectedness of water throughout nature and our lives.

For an activity like this, I used a completely different pattern of discourse than I normally would. I had constructed my own concept map for this material, and I had an example of one from the previous year. Because of this, I knew exactly where I wanted the discussion to go and how the ideas would connect. I had an overall goal for this activity and the structure of the concept map, but didn't want to directly tell the students or force them to my conclusions. Instead, I wanted to guide them and allow them to reach this conclusion on their own. In order to successfully and effectively manage this situation, I needed to carefully plan the discourse.

As I mentioned earlier, the discourse of this lesson very closely matched the ideas about class discussion laid out in the book *Teaching and Learning Through Discussion*. They gave eight tactics for effective use of discussion in your classroom. They are: priming the pump, accepting, probing, wait time, focusing, energizing, referring to previous student remarks, and launching. Of the eight tactics for effective class discussion, I found obvious examples for five of them in my lesson. Without knowing that they had been given formal names in research, I had used the tactics of priming the pump, accepting, focusing, probing, and the use of previous student remarks. I am not counting my use of wait time because it is hard to show examples of that in a transcribed audiotape.

To '*prime the pump*' of my students, I had them make a list of everything they knew about water: what they use it for, what they do with it, what they do in it, etc. I gave them seven or eight minutes to individually make as long a list as they could; this way they all had something to share during the discussion. Also, since this lesson was the first one for our water unit, it was designed to get the students thinking about water and how it connects to our lives.

Once each student had a list of ideas about water, we started the discussion. The tactic that I displayed during this part of the discussion was *accepting*. At the beginning of the lesson, I set up ground rules that established an open, accepting climate for all students. I started out by taking all ideas that students offered and wrote them on the board. Then later we came back and categorized them. The belief behind this action is that, if the teacher does not reject any student's ideas, then the others will be more willing to contribute. As the lesson continues and more and more students are contributing, I then start to reject certain ideas if they do not fit into our concept map. This can be seen by the high concentration of teacher responses from the *encourages participation* criterion. This high number represents the comments made that affirm or accept student responses.

The next tactic that I exhibited during this lesson was *focusing*. Focusing involves harnessing all the energy and ideas of the students and leading them in the direction I want the lesson to go. This is not a form of manipulation, which has negative connotations associated with it. Here is an example from my audiotape:

T:	What about other organisms, not just humans?
S1:	Fish.
T:	What about fish?
S1:	They live in water.
T:	What larger name could we give this heading then?
S1:	Environment?
T:	Okay, maybe try a term we have used before—think back to around Christmas time . . .
S2:	Habitat.
T:	Good, does everyone remember what that is?
S2:	It is a place where something lives.
T:	Alright, let's use habitat then.

Here I am allowing the students to construct the concept map and connect ideas, but the end product turns out just as I had planned. To me, this is the fun part of teaching; it really feels that you are helping the students make connections in their heads. A discussion like this obviously takes on the personality of the class.

Another of the eight tactics I found an example of was *probing* where you ask the student(s) to explain their answers more fully, or to add details to their response to promote deeper thinking on the subject.

S1:	Water sports.
T:	Oo, good. That would include Nick's idea of jet skiing and lots of others.
S2:	Skiing.
T:	Yes, water skiing would be included too.
S2:	No, skiing.
T:	Oh—snow skiing—Good. You got me there.
S3:	But that doesn't have anything to do with water.
S2:	Uh huh, snow is frozen water.
T:	Good! I think we just made two new categories. In addition to water sports we now have . . .
S4:	Snow sports.
T:	Plus another large idea . . .
S2:	Frozen water!
T:	Exactly, the different states of water. Let's put that under a new heading called Properties.

This tactic can be used to fulfill one of my goals for this lesson, which is to see where my class stands in terms of content knowledge about water. I can do this by asking them to explain their ideas or to connect them to something else. Doing so can serve a dual function—to act as a preassessment for the water unit, and to get their thought processes ready for thinking about water. It can also help them to make new connections about water before we start adding a lot of new material in the unit.

The final tactic I would like to discuss is the *use of previous students' comments*. With so many people throwing out ideas, I needed to *softly* reject some of them in order to keep the discussion moving in the direction I wanted. Later, the situation would arise where a past student's comment would be relevant. I would then allow the student to restate their ideas and categorize it on our concept map. This helps to show the student(s) that their idea wasn't incorrect, just that it fits better somewhere else. In fact, it shows them that their idea was important enough to come back for. This can lead to an increased level of contributions because a lot of the risk in opening yourself up to criticism has been removed.

Activities

1. Plan a discussion using one of the classroom activities described in this chapter. Describe the activity you would use and then say what kind of student responses you would anticipate based on the activity.
2. Plan discussions using the three other types of classroom activities. Again anticipate what type of comments your students would be likely to make.

Study Group Activities

3. Bring a lesson plan to the study group that has relied on a lecture or relies heavily on teacher guidance. As a group, discuss ways in which the teacher and student discourse interactions could be changed by introducing an activity. After you have finished discussing all the lesson plans, examine the solutions you have proposed. Can you draw any kind of conclusions about which solutions work best in which situations?
4. Use the same lessons you changed in #3 and create two discussions. One discussion should lead to the concept (inductive discussion) and one discussion should apply the concept (application discussion).

part three
Keeping Students Involved

The third section of the book is intended to show readers how to keep students involved in discussions by creating a supportive climate. Discussions arise from within myriad daily interactions with students, including giving directions, handling discipline issues, and providing one-on-one support for students. Understanding specific ways of talking that contribute to a supportive atmosphere can help assure a more consistent and enduring success with a discussion-based approach to teaching. Chapter 6 will show teachers how they can support discussions by building positive relationships with and among students, through the use of accountability strategies, and through group work. Chapter 7 will address providing individual support for students whose cultural and linguistic differences may provide special instructional challenges.

six

Building a Climate for Discussion

Framing Discussion

Carefully read the transcript excerpt below. In the excerpt, Mr. Sanchez is helping his fourth grade student brainstorm ideas for a paper on a Native American named Montezuma. The purpose of this support is to help the student generate ideas for both the paper and the ensuing discussion. Like whole group discussions, one-on-one interactions have predictable patterns with a beginning, middle, and end. The interaction below can be broken down into five steps, including:

1. assessing the level of student understanding;
2. connecting the current problem to previous student experiences;
3. engaging students to apply their previous knowledge to extend and expand their knowledge;
4. acknowledging or affirming student thinking;
5. giving encouragement and/or suggesting how the student is accountable.

After you have finished reading, discuss the following questions.

1. What kind of emotional support does Mr. Sanchez provide? How does he build relationships?
2. What kind of cognitive support does Mr. Sanchez provide?

3. How does he make connections with Karen's previous knowledge? What kind of discourse moves does he use?

4. What strategies does Mr. Sanchez use to encourage Karen to think for herself?

5. In what ways does Mr. Sanchez challenge Karen?

1. Assess the Student's Understanding

Mr. Sanchez:	Karen?
Karen:	I still don't get what you meant by summarizing the main points.
Mr. Sanchez:	Not a problem.
Karen:	I already thanked the reader.
Mr. Sanchez:	You thanked the reader already?
Karen:	Yes.
Mr. Sanchez:	Did you suggest your additional resources?
Karen:	No. I want to create a catchy slogan.

2. Connect the current problem to previous student experiences

Mr. Sanchez:	Okay. Somehow we have to find a way to leave a lasting impression on the reader. Have you ever read a book that was so good that you never forgot it?
Karen:	No.
Mr. Sanchez:	Early in the year we started reading *Tales of a 4th Grade Nothing*. Okay? That was a story about Fudge. The entire class loved it so much you all asked me to get the sequel *Super Fudge*. *Tales of a 4th Grade Nothing* was so good that you wanted to read more about that person. Okay? You have to find a way to make what you're writing so good that a person's going to want to keep reading more and more about it. That's why you're suggesting additional resources. Okay? But before we get to that part we gotta find a way to sell what we're writing. What do I mean by that? You have to convince the reader that they have never read anything as wonderful as when they read *Carlos Montezuma* by Karen Whitely.
Karen:	I don't know a catchy slogan.
Mr. Sanchez:	Do you have a suggestion? Montezuma.
Karen:	I don't know.
Mr. Sanchez:	What does the last name Montezuma sound like? What's the familiar word you hear in there? Your stepdad has a brand new car, right?
Karen:	Yeah.
Mr. Sanchez:	Does he drive real fast in it?
Karen:	My mom's got a new car.
Mr. Sanchez:	Does she drive real fast in it sometimes?
Karen:	No, but we got a new pontoon boat that she drives real fast.
Mr. Sanchez:	Okay. Does that spark any ideas?

Karen:	I don't know. When you picture the Montezuma castle . . .
Mr. Sanchez:	That's a good start. Let's work with that now. Have you ever watched TV and then a commercial catches your interest? Let's think of this conclusion as your commercial to your paper. Okay? Now one of the purposes of a commercial is to advertise a specific product to make it sound as if it's the best product. If you're ever going to buy window cleaner, buy Windex. Windex is the best one. They have all these catchy songs and slogans to make you remember Windex. For example, Mr. Clean, the floor cleaning agent. Everyone's kicking the bucket "Mr. Clean is the man behind the shine. Is it wet or is it dry." You've heard that before, right? How did I remember that song if nobody ever gave me a copy of what they're saying in the commercial?
Karen:	Because you saw it.
Mr. Sanchez:	Because I saw it and what else?
Karen:	You liked it and ???

3. Engage students in applying their previous knowledge

Mr. Sanchez:	There you go. Now here's your challenge. You need to be a commercial creator on paper. You need to come up with a catchy slogan that will sell *Carlos Montezuma* to whoever's reading it, to the point where they want to learn so much more about it that they're going to look for your additional resources that you include in your conclusion. Okay?
Karen:	I still don't know a slogan.
Mr. Sanchez:	It sounds to me like you want me to create one for you.
Karen:	No. I need an idea.
Mr. Sanchez:	You need an idea. All right let's focus on how the name sounds for a moment. The castle was one idea.
Karen:	Or you could think of mountain. "Every time you hear a word like Mount, like Mount Rushmore, think of Montezuma."

4. Acknowledge/affirm student thinking

Mr. Sanchez:	So what would be the connection now? Now we're getting somewhere.
Karen:	That the word "mount" like Mount Rushmore, you'd think of it.
Mr. Sanchez:	So you're making a connection between him and mountains. If you can find a way to make that connection, you have your catchy slogan. That's the trick. She showed you a name of a memorial that had Mount Montezuma in it. Somehow you have to go from that to helping to make a connection between remembering Carlos Montezuma. Another example—you may want to suggest that the

> reader zooms to the library to learn more about Carlos Montezuma. However, you want to remind the reader to remember that name. That's your challenge now. It may not come to you all at once, but you gotta think about it a little bit. When it comes to you, you'll know it because it'll be your original idea.

Karen: How do you summarize?

5. Give encouragement and/or suggest how the student is accountable

Mr. Sanchez: How do you summarize the main points? The ideas that you talk about within the body of your paper, those are the points you're going to summarize in a sentence or two. You're going to remind the reader of the importance of the person you just studied. Okay? Any other questions? You got it? I'm gonna come back and check with you in about five minutes and see where you've gotten, okay? All right. Make me proud.

Introduction

Discussions occur within a larger context of classroom activities and are built upon the brief conversations that occur on a daily basis between teachers and students. During those interactions, teachers can nurture relationships with and among students that carry over into small group and whole group discussions. For example, in the one-on-one interaction above, Mr. Sanchez pays careful attention to Karen's concerns, asks probing questions to explore and clarify the nature of her difficulties, and helps her make connections to her previous personal experiences. At every step, he reassures and encourages her, while simultaneously challenging her and holding her accountable.

Enhancing the quality of interactions like these can make a significant impact on the willingness and ability of students to participate during large group discussions. The purpose of this chapter is to show teachers how to improve classroom discussions by building and fostering relationships. The first half of the chapter will focus on how teachers can build relationships *with* students, and the second half of the chapter will focus on building climate by fostering relationships *among* students.

Building Discussion through Relationship

A healthy relationship between teacher and student promotes a comfortable classroom atmosphere, one in which students enjoy contributing to the discussion, and the teacher can challenge students without making them feel insecure. Sidorkin (2002) asserts that having a relationship with the teacher may be the single most motivating influence for students, and numerous other authors have discussed the importance of caring to the learning process (e.g., Noddings, 1984, 1992). To cultivate that relationship, teachers need to show personal interest, actively listen, be respectful at all times, and find ways to challenge their students.

Showing Personal Interest

Teachers should continually demonstrate their interest in students by what they do and say, beginning on the first day of class and continuing throughout the year. Examples would include greeting students at the classroom door, smiling at the right time, using the students' names, giving appropriate encouragement, providing personalized feedback on student work, and engaging them in a personal conversation before or after class. These interactions become the launching pad for the interactions that take place during a discussion. As a high school teacher, it was not unusual for me to start a discussion by first asking about the prom, Friday's football game, or a recent assembly.

Often teachers can show their personal interest in students by interjecting a more personalized question or comment into more business-like interactions. These brief exchanges can occur during whole class discussions, as students work in groups, or when helping individual students. For example, in the transcript excerpt below, Ms. Lowell allows a brief digression during a whole group discussion to insert a comment that acknowledges and reinforces the personal side of her relationship with a student. The teacher's initial comment about Carly, a character in a novel called *Pinballs*, is intended to help her students empathize with the character. Trying to put themselves into Carly's situation prompts two students to introduce personal comments into the discussion. The teacher chooses to engage in a brief personal interchange, then returns quickly to the topic of discussion.

Ms. Lowell:	Yes, you build that trust. I begin to trust all of you and hopefully you are doing the same for me. Put yourself in Carly's position. All of a sudden tomorrow I'm going to move into your house, David. I'd be scared to death. I know the Nielsons a little bit, but not enough to make myself comfortable in your house.
Sandy:	I have a big dog.
Ms. Lowell:	You have a huge dog; that thing's a pony.
Sandy:	Our house is too messy for you to come in.
Ms. Lowell:	Oh, really? So I really wouldn't be invited in, is that it? What else?
Karen:	Two months ago my mom told me to clean my room and then it took her two days to clean the house.
Ms. Lowell:	Thinking back to the question, why do you think Carly was the way she was to those three? What did you put down?

This example is representative of many similar types of teacher and student interactions. They may involve an inquiry about the student's health, mood, a recent vacation, an extracurricular activity, or any personal concern. Typically, teachers limit these to short digressions by quickly returning to the task at hand. In that way, the teacher is able to maintain the business-like tone of the lesson, while reinforcing her personal interest in the students.

Active Listening

Teachers can also communicate a personal interest in students by listening closely to what they have to say. Gordon (2003) has suggested several techniques for developing better listening skills. The first is to remain silent. By simply not talking, the teacher is offering an invitation for students to speak further. In lieu of verbalizing, teachers can show their interest in students through their posture, proximity, body movements, and other nonverbal communications. Second, teachers can show they are listening through *acknowledgement responses*, such as "I see," "Uh huh," or "Right." Third, they can use *door openers*, which are comments that invite students to say more, such as "Would you like to tell me about it?" or "that sounds interesting. I would like to hear more about it." Fourth and finally, the teacher can practice *active listening*, by listening empathetically to student concerns, then summarizing and restating what the student has said. This assures the student that the teacher is actively engaged in the problem, while also helping her to fully articulate her feelings. For example, a student in the following example is explaining a concern about the effort of a classmate in his cooperative group.

Ramone:	I don't like Denny, and I don't want him to be in my group any more.
Ms. Gibson:	Why? What's wrong, Ramone? [*Door opener*]
Ramone:	He was absent the week we worked on the project in class.
Ms. Gibson:	Uh huh. [*Acknowledgment response*]
Ramone:	During group time yesterday, he would only talk to Anna, and I had to stay up until 10 o'clock last night gluing the teepee poles together.
Ms. Gibson:	So you are saying that you feel Denny isn't helping enough in class, and you feel that is not fair because you have to make up for it by doing extra work at home. [*Restating what the student has said*]
Ramone:	Yes, I don't want to be in his group.

When actively listening, teachers should empathize with the student's problem and help them to clearly articulate it. With the emotional and cognitive support of a trusted adult, students are better able to think through their problem and develop their own solutions. However, Gordon cautions teachers against lecturing, preaching, advising, criticizing, or using several other forms of ineffectual communication. Each of these has the potential to block communication with students, which will inevitably affect student participation during whole class discussions.

Being Respectful

One key to building a climate for discussion is to be respectful of students and their concerns at all times. The most difficult, and therefore the most important, time to remain respectful of students is when there is a conflict between teacher and student. At these times, teachers are most likely to resort to the use of judgmental language, which can be extremely damaging to the classroom climate. Gordon refers to judgmental language as *noncongruent communication*, e.g., "This class is being too loud as usual. Please try to keep it down." In this case, the teacher has labeled the class's character, rather than addressing the situation. A second example of noncongruent communication is the You-message. You-messages are judgmental in tone and address the student's character rather than their behavior: "Please quiet down. You are not taking this project very seriously." The situation is worsened if the teacher's inferences are wrong. There is always the chance the students are being noisy because they are highly engaged or because a silverfish has unexpectedly emerged from the wall and run across the floor.

In contrast, teachers can address a noisy classroom by using *congruent communication*, "It needs to be quiet so everyone has a chance to concentrate on their writing." In this case, the teacher gives the class a reason (improved performance) for limiting their talking. Congruent communication emphasizes the students' behavior instead of their character. A second example of congruent communication is the I-message. In contrast to You-messages, I-messages enable teachers to confront student misbehavior and express their feelings without becoming accusatory. For example, the teacher might address a noisy class by saying, "Please quiet down. I cannot concentrate on what I am trying to say when there is so much noise." Because they are based on the teacher's perceptions and are rooted in observable facts, students cannot easily dispute I-messages. In addition, the I-message can be used as the first step to further action if the student proves unresponsive.

Providing One-on-One Support

Teachers can also show a personal interest in students as they provide one-on-one support. When providing one-on-one support, the most effective approach combines challenge, sensitivity, and responsiveness with sound instructional techniques to foster both emotional and cognitive growth in students (Lepper, Drake, & O'Donnell-Johnson, 1997). The example at the beginning of the chapter illustrated an interaction solicited by the student. In the example below, Mr. Sanchez is giving unsolicited feedback on previously completed work, a paper on a famous Native American. In this case, the teacher should begin by (1) acknowledging or praising the current level of student achievement, and (2) giving specific feedback on the student's work. Mr. Sanchez initially gives the student feedback on his introductory paragraph, then tries to provide some directions regarding the future direction of the paper. The italicized lines indicate Mr. Sanchez is reading from his student's paper.

1.Acknowledge/praise the current level of achievement

Mr. Sanchez: I am very, very impressed. You worked on this for a long time yesterday for homework. It's amazing to me what you can do when you put your mind to it. This is one of the best introductory paragraphs I've heard today thus far.

2. Give specific feedback

> What's original about it is, you didn't do it in the same order everyone else did. You changed the order. You let the reader know right off the bat that *I'm going to invite you to see what I've learned about this famous Native American.* That's a fantastic introductory statement. *Take a fun quest and listen to what I have to say. I'm studying . . ..* This is just fantastic work. You've covered all the different components of the introductory paragraph I was asking you about.

3. Challenge the student to extend the current level of achievement

> So from here, we're gonna go into the body. Where's the body of your paper now? Here you're just repeating the same information. *My name is Donny and I'm going to be talking about John Ross.* Here we have a number 2. That's where the body of your paper begins. What I'd like to see you do with the body, since you finished with your introduction now . . . remember the time line that you did on John Ross? I would like you to discuss his birth.

Donovan: I did.

Mr. Sanchez: Okay. Discuss one or two significant events that happened in his life.

The interaction between Mr. Sanchez and Donovan continued further in a fashion similar to the example given at the beginning of the chapter. In the last two steps of the interaction, Mr. Sanchez gave encouragement and set goals for Donovan. These steps have not been included here because they were illustrated in the previous transcript excerpt.

Building Relationships Among Students

The classroom climate for discussions is also dependent on the quality of student interactions. Students who are frightened or intimidated or perhaps even indifferent toward their classmates are less likely to contribute to class discussions. Consequently, promoting positive student-to-student relationships is a way to enhance classroom discussions. Starting on the first day of class, teachers should begin building these relationships through their talking, by the expectations they set, and through the use of cooperative learning.

Procedural Talk

All student-to student interactions occur within a framework created by the teacher's talking (Bellack, Kliebard, Hyman, & Smith, 1966; Mehan, 1978, 1979). Through procedural talk or, more simply put, giving directions, teachers create spaces or frameworks for specific classroom events, such as a whole group discussion, working in groups, or conducting an inquiry. For example, in the transcript excerpt below, a middle school mathematics teacher is setting the conditions for her students to engage in small group discussions. She gives direction for what students should do, sets some criteria for finishing, and cues them to what they should be thinking about.

Ms. Brady:	All right. I still don't see that some people have on their sheet that looks like—let's see—you got it, Sam. You are on the ball. We're going to do a little practice for what we're going to do when we have our final project, which I think we'll introduce on Friday, okay? And that is, we'll look at what you did here and those people that were still struggling with it, I hope that you take the opportunity, when we get the chance, to ask me some questions and ask your partner some questions. Ian, are you lonely today? No? You're going to be partnered up with John and Brittany, okay? Just so you know.
	Okay, what we're going to do is you're going to look at your partner's work and you guys are going to compare and try to decide who had the best possibility for designing a pop can. Whose was best? Okay? That's pretty much it. Whose you think you should build. Now, what I want you to do, and we'll do this eventually all together, is that you're going to write down what kind of criteria you used to decide that. And I'm not going to give you any ideas right now of what that would be, but ways to judge whose was the best. Each partnership will share one pop can solution. There are an infinite number of solutions, by the way. Infinite. Many more than the twenty-one people that are here, okay? So. Rachel, do you know what you're going to do? Do you know what I want you to do? Okay, what do I want you to do?
Rachel:	You want us to compare answers and decide whose is better, then give the criteria.
Ms. Brady:	Tell me how you decided, okay? The thing I am going to remind you of is that the current pop can volume in cubic centimeters is approximately three hundred and thirty-nine and twelve hundredths cubic centimeters. That's the same as saying twelve ounces. Doesn't sound the same, but it is the same. Twelve ounces is about 339.12 cubic centimeters. Everybody know what I want you to do? If you have questions as a partnership, ask me. Don't ask me until you talk to your partner. Let's say that one of your partners got it done and somebody else didn't.

Procedural talk is most effective when it is clear and concise enough so that students know just what to do. This eliminates or reduces the need for further talk or management interventions. While procedural talk is essential for students to function effectively in a classroom, its importance is secondary to the curricular content (Edwards & Mercer,

1987). Achieving worthwhile discussions depends in part on minimizing procedural talk in order to maximize the discussion of the curricular content. Yet some procedural talk is essential and, without mastering this form of classroom discourse, effective discussions are not possible.

Setting Expectations

My chief concern at the beginning of a course is to rapidly build an atmosphere for discussion by setting expectations and establishing classroom norms. In my high school English classes, I would began talking on the first day of class about the importance of discussion for building reading comprehension. As a professor of teacher education, I tell my preservice teachers they are future teachers, that they will be expected to talk as a teacher, and that I expect them to contribute to the discussion. Simply letting students know that you value their contributions to the discussion can go a long way to fostering participation and establishing positive behavior patterns.

Initially, I worry less about achieving curricular objectives and more about building climate. I will choose topics on which my students are fairly knowledgeable, in which they are very interested and, if possible, which address one of the primary themes of the course. However, at the very beginning of a course, I am not as concerned about the topic as I am about the quality of the discussion and the amount of student participation. Accordingly, I offer incentives and/or extend the length of the discussion for the express purpose of encouraging more participation.

I also like to get the class on its feet right away, so I begin moving them around immediately. One purpose of this movement is to meet as many of their classmates as possible and thereby reduce the anxiety of talking during discussion. A second purpose is to establish classroom routines for moving in and out of group discussions. To acclimate students to these transitions, I randomly group students together in a variety of ways, e.g., based on the color of their clothes, random counting, or self-selection.

Establishing routines for moving in and out of groups helps reduce the need for giving directions or relating procedures. With a little practice, students can make transitions without the lengthy explanations usually needed when a new activity is introduced. Another advantage of establishing routines is they can be modified with a minimum of directions. However, these benefits diminish with overuse. Without some variety, your students may perceive them as boringly repetitive, thus inhibiting both motivation and productivity.

Cooperative Learning

One of the most effective approaches for structuring small group work is cooperative learning, which has been shown to improve student achievement and to foster student-to-student relationships. Cooperative learning groups are structured according to the following five principles.

1. Individual accountability: Students are held individually accountable for their work and their behavior in small groups.
2. Positive interdependence: Some classroom incentives should be structured to promote responsibility for the quality of classroom interactions, e.g., if every single person participates during the discussion, everyone will receive a bonus point.
3. Face-to-face interactions: When working in a small group setting, students should position themselves so they can discuss in face-to-face interactions.
4. Teach collaborative skills: Teachers should explicitly teach their students how to work together in small groups.
5. Group processing: Students should spend some of their time in groups reflecting on how they interact as a group.

Holding Students Accountable

Individual accountability and positive interdependence are critical to the success of cooperative learning groups (Slavin, 1995). Strategies for holding students individually accountable include summative assessments like tests, written reports, and essay questions. More formal strategies will motivate most students, who tend to perceive traditional assessments as weighty and important. However, since these types of assessments occur at a distance in time from the discussion, they lack the immediacy of less formal accountability strategies. They also take longer to grade and record.

Informal Accountability Strategies

Informal accountability strategies may be less utilized by teachers. But because they require less time and effort, they can be very helpful for encouraging students to talk without unduly burdening the teacher. One example would be the practice of cold calling, i.e., calling on students who have not raised their hands. Even students who aren't called upon feel accountable because they know they may be asked to respond at any time. Another less formal strategy during group work is to tell a student, "I am very interested in your work. I will check back in ten minutes. I really want to see what you have done." A third approach is to have students write down their contributions to the discussion on an index card and collect them. Later, the students could be asked to reflect on their participation in a journal entry. Other less formal ways to hold individual students accountable include awarding bonus points, journaling, or giving students a class participation grade.

Positive interdependence is often created as part of the way the groups are structured. Three well-known group structures that promote positive interdependence are think–pair–share, numbered heads, and jigsaw (Brookfield & Preskill, 2005). Each of these approaches is structured to promote positive interdependence. For example, in think–pair–share, students brainstorm on their own, then share with a partner, then report to the whole group. In numbered heads, every student is assigned a number; then, after the small group discussion, the teacher designates a number, and the group member whose number is called answers for the whole group. In jigsaw, students are organized into heterogeneous groups of three to six students. Each student is assigned a part of the lesson, works independently to become an expert on a portion of the lesson, and is accountable for teaching the information to others in the group as well as mastering the information other group members have provided.

Whatever accountability strategies you choose, it is important to use them very gently, because coercion is a poor substitute for the easy give and take that should characterize a discussion. Too much grade pressure on group performance can cause relationships among group members to deteriorate. It can heighten anxiety to unacceptable levels and make students feel that they are too dependent on the behavior of others. For example, two members of a group could become very resentful of less diligent peers if their group grade does not reflect their individual effort. Therefore, it may be better to soften the grade pressure by creating positive interdependence through less formal accountability strategies, e.g., numbered heads, assigning roles to group members, or giving students the chance to win bonus points.

Accountability strategies may be more important earlier in the year when students are a little more reserved about participating. As students become more comfortable in your classroom, the need for accountability strategies will probably lessen. The longer students spend in an atmosphere that promotes active involvement in discussions, the more they will begin to participate automatically, without thought of reward. Your goal is to create an atmosphere that impels students to talk because they want to talk.

Teaching Collaborative Skills

The last three of the five cooperative principles address the importance of teaching collaborative skills to students, a process that should begin the first day of school. As soon as the students walk in the door, they can be cued to the principles and strategies associated with cooperative learning through posters and bulletin boards. Teachers can also introduce collaborative skills through games that are specially designed to enhance collaborative skills, through a variety of group exercises that emphasize cooperation and interpersonal skills, or through highly motivating activities that are designed to elicit a high level of student participation and interaction. These types of activities can accomplish several purposes simultaneously, including establishing class norms, providing students with an opportunity to get to know their classmates, and also introducing the subject matter.

Throughout the year, the teacher can reinforce collaborative skills by giving students an opportunity for group processing. Group processing occurs when group members discuss, describe, and reflect on the group's interactions. A variety of approaches are possible. For example, the teacher might ask during an informal discussion "What did your group do in order to be successful?" or "What positive things did your group members do to get the job done?" Another approach would be to let them discuss among themselves, guided by questions on a worksheet. A third approach might be to have group members respond to a survey about their group's functioning. A fourth approach would be to assign each member of the group a role to perform within the group. One member's role would be to observe the frequency with which each member engages in the targeted skill. Assigning a grade or giving a reward to groups whose members demonstrate competence with collaborative skills could also further validate their importance.

What Teachers Need to Know

The purpose of this chapter was to make teachers aware of some fundamental, albeit indirect, influences on the quality of whole group discussions. It was intended to show that the environment for discussions can be enhanced by building relationships with and among students. Teachers can build relationships with students by adopting caring dispositions and behaviors, such as showing personal interest in students, actively listening to students, and being respectful to students. Discourse moves that complement caring dispositions and behaviors include congruent communication, I-messages, and blending challenge with affirmation during one-on-one interactions.

Relationships among students begin with the teacher's procedural talk, which creates a framework for talking in small groups. While procedural talk is important, it should be minimized by setting expectations early in the year, creating routines, and using cooperative learning principles to structure small group work. The five principles of cooperative learning can be divided into two primary approaches: holding students accountable and facilitating collaboration. Accountability strategies are applied on an individual and group basis. More formal accountability strategies include tests, projects, or written papers; or the strategies can be more informal, such as reporting out from a group, being assigned a role in a group, or documenting class participation. Facilitating the use of collaborative skills occurs by encouraging face-to-face interactions, directly teaching collaborative skills, and providing time for group processing.

Application Discussion

A primary theme of this chapter has been that discussions are constructed from many elements. The purpose of this application discussion is to gain an appreciation of how these separate elements are integrated into a single discussion. So, as you read the teacher reflection below, try to identify as many of the teacher's strategies as you possibly can. Consider relationship building, preparation and accountability strategies, group work, discourse moves, providing help for individuals and small groups, and the direction of the discussion. After you finish reading, answer the questions below.

1. What strategies were employed as part of this discussion?
2. What kind of changes did the teacher make from the first to the second discussion? What effect did these changes have on the discussion?

3. Compare the discussion described below with a typical discussion that you have led or in which you have been involved. What similarities did you find? What is different?

Introduction

Fortunately, I had an opportunity to work with two groups of seventh grade high ability readers. I met with one group and presented the lesson about as I normally would. Then about two weeks later, I was able to meet with a second group with the same lesson. What has transpired is the foundation of this last paper. I was able to make changes in my presentation to significantly influence the student discourse in the lesson. The two lessons are compared in the paper.

Activity

The activity is a short unit associated with the Junior Great Books' approach to understanding literature. The reading is entitled "High School Graduation" and written by Maya Angelou. It is a portion from her autobiography *I Know Why the Caged Bird Sings*. This class consists of twenty-nine seventh grade students. The class is Reading to Learn. The students are taught reading strategies to improve students' reading scores. Students are ability leveled by DRP (Degrees of Reading Power) scores. Both groups are top reading ability classes.

Usual Classroom Discourse

The normal routine for this activity is a very brief intro to reading a story from the literature book. Students are assigned to read the story individually. They are given class time to read. The following day, students are asked, "What is this story about?" These students are asked to round out their circle of students, so everyone could see one another during discussion. Questions are IRE triad. Students are called on soon after their hands go up. Very little wait time is given. There are about one to three students who always have their hands raised. One of them is usually called upon to answer. The answers are quality. It appears that the others don't bother to raise their hands because they know one of the three will undoubtedly be selected to answer and will answer correctly. There were two days of discussion, which was dominated by two or three students. There were no specific references made to the story. Ideas and major themes of the story were tossed out. Students were asked to pretend they were the main character in the story, Marguerite. She would be the valedictorian and would be giving the address following Donleavy's speech. "What would you say in your address?" This was given as a writing assignment with rough drafts due the following day. The quality of the essays was mediocre.

Restructured Activity

The second group of students has a new format. I am warmly introduced to the class. I had already done a Mock Trial unit with all of these students earlier this year. But I have never had this same group of students together before. They seem happy to have me back. I make some small talk with students as I begin to maximize the student participation by asking, "What kind of reading do you like to do?" Immediately hands go up as I see there are some definite avid readers. As I receive types of reading, I ask a quick follow up question of, "Who is your favorite author?" "Which book is your favorite?" As several students contribute to the conversation, one student cites realistic fiction as a favorite type. We talk about what that really is and get to nonfiction, and this story is part of an autobiography. I tell them that this story is called "High School Graduation." Books are handed out.

Each student is given a large 6" × 8" card to record questions as they read the story and/or vocabulary words they do not know or understand. The next session, the "priming the pump" strategy is used to elicit more student participation. Students are asked to write on their card a quick summary of the story. By doing so, this helps the student to think through the events of the story and gives accountability. Hopefully, the pump is primed and ready to go. One to two minutes is allowed. Then I ask, "What is this story about?" Hands go up in two to four seconds. After a quick response, I say, "Then what?" Other students are called upon, and the story keeps moving as I keep saying, "What happens next?" This questioning technique is used to focus and facilitate their thinking. The sequence of events naturally leads to having the guest speaker, Mr. Donleavy. We discuss if he were invited especially for this event or if he asked to be invited, since he is a politician. Students agree he was not invited. The idea of an emotional roller coaster is used as an analogy. "Where are the places in the story that show Marguerite has closeness with her people or separation from her people?" "Why do you think she feels that way?"

The topic of Henry Reed giving the valedictory speech is discussed after the question, "Why do you think he chose this title, 'To be or not to be?'" A student gives an elaboration in regard to Hamlet. We discuss Hamlet's dilemma and ask for opinions. As that point of interest wanes, I ask students to locate specific text where Marguerite feels connected to her people and/or separated from her people. After a couple of examples cited by students, the end of our thirty-minute time slot is realized. Students are asked to think about how they would feel if they were Marguerite. Our discussion would continue tomorrow.

At the beginning of the next session, I open with comments about the author's purpose in his/her writing. "Why do authors write?" This is an open framing for discussion. "What does the author want us to know from reading this story?" "What are some larger themes in this story?" As students respond with ideas, these are written on the board. Themes included courage, perseverance, and racial prejudice. The question is posed, "Why does Donleavy's speech make Marguerite start to hate the whole human race?" Students are asked to cite specific excerpts which support their answer. They are given ten minutes to find samples. Since these students have done work similar to this with me in Mock Trial, I remind them of the same skill of finding facts to support your answer. Students give a few examples when time runs out.

The following class session opens with a teacher discourse on the evaluation criteria for this unit. Students are reminded that there would be a written assignment made one day next week. When students turn in their papers, they would also include all of the hand-out materials that they had been given to assist them with this unit, i.e., 6" × 8" card, pink note taking sheet, and the discussion questions sheet. Interestingly enough, the time that followed seemed much more productive than before. Students more readily volunteered to answer questions and to give their opinions. That was exactly my purpose in giving that particular elaboration. The students would be held accountable for how these tools were used.

Students will be given three choices for a writing topic. The first group was only given one choice to write a valedictory address following the Donleavy speech. The second group will discuss other major themes of the story such as prejudice and bias. In this application portion of the discussion, students will be asked if they know anyone personally who can identify with bias and prejudice that is portrayed in the story. The purpose here is to open up the discussion for more participation. Hopefully, a meaningful discussion will follow.

The questions for writing prompts are "In writing this story, do you think that the author primarily wants to change the attitudes of white people or the attitudes of black people?" "How are the problems that young African-American graduates face today like and unlike those that Marguerite faced?" "Why has an equal, quality education for all been so difficult to achieve in America?"

Reflections

The improved approach includes purposeful attention to establishing a positive classroom climate. We all know one another from a previous unit earlier in the year. Making a conscious effort to chitchat with them before everyone gets into the room is a new improvement for me. I would normally remain separated from them before class starts. After two days of discussion, students' responses only yielded twelve and thirteen students participating out of twenty-eight present. With this type of open discourse, I had expected more students to respond. More wait time was given than usual, which proved to be successful. I may have been too eager to call on students who responded. In retrospect, I would have made a more conscious effort to relate to specific text sooner in the discussions. Students really need more time to read and contemplate the text.

After essays are turned in, I will show this story portion of the movie *I Know Why the Caged Bird Sings*. I think it is always enlightening to read and watch the same text.

Doing this unit the second time has been much more rewarding than the first. I feel that I was definitely much more attuned to trying to teach well. I was more focused on trying to get the students to participate and to get them to do some real thinking. I am doing another similar unit with sixth graders next week. Hopefully, having had these experiences in classroom discourse will positively advance my professional teaching.

Activities

1. Video or audiotape yourself working one-on-one with your students. Analyze the pattern of talk and compare it with the model suggested in this chapter. Devise a plan or a series of strategies for improving your one-on-one support of students.

2. Think of five discussions that you have led. Consider the strategies for building a positive climate discussed in this chapter. Which ones do you routinely address? How could their use be further expanded? What could you do to include the ones you don't use?

3. If you have not led your own discussions, think of two or three discussions in which you have participated. Consider the strategies for building a positive climate discussed in this chapter. Which ones were most often addressed? Which ones were least often addressed? How could their use be expanded? What additional strategies could have been incorporated?

4. Develop a plan for improving the climate surrounding your discussions. Then decide how you will collect and analyze data to evaluate your plan.

5. Design an accountability strategy for one of your discussions. Include multiple strategies including both formal and informal strategies. How will your strategies facilitate student thinking? In what way are your students accountable for their content knowledge? How are they held accountable both individually and as a group?

Study Group Activities

6. Bring your plan or your data to the study group and share your ideas or your data for facilitating teacher–student and student–student relationships, one-on-one instruction, and accountability. Make a list of strategies so that teachers can reference them.

7. Bring a transcript, an audiotape, or a videotape of your one-on-one talk with students and analyze it with your study group.

seven
Supporting Cultural and Linguistic Diversity

Framing Discussion

In the preceding chapters, you have learned a variety of different strategies for designing and leading a discussion. In this chapter, you will learn how to enhance those strategies to better support culturally and linguistically diverse (CLD) students. Read the description of the CLD class of second graders given below. Then use that information to answer the following questions and design a discussion on the solar system. At the end of the chapter, you will be asked to add to your original strategies.

1. What kinds of diversity are present in this class?
2. Design a discussion that would address the diverse needs of the classroom described below. Consider the activities, small group work, accountability strategies, the direction of the discussion, and the discourse moves that you anticipate using in this discussion.
3. Which of your strategies would be especially helpful for CLD learners?

Purpose and Desired Outcomes

In second grade, a district goal/objective is that each student will learn basics about the solar system. Students need to know about objects in the sky (sun, moon, and stars) and about the properties of Earth and space. "Postcards from Pluto" was a story in our reading basal. Many facts about all the planets were given within the story. I want my students to be able recognize the differences and similarities among planets and to be able to find nonfiction information within this story.

Participants

My entire second grade class of twenty-six children will be involved in this discussion. Within my classroom, I have ten girls and sixteen boys. There are fourteen African-American students, six Hispanic students, and six Caucasians. They are from middle-to low-income backgrounds. Two of the Hispanic students are also English as a second language (ESL). My students' abilities range from reading at an early first grade level to a handful of students reading at a fourth grade level. The range of student abilities makes many lessons/discussions quite challenging. My class has adapted to each other's abilities, rarely making fun of another classmate's work or words.

Setting

We have had several stories within this anthology book containing information about the solar system. The students have done small group discussions and assignments pertaining to this topic. In our social studies lessons, we have been talking about the Earth's rotation and the changing seasons that happen as a result of the Earth spinning. The students are very excited and curious about the topic. They come up with some great questions and ideas. As a result, the majority of the class is very focused and willing to share their thoughts and ideas.

Introduction

A discussion-based teaching approach is inherently well suited to meet the diverse learning needs of the CLD students in the classroom described above. First and most important, it provides students with opportunities to practice their emerging language skills during small and large group discussions. Exposing students to diverse ways of speaking and thinking benefits both diverse and mainstream students (e.g., Heath, 1982; Gallas, 1994). Second, asking open-ended, divergent questions can create opportunities for assessing, understanding, and making better connections with your students' cultural background. It also facilitates the "inductive, interactive, and communal" communicative styles of many African-American, Latino, Native-American, and Asian-American students (Gay, 2000, p. 93). Third, discussion-based teaching provides opportunities for teachers to build relationships, to give individualized feedback, and to scaffold student thinking. The purpose of this chapter is (a) to help teachers become more aware of the special concerns related to providing instruction to CLD students, (b) to illustrate how discussion-based teaching can benefit them, and (c) to introduce strategies that can further enhance the benefits of discussion-based teaching.

An Increasingly Diverse Population

The classroom described in the example above is becoming increasingly more common as the student population of the United States becomes increasingly diverse. Of the 48 million students enrolled in public, elementary, and secondary schools, nearly forty-three percent are Asian, American Indian, African American, or Latino (National Center for Educational Statistics (NCES), 2004a). Of those forty-three percent, most are enrolled in urban schools; the hundred largest school districts in the country have a minority enrollment of seventy percent (NCES, 2006). The number of school age children (aged 5–17) who speak a language other than English at home grew from 3.8 million to 9.9 million between 1979 and 2004, an increase from nine percent to nineteen percent. That represents a 162 percent increase in the number of children who speak a language other than English in comparison to an eighteen percent increase in the total number of school age children. During that same time period, there was a 114 percent increase in the number of children who speak English with difficulty (NCES, 2004b).

These numbers reflect the increasing diversity of the U.S. population. According to the U.S. Census Bureau, the percentage of the white population declined from eighty percent to seventy-five percent of the total population from 1990 to 2000, a decrease offset by an increase in the Asian population from 2.8 to 3.6 percent, and an even more dramatic increase in the Latino population from 9 percent to 12.5 percent of the total (U.S. Bureau of the Census, 2001; Gibson & Jung, 2002). The African-American population remained relatively stable (slight growth from 12.1 percent to 12.3 percent), as did the American-Indian population (0.8 to 0.9 percent). Nearly nineteen percent of the total U.S. population now speaks a language other than English at home, with over half of these speaking Spanish (U.S. Bureau of the Census, 2005).

A Mismatch Between Home and School Culture

CLD students may face special challenges in school, because they do not understand English, because their cultural values don't align well with mainstream American classrooms, or because they are disadvantaged by subtle, hard-to-detect differences in their understanding of language. For example, a landmark study by Heath (1982) established a relationship between student patterns of interaction at home and their success in school. In her study, Heath found that performance in school was related to three distinct interaction patterns found in three different communities: Trackton, a black mill community; Roadville, a white mill community; and Maintown, a community of professional and business people. Students from the Trackton community had the most difficulty in school. Immediately upon entering school, they quickly fell behind and, by third grade, had established a pattern of failure from which they never recovered. The students from Roadville were successful in the early grades but, around the fourth grade, they began experiencing difficulties. Only the students from Maintown were able to experience consistent success in school.

Heath found distinctly different patterns of adult-to-child interactions in each of these three communities. For example, in the Trackton community, children were invited to make analogies, tell stories, or provide descriptions. Parents rarely asked their children the kind of direct questions common to a classroom. Thus, they were completely unfamiliar with the pattern of questions and answers typical of classroom recitations. Consequently, they performed very poorly in response to the predominant use of recitation questions they encountered in the first three grades.

In contrast, Roadville parents emphasized questions that required short answers, like naming objects or parts of the body. Thus, Roadville children fared very well during the early grade levels when the teachers asked a high number of short answer comprehension questions. In the later grades, however, Roadville students were less able to answer more abstract, hypothetical questions and often failed to see their relevance, e.g., "How would you change the ending of the story?" or "Which character would you like to invite to dinner and why?" As these types of questions became more prevalent in the upper elementary grades, Roadville students dropped in performance.

In Maintown, parents provided detailed verbal commentaries on their children's actions, they related information read in books to the outside world, and they encouraged questions and intellectual exploration. When they arrived at school, Maintown children were acclimated to both recitation questions and the more abstract hypothetical questions that began around fourth grade. As a consequence, Maintown students were more in sync with the discourse common to schools, and were the only group of the three to be consistently successful in school.

Cultural Differences and Discussion

Initially, the difficulties of students from minority cultures were viewed as indications of a cultural and linguistic deficit. The poor performance of CLD students was attributed to a lack of language enrichment within an impoverished home environment. Labov (1972) dispelled this misconception in a seminal study predating Heath's work. Labov's study attributed the difficulties of CLD students to a mismatch between the expectations of school culture and the child's dialect. For example, Labov found the single syllable answers of an eight-year-old black male were expanded and transformed when interviewed in a more informal and comfortable setting outside the classroom. He concluded that the child had not been linguistically deprived by his inner city environment; rather, the child's rich store of linguistic resources was largely unusable in a school setting.

Since Labov's original work, there has been an increasing recognition of the pervasive and deep influence of culture on learning and thinking. Cultural influences encompass a very broad range of social interactions, including "the ever-changing values, traditions, social and political relationships, and worldview created and shared by a group of people bound together by common factors (which include a common history, geographical location, language, social class, and/or religion) and how these are transformed by those who share them" (Nieto, 1996, p. 390).

Topic-Centered Discourse and Associative Discourse

The impact of cultural influences on individual thought processes and behaviors can be very deep and very powerful. Differences among cultures can lead to differences in body language, the meanings of gestures and words, and communicative styles. These differences can vary significantly among cultures and are cultivated almost from the moment of our birth. Nearly all babies under the age of six months can distinguish vowel sounds in any language; by the age of ten months, they can distinguish the vowel sounds only in their native language. Even as early as four days old, babies show a preference for their native language (Pinker, 1994).

Often, we are unaware of these differences and the potential bias associated with them. A case in point is the difference between white teachers' expectation for a topic-centered discourse and the preference of African-American, Latino, and Native-American students for a more topic-associative discourse. When guided by a topic-centered discourse, speakers focus on one issue at a time, arrange facts and ideas in a logical linear order, and articulate explicit relationships between facts and ideas. The structure of topic-centered discourse is similar to the structure of expository writing, descriptive writing, and the speech commonly used in schools. In contrast, a topic-associative discourse is episodic, anecdotal, thematic, and integrative.

To a white teacher, the topic-associative narrative of an African-American student can appear shifting, unassociated, and even incoherent. Relationships among segments of the discourse are implied rather than explicitly linked. Thinking and speaking appear to be seamless and circular rather than linear and clearly demarcated. Thus, when evaluating a topic-associative discourse, white teachers may be more likely to infer a low achieving student and predict future difficulties for the child. In contrast, black teachers are more likely to appreciate both topic-associative and topic-centered discourse as logical and well structured (Michaels & Cazden, 1986; Cazden, 2001).

The important point here is not to determine the best way to tell a story, although it should be noted that Gee (1989) has argued that the topic-associative style is the more complex and subtle of the two narrative styles. What is crucial is our awareness of potential differences. As teachers, we need first to be careful not to interpret differences due to culture as signs of inferior functioning and, second, we need to develop strategies that help children make the necessary connections between their home environment and the skills needed to be successful in school and society (Delpit, 1995; Nieto, 2002).

Culturally Congruent Teaching

Adjusting our teaching approaches so that they better align with the cultural heritage of students can improve achievement. For example, studies of Head Start programs (e.g., Piestrup, 1973; Hall, Reder, & Cole, 1979; Howard 1998) have found that literacy skills can be improved by using African-American communication styles such as "dramatic presentation styles, conversational and active participatory discourse, dialect, gestures and body movements, rapidly paced rhythmic speech, metaphorical imagery, and reading materials about African American culture and experiences" (Gay, 2000, p. 87). In another study, Foster (1989) showed that a community college teacher's use of a culturally congruent communication style led to better recall, concept mastery, classroom dialogue, and increased motivation among African-American students. At the middle and high school level, Lee (1991, 1993) used a speech form called *signifying*—the use of exaggeration and humorous insult to put down another speaker—to teach critical thinking skills to African-American students. First, the students analyzed examples of signifying dialogues, second, they analyzed two scholarly articles on signifying, third, they created their own signifying dialogues in groups and, fourth, they applied the knowledge they had gained to the use of figurative language in literary criticism. Thus, the existing verbal skills of the students were recognized, validated, and used as a connection to the technical language of literary criticism.

Similarly, a group of Hawaiian students improved from a mean score at the 27th percentile on standardized reading tests to a mean score over the 50th percentile by altering instruction so that it was more culturally congruent (Jordan, 1985). Changes included letting the children help each other in small groups, relating the readings to the previous experiences of the children through brief discussions, and addressing the class as a whole group rather than singling out individual students. They also allowed students to respond in a variety of speech patterns that are indigenous to Hawaiian, albeit atypical for a classroom. Teachers encouraged students to give choral responses, to tell stories collaboratively, and to use overlapping speech (a student begins to talk before the speaker has completely finished). The teachers also found that the most effective classroom management strategies involved a blend of warmth and strictness.

The program worked so well that it led researchers to try a similar approach with a group of young Navaho Indians (Vogt, Jordan, & Tharp, 1987). The Navaho students shared a number of similar characteristics with the Hawaiian children. They worked best in small groups and responded better when individuals were not singled out. However, the same program yielded dramatically different results when transplanted from Hawaiian to Navaho culture. In contrast to the overlapping and joint responses of the Hawaiian children, the Navaho students opted for a pattern of individual turn taking. The Navaho children also did not respond well to the strict disciplinary approach taken with Hawaiian children and were willing to engage in protracted battles with the teacher to resist it. Finally, they would not work together in small groups. Navaho children of the opposite sex do not play with each other after the age of eight. However, after the groups were reduced to two or three students of the same sex, the children began to help each other.

To avoid being surprised by unexpected differences, teachers need to be aware of the potentially striking differences among cultures. The following descriptions are intended to help you increase your awareness of potential differences among Asian-American, Native-American, African-American, and Latino students. They are in no way intended, however, to serve as convenient labels by which to stereotype students.

Asian Americans

A discussion-based approach may be new and uncomfortable for some Asian Americans. If they have had school experience previous to the United States, they may be accustomed to learning through listening, observing, reading, imitating, responding to teachers' questions based on lectures and notebooks, and taking tests that require only the recall of factual information (Cheng, 1996). In Asian classrooms, volunteering information can be considered overly bold. Thus, Asian Americans may not feel comfortable offering their opinion, challenging others, or taking risks during a discussion. In general, they may be more oriented toward maintaining group harmony, more restrained about taking oppositional points of view, and consequently, less direct than Westerners. They may tend to display hesitancy and verbal ambiguity in order to avoid confrontation, the expression of negative feelings or opinions, making spontaneous or critical remarks (Matsuda, 1989; Gay, 2000), or even using the word "no" (Wierzbicka, 1991; Coker, 1988).

When working individually with Asian-American students, teachers should also be aware of key differences in nonverbal messages. Many Asian students have been raised according to traditional values, which include deferring gratification, saving face, being respectful of elders, taking responsibility for relatives, and cultivating self-discipline. They may be self-effacing, presenting a modest appearance to avoid drawing attention to themselves, and avoiding eye contact as a show of respect. Consequently, Asian-American students may appear unfriendly when the teacher offers a greeting. Other nonverbal messages could be misinterpreted as well: Asian students may frown as a sign of concentration rather than displeasure, and they may giggle when they are embarrassed or don't understand. The latter should not be mistaken as lack of seriousness or a sign of disrespect.

Native Americans

Native Americans comprise another group that may not seem to be very talkative to their Anglo teachers. Students may demonstrate a great reluctance to participate either in front of a large group or within a small group such as a reading group. In Native-American culture, there is no naturally occurring situation in which a single adult authority regulates who speaks, when they speak, at what volume they speak, and to whom they speak. Consequently, Native-American students may not acknowledge the teacher's authority to ask questions, and regard students who do answer them as show offs. To maximize student participation, teachers of Native Americans may want to let students discuss at their own pace in small groups. Native-American students seem to respond better to teachers if individuals are not publicly singled out to recite before the group, if their answers are not publicly evaluated by the teacher, and if the teacher interacts with individual students in a smooth, slow, deliberate, and economical manner (Phillips, 1972).

African Americans

African Americans could have a more assertive, participatory, communicative style than either Asian or Native Americans. In their discourse interactions, they may be accustomed to gaining access to conversations through "personal assertiveness, the strength of the impulse to be involved, and the persuasive point of the power they want to make" (Gay, 2000, p. 91). Thus, they are more likely than other students to challenge authority (Kochman, 1981), and they may contribute to a discussion by calling out responses (Weinstein, 2007), a tactic that teachers could find disruptive or rude. (For an example of a teacher who was able to successfully incorporate call outs into his class discussions, see Dillon, 1989.) They are also more likely to think of discussion as a verbal competition with definite winners and losers. This may conflict with the expectations of white teachers who are expecting a less dramatic, more cooperative discourse. Consequently, the more emotional, assertive, and adversarial style of African Americans could be seen as confrontational, divisive, and inflexible by white teachers.

Latino

Engaging Latino students in discussion depends in large part on establishing a personal relationship. As the largest minority group in the United States with the second highest dropout rate, Latino students could become more strongly connected to the school community through a relationship with a caring adult. Such a relationship could help overcome the negative images that Latino students have of school and teachers, as expressed in the following statements taken from the Harvard Longitudinal Immigrant Student Adaptation Study: "Most Americans think we are garbage" (made by a fourteen-year-old Dominican boy) and "They treat immigrants like animals. There are a lot of racist people" (made by a thirteen-year-old Mexican girl) (Suarez-Orozco, Suarez-Orozco, & Doucet, 2004, p. 428). Teachers need to be aware that, for Latino students, establishing a relationship or "setting the stage" is an important part of working with others, so that what could appear to be off-task behavior within a small group is actually a necessary first step.

Summary

The descriptions above are intended only to make you aware of the potentially striking differences that can occur among groups with different communicative styles. It is important, however, not to assume that individuals in any group will conform to a single description. Cultural and linguistic patterns are constantly evolving and changing, and there is considerable individual variation within and among cultures. Many students may appear to be from similar backgrounds but, in reality, share very few commonalities. For example, the term "Asian American" covers a wide variety of national, cultural, and religious groups, more than twenty-nine of which differ in language, religion, and customs (Feng, 1994). Furthermore, differences in their socioeconomic status, parental education, and parental literacy may also influence discussion behaviors (Olneck, 2004). For example, Lubienski (2000) has suggested that middle class students may be more comfortable expressing and defending their positions, while lower socioeconomic status (SES) students feel apprehensive about exchanging conflicting ideas and desire more teacher direction. Finally, some researchers entirely dispute the validity of attributing a particular learning style to any group of people based on the isolation of a few characteristics (Irvine & York, 1995).

Enhancing Discussion-Based Teaching for CLD Students

Discussion-based teaching offers numerous advantages for CLD students. One purpose of this section is to explore those advantages by revisiting some features of discussion-based teaching that are particularly well suited to addressing the needs of diverse learners, such as relationship building, connecting students to their previous experience, and collaborative learning. A second purpose of this section is to introduce a few additional techniques for enhancing discussions with CLD students, such as providing more visual information, using a guarded vocabulary, and letting CLD students use their native language or dialect.

Building Relationships

Negative emotional responses can interfere with the tacit or unconscious acquisition of language. Simply put, a dislike for persons or situations can cause an aversion that prohibits language learning. If a second language learner is uncomfortable, is exposed to constant criticism, or doesn't trust their teacher, there is less of a tendency to emulate the teacher's language. Since much of language acquisition occurs tacitly or unconsciously through naturally occurring verbal interactions, creating and maintaining positive relationships with students is critical to the learning of language. Students who are highly motivated and have high self-esteem and a low level of anxiety will perform at a higher level and acquire new language much more quickly. Therefore, cultivating positive relationships increases the chances that students will learn standard English or will acquire English as a second language (for further explanation of the Affective Filter Hypothesis, see Krashen, 1982).

You can enhance your relationships with CLD students by communicating the expectation that all students can succeed and showing them that you are eager to help and that you value their culture. Therefore, it is important to learn about the values, traditions, and customs from which your students come. One approach is to collect background information through a survey—or even better to make home visits. Home visits can be extremely enlightening in regards to the cultural and linguistic practices that guide the household and thus the student's thinking and speaking practices. They can also help establish supportive relationships with parents and provide opportunities for teachers to communicate with parents about their child's experience. That can be especially helpful for newly arrived families, who may value education and support their children but have little knowledge of their child's school experience (Suarez-Orozco et al., 2004). In summary, Ladson-Billings (1994, p. 55), lists four dimensions of relationship that characterize culturally relevant teaching:

1. Teacher–student relationship is fluid, humanely equitable, and extends to relationships beyond the classroom and into the community.
2. Teacher demonstrates a connectedness with all students.
3. Teacher encourages a "community of learners."
4. Teacher encourages students to learn collaboratively. Students are expected to teach each other and be responsible for each other.

Cooperative Learning

Engaging in cooperative learning tasks is widely recommended for CLD students (e.g., Hertz-Lazarowitz & Calderon, 1993; Slavin, 1995). Talking in cooperative learning groups before the discussion offers several advantages. First, it promotes cognitive development by integrating language acquisition with content learning. Second, it facilitates second language acquisition by multiplying the amount and variety of student talking. This exposes CLD students to a greater variety of peer models, gives them more chances to speak expressively, and lets them take more risks without fear of embarrassment in front of a large group. Third, it can promote understanding among diverse individuals by providing a vehicle for sustained interactions among students. All students will benefit by exposure to diverse perspectives and alternative ways of thinking.

Connecting with Previous Experience

Discussion-based teaching also provides numerous opportunities for teachers to link the curriculum to students' out of school experiences. This is especially important for CLD students, who often experience difficulty connecting what they are learning in their new culture to their native culture. This lack of connection can pose a serious obstacle to learning.

> The depth, interconnectedness, and accessibility of prior knowledge all dramatically affect the processing of new information . . .. Students must connect their own prior knowledge with new information continuously, while teachers must understand how well students are making those connections.
> August and Hakuta cited in Herrara and Murry (2005, p. 37)

With a discussion-based approach, teachers can uses "cultural referents" as an entry point to engaging with academic concepts. For example, Ladson-Billings (1994, p. 18) suggests a fifth grade teacher could begin a lesson about the U.S. Constitution by discussing how a local church or African-American civic association was organized using bylaws and articles of incorporation. The teacher could begin the discussion by asking students about their personal experience of such institutions and giving them a chance to elaborate about them. Their responses are a potentially rich source of information that can enhance your relationships with your students while simultaneously informing your awareness of cultural differences. As they talk about their experiences, look for connections to your learning objectives. Making these connections will not only help students understand the role of documents in organizing new institutions, they will also see their people as role models for creating and leading those institutions.

Preparation

When using activities to prepare CLD students for a discussion, it is best begin them with more contextualized information and gradually move to decontextualized information. Learning in a more context rich environment would include activities like context embedded sketching, drawing, hands-on activities, responding to easy guidelines with illustrations; one-on-one discussions; simulations, illustrations, and other how-to examples; a lesson illustrated by a video clip; science experiments; reading a map; following a route; reenacting historical events; and doing multiplication using cuisenaire rods. CLD students learn better when new information is contextualized through activities. Participating in shared activities can illuminate the meaning of language by providing CLD learners with more points of connection with their prior learning, helping them to build new experiences as a reference point, and encouraging higher order thinking skills.

In contrast, it is much more difficult for CLD learners to process new information from highly abstract, decontextualized learning tasks. Decontextualized tasks focus mainly on more symbolic forms of information and less on pictorial or sensory forms of information, such as responding to an email, responding to a message left on the table, responding to guidelines without the aid of illustrations, completing standardized classroom assessments, reading a chapter in a textbook, writing an essay, explaining the Pythagoras theorem and other math concepts, deriving the square roots of numbers and other complex math equations, and learning from classroom instruction via a lecture format. Without the context from which these tasks were derived, it is difficult for CLD students to make connections with prior knowledge structures needed for complex problem solving (Herrera & Murry, 2005).

Provide Visuals

During the discussion, teachers can support CLD learners by supplementing concepts and processes with additional visual information, such as photos, media, computers, drawings, charts, tables, and diagrams. The use of visual aids addresses multiple learning styles and may increase the relevancy of instruction for CLD students (Herrera & Murry, 2005). By providing visual links to key concepts and vocabulary, visual aids can benefit the comprehension and retention of content material for all students.

Use Guarded Vocabulary

Using guarded vocabulary does not require speaking unnaturally or raising your voice. Instead, teachers can make a few small adjustments in their speech patterns to facilitate the understanding of second language students. Some examples of guarded vocabulary include the following (from Herrera & Murry, 2005, p. 255):

- slowing the rate of speech;
- emphasizing word enunciation;
- inserting more pauses;
- using shorter sentences with simpler syntax;
- using more consistent vocabulary with appropriate repetition, such as patterned stories, songs, raps, or chants.

Teach Strategies

Explicitly, teaching strategies can be very empowering for CLD students because they often lack the tacit understanding of grammatical rules that native speakers possess (Delpit, 1995; Garcia, 2005). For example, many of the language gaps described in Heath's study of Maintown, Roadville, and Trackton were successfully addressed by designating the children "language detectives" and encouraging them to investigate their talking at school and home (Heath, 1983). Their increased awareness of language patterns helped them overcome the cultural barriers they were encountering in the classroom. Similarly, CLD students should be given explicit instruction on classroom discourse moves, e.g., asking questions, synthesizing ideas, and facilitating discussion. Refer to part I of the book and most especially chapter 2 for more specific descriptions of strategies that facilitate student talking.

Allow Use of their Native Language

There are several benefits to letting CLD students use their dialect or native language at appropriate moments in the classroom. First, our native language is a key element of our identity, and the possibility of losing it can be threatening. Letting students use their language may improve their self-esteem, thus providing the emotional support needed to accelerate their learning of English (Delpit & Dowdy, 2002). Second, limiting classroom communication to English is especially difficult for students who are not yet proficient. A lack of proficiency in English not only inhibits understanding of the subject matter, it can interrupt the development of numerous communication skills and thinking processes that are fostered through verbal interactions with parents, teachers, peers, and others. It typically takes five years of schooling to close the achievement gap between second language learners and native speakers. If a lack of language proficiency prohibits these verbal interactions, then CLD students can be deprived of vital stimulation needed for cognitive growth and development.

Third, the most successful CLD students are typically fluent bilinguals (Walsh, 1991; Zentella, 1997). Although, some immigrant students reject their language and speak only in English, the most adaptive identity involves code switching, which refers to the students' ability to use the most appropriate language demanded by the context (Suarez-

Orozco et al., 2004). CLD students have greater comprehension when they make strategic use of both languages to construct meaning from text (Herrera & Murry, 2005).

Providing Individual Support

One of the most important themes of this chapter has been that interactions with CLD students may not be as they seem, i.e., teachers and students from differing cultures may not interpret words, gestures, or actions in the same way. Furthermore, it is very hard to predict when these differences will occur, as it is natural to believe that others can see and hear what appears to be so obvious to us. Therefore, as an initial step to addressing potential miscommunications, teachers must be aware that their thinking may differ from students' in ways that are subtle and difficult to detect. To expose these differences, teachers must consciously maintain an awareness of potential differences and explicitly monitor their communication. The recommendations and questions below have been adapted from Barrera and Corso (2003).

Listen Mindfully

To better detect cultural differences, teachers should carefully observe themselves as they interpret and respond to their CLD students' words, gestures, and actions. By constantly questioning themselves and their interpretations, teachers can remain open to alternative interpretations. Questions teachers could ask themselves include:

1. Is there more than one way to look at this interaction/situation? How else could I interpret it?
2. Have I rushed to judgment or have I paused and considered alternative ways of interpreting the situation?
3. Is there any information I could be missing? Have I tried to collect additional information before drawing a conclusion?
4. Have I questioned my own assumptions regarding situations/interactions like these? Am I too preoccupied with my goals, interpretations, and judgments?
5. Have I considered the situation from my students' point of view and how they may be interpreting my actions?
6. Have I tried to observe how others seem to be responding to my words and actions?

Remain Nonjudgmental

Teachers should also cultivate a nonjudgmental attitude toward perspectives that differ from theirs. Attributing lesser value to the contributions of others can interfere with understanding. Instead, try to establish interactions that allow equal voice for all perspectives (i.e., avoid giving greater weight to one perspective over another). Teachers should try to put themselves in the place of the learner, then use their imagination to see the world through his or her eyes. Experiencing empathy for another often leads to insights regarding their thinking. The following are questions that teachers can use to cultivate a nonjudgmental disposition:

1. What is positive about this student's behavior?
2. What is this student adding to the small and large group discussions?
3. What can my other students learn from this student?
4. What can I learn from this student?

Search for Differences

Another way of discerning differences with CLD students is through explicit questioning. Rather than automatically relying on an initial impression, the teacher can seek further clarification by asking students to more fully elaborate their thoughts.

1. What does this mean to you?
2. Could you explain what you mean a little more?
3. Could you explain what you want a little more?

Probe Initial Responses

If students' initial responses still have not fully revealed their thinking, further probing may be necessary to bring unexpected differences to light or enable teachers to test their understanding of student thinking. Teachers could ask questions such as the following:

1. Let me see if I understand what you mean. Are you saying that . . .?
2. Could you give an example of what you mean?
3. What you're saying reminds me of another situation. Am I right in thinking it is like . . . (make a comparison)?

Help Others Search for Differences

It is likely that students will experience similar challenges when trying to interpret their teachers' behavior. Thus, teachers could facilitate communication by helping others to interpret their actions. This could help CLD students clarify their understanding of the teacher's perspective. Specific questions to ask CLD students could include:

1. What do you think I mean when I say or do this?
2. Could you explain what I said in your own words?
3. Could you tell me what you are thinking when you see me do or say . . .?
4. What do you think I am asking you to do?

Making communication more explicit by listening and asking questions can give teachers insights into students with differing cultural backgrounds, as well as helping them better communicate respect and understanding.

What Teachers Need to Know

Differences in cultural and linguistic backgrounds can lead to significant differences in the way students interpret actions and words. This puts some students at a significant disadvantage to others. Discussion-based teaching can offer several means for addressing this discrepancy. It provides an inductive approach to instruction, introduces new learning in a context rich environment, and offers students an opportunity to develop shared meanings through shared activities. Verbal interactions can be increased by talking in small groups before the large group discussion, thus providing an opportunity for all students to benefit from learning in an environment rich with linguistic diversity.

Teachers can enhance the benefits of discussion-based teaching for CLD students by adopting some additional strategies, including gathering background information on CLD students, providing context rich activities, providing more visual resources, developing explicit questioning strategies to expose subtle differences in values and the interpretation of language, and teaching CLD students specific strategies for coping with cultural and linguistic differences. Although these strategies are all intended to provide additional individual support for CLD students, they also offer benefits for other students as well.

Application Discussion

Return to the framing discussion at the beginning of the chapter, review your discussion design for the class of second graders, then answer the following questions:

1. How could you learn more about the students' background knowledge before the discussion began?
2. How could you better prepare the CLD students for the discussion?
3. How could you create opportunities to interact individually with CLD students before the discussion?
4. What kind of questions could you ask students to expose hidden misunderstandings in this discussion?
5. How could you enhance the discussion for CLD students?

Activities

1. Create a questionnaire for the purpose of gathering background information from students.
2. Select a student in your class with a different cultural background from yours. Design a series of questions intended to help you learn more about his or her background.

3. Audio or videotape yourself while interacting with the student in question 2. Then analyze the videotape and write a teacher reflection like the ones you have read in this book.

Study Group Activity

4. Share your reflections and your strategies for interacting with CLD students with other study group members.

Part four
The "Bow Tie"
A Model for Conceptualizing Discussion-Based Teaching

You began this book by reading about individual discourse moves in part one. In part two, you learned how to combine those discourse moves into single discussion patterns. In part three, you learned how to keep students involved through relationship building and providing support for individual students. In part four, you will learn how to combine all of those components into a unit plan for discussion. This unit plan will be based on a template for discussion called the "bow tie". The bow tie is a conceptual model that will help you identify the most likely places in your teaching units for opening up the discussion.

Three types of discussions will be introduced; each of them can be associated with a specific place within a teaching unit: (a) framing discussions or discussions that draw on students' previous knowledge to open a unit, (b) conceptual discussions or discussions intended to introduce new concepts, and (c) application discussions or discussions for the purpose of applying new concepts in real world settings. These discussions can be distinguished by differences in their location, their direction, the level of preparation needed before discussion, the type of accountability strategies needed, and their patterns of discourse moves. Chapter 8 will provide an overview of the "bow tie." Chapters 9, 10, and 11 will discuss the elements of framing, conceptual, and application discussions respectively.

eight
The Bow Tie

Framing Discussion

In the reflection below, a ninth grade environmental science teacher describes how he redesigned a unit on waste management in order to incorporate more discussion. As you read, consider how the teacher restructured his activities, grouping arrangements, accountability strategies, and his discourse moves. Also pay attention to the three different types of discussions he describes. After you have finished reading, answer the following questions:

1. What changes did the teacher make in preparing his students?
2. What changes did the teacher make with his grouping arrangements?
3. What changes did the teacher make with his accountability strategies?
4. What changes did the teacher make with his discourse moves?
5. What differences do you see among the three types of discussions he describes?

Activity Modification: Changing a Closed Discourse to an Open Discourse

There are many ways in which a discussion can be used in a classroom—to teach a concept, examine an issue, or just to share ideas. There are also many ways to structure a discussion, all dependent upon your goals for the lesson. Sometimes, it is more beneficial to have a "closed" discussion where you are looking for a specific set of answers. Other times, it is more effective to have an "open" discussion that explores a larger set of potential answers.

I believe that too many times a closed discussion is used when a more open discussion would not only be more effective, but also promote more student thinking. Many teachers may not employ open discussion as often as they should because they may not like the "risk" involved, or may not want to put in the little extra effort needed to successfully execute an open discussion. However, it is my belief that the overall enhancement of student thinking far outweighs these "perceived" difficulties. It is important that more closed discussions be converted into open ones. And I will present a specific example of me doing just that.

Closed Activity

The activity I have chosen to modify comes from the waste unit of our environmental science class. This is the required science class for all freshmen, so there is quite a variety of the type of students you will have in your class. Our environmental science course is only in its third year, so the curriculum is still not completely set. This particular activity came with the original packet of suggested activities from the curriculum development committee.

In this activity, students will be looking at how much packaging certain products have. Specifically, they will be analyzing the price per ounce of different sized containers of Froot Loops®. In preparation for this activity, the teacher needs to go to a supermarket and get the price and size of different Froot Loops boxes. There are usually three sizes: the regular box, the large box, and the very small individual box. The students then do the math to determine which of these is the cheapest in price per ounce, and graph the data. The overall theme of the lesson: the larger the box, the cheaper it is per ounce.

It is obvious to me that this activity is begging to be modified; it is too boring and one dimensional. First of all, it is only looking at one kind of cereal. Froot Loops has few generic counterparts that would definitely contribute to the complexity of the lesson. Second, only one factor of the price of the cereal is being looked at: the size of the container. There are many more factors contributing to the price of a product than just the size of the container.

As a result of the limited nature of this activity, the discourse will be rather limited as well. Everything is based on right and wrong answers. The majority of the activity is the math and the analysis of the price per ounce. Obviously, for this math, there is either a right or a wrong answer. Even the discussion at the end of the activity will be made up of low level, simple responses to answers about the fact that the larger the boxes are the cheaper the product is per ounce. The only higher level questions you can get out of this lesson are about why this situation exists, but even these responses will be rather dull.

Open Activity

I modified this activity in such a way that it would more closely resemble the model for discussions that Dr. Henning presented to us in class. This model starts with a very open framing discussion that is designed to maximize student involvement and pull all the students' ideas together. This is followed by a more closed discussion where conceptual information is added to make the discussion more specialized and specific. Finally, an open discussion is used again to apply this conceptual knowledge to a new situation. The way this lesson was previously designed only emphasized the conceptual component of this model.

In order to open up this lesson to more unique discourse, I first changed its structure. First, I involved more than one brand of cereal. I found as many different kinds of Froot Loops, Tootie Fruities, or Froot Rings I could in as many different containers as possible (seven in total). Second, I actually bought the cereal so as to have visual aids for the discussions and a printed receipt to add to the analysis. Finally, I added an open discussion to the beginning and the end of the activity so that it would more closely fit Dr. Henning's model.

Framing Discussion

The purpose of the framing discussion at the beginning of the lesson is to introduce the idea and get the students thinking. It attempts to narrow down the broad personal experiences of everyone in the room to a particular topic or details of the lesson. In this specific activity, I started by placing a box of Froot Loops on the front table and handed out the five discussion questions. These questions asked the students to list different types of packaging, what are the functions for packaging, and are all of these functions necessary. The purpose was to narrow down their thinking to just the packaging aspect and its possible functions. They were given time to brainstorm these ideas individually, then we snowballed.

Snowballing is a certain type of participant structure where students are first asked to respond to questions or ideas as individuals. After a few minutes, they join with another person to discuss their ideas. Later, these two join with another two, and eventually you are discussing as a large class. For the student who is less willing to contribute, this is a chance for them to share ideas in smaller less threatening groups first before the large group discussion. Hopefully, this will lead to an increased level of participation once the class is discussing as a whole.

During the framing discussion, my particular choice of discourse moved things along in a coherent manner. Since the concept of product packaging can be very broad, I used cued elicitation to highlight particular aspects I wanted the discussion to focus on. At first, I did not reject many responses because I wanted to keep the discussion as open as possible, and I wanted to promote as much participation as possible. Many times, I needed to reformulate the students' ideas in order for them to more closely fit with the direction I wanted the discussion to go. Reformulation also took place in order to attach vocabulary to the ideas we would be covering in the activity.

Conceptual Discussion

The conceptual discussion is designed to focus the lesson even more and to reach direct outcomes. This is the area where there will be "right and wrong" answers. For the Froot Loop packaging activity, this section is basically the same as the old activity. The students are shown the printed receipt for the cereal and crunch the numbers (no pun intended) to determine the price per ounce. This data is then displayed in a graph. Obviously, because of the math, the discourse will be extremely closed, and there will be wrong answers. No analysis of these numbers takes place, just strictly finding the mathematical answers.

Application Discussion

The application discussion component of this type of lesson is meant to apply the information learned in the conceptual discussion to the real world. It is designed to open the discussion back up and allow for more sophisticated talk about the concept. This discussion can be used by the teacher to bring up more in-depth points, or as an assessment of the students' learning of the material from the conceptual discussion. The specific purpose of the application discussion for the Froot Loops activity was to relate the concepts to our waste unit. I wanted to show that not only does excess packaging cost more, but it doesn't help our waste management problems either.

In order to relate these concepts to the students' lives, the discourse needed to be open. In fact, this part of the lesson was even more open than the framing discussion at the beginning. My questioning was much more broad and I accepted many kinds of answers; basically, I wanted to see which direction the class would take the discussion. I also asked for much more elaboration because I wanted to explore the thinking processes behind the student responses. My intent was to help the students connect the ideas from the lesson with their everyday lives. This is one of the overall goals for the environmental science course. I also wanted to get a feeling for their overall understanding of the concept.

Conclusion

I believe that structuring a lesson or a discussion so that it contains a framing, conceptual, and application component is very effective. It exhibits a natural flow or progression of thinking that the students can follow. As I have thought more about this structure for lessons, I have realized that many times I have used a format similar to this but not quite as developed. To me, this means that I have been doing something right, and it raises my confidence in my teaching ability. However, by the same token, it shows me that I can still greatly improve and can further develop any existing and future lessons to increase student learning.

Introduction

The teacher reflection above illustrates a model for creating discussions across a unit of instruction. The name "bow tie" makes reference to a cyclical pattern of open, closed, and open discourse patterns that resemble a bow tie when represented schematically (see Figure 8.1). The underlying assumption of the bow tie model is that the most desirable classroom discourse will alternate between teacher guided discussion and high levels of student participation. The bow tie identifies the most opportune times to maximize student participation, as well as the times that teacher guidance is most needed. Thus, it can help alleviate the difficulty teachers may experience when planning for discussion-based lessons, especially teachers who lack experience or those in subject areas that have traditionally sponsored a more teacher directed dialogue (e.g., math and science).

The Basis for the Bow Tie

The bow tie is a conceptual tool. It originates from my own teaching practice, from the observations of teachers, from conversations with teachers, and from working with teachers to improve their classroom discussions. It is intended to provide a systematic approach to planning discussions at the unit level. However, it is not intended to preclude or preempt other approaches to planning discussions.

The description of the bow tie is consistent with Habermas' (1984–87) theory of communicative action, which describes how students move from their everyday experience and language to more technical academic concepts and language. There are three essential parts to Habermas' account, beginning with the conversational skills students bring from their everyday life, followed by a gradual acquisition of more technical language and concepts in school settings, and eventually an integration of those new concepts into conversations outside of the school setting.

The language of our everyday life, or "lifeworld," serves as the initial basis for the more formal and technical discourse that occurs in disciplines such as mathematics,

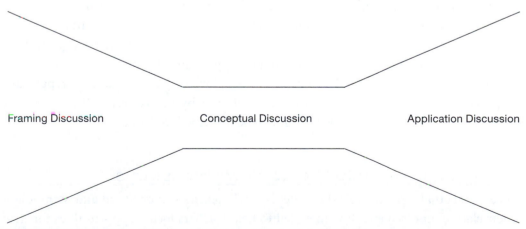

Framing Discussion   Conceptual Discussion   Application Discussion

FIGURE 8.1 The "bow tie" model of open and closed discourse.

political science, and English, or professions such as education, law, medicine, and science. The technical discourse in each of these fields is more formal and objective than everyday language. For example, a layperson may speak of a student as being "rude" or "obnoxious." In contrast, an experienced teacher might refer to the same child as "lacking in social skills." The teacher's more professional and objective description of the problem suggests a solution path—work on the student's social skills. The more subjective description of the layperson is essentially judgmental and nonproductive.

Over time, concepts associated with a professional vocabulary work their way back into the lifeworld, where they are gradually absorbed and made part of everyday talk, with the potential to influence the lifeworld experience. For instance, consider how the scientific term "positive reinforcement" has become a part of everyday language. The commonplace idea that people work for rewards became objectified and formalized as "positive reinforcement" through scientific research on behavioralism. While initially used only in a scientific setting, this term has gradually become part of the lifeworld vocabulary and, in so doing, has redefined our original conception of working for rewards.

Overview of the Bow Tie

There are three types of discussions in the bow tie model: (a) framing discussions or discussions that draw on students' previous knowledge to begin a unit, (b) conceptual discussions or discussions intended to introduce new concepts, and (c) application discussions or discussions for the purpose of applying new concepts in real world settings. These three types of discussions can be distinguished by differences in their location in the unit, their direction, their preparation and accountability strategies, and their discourse moves.

This model is an extension of the inductive and deductive discussion patterns presented in chapter 4. The framing discussion, which is the opening discussion in the model, is an inductive discussion, i.e., one that moves from student experience toward new learning. Similarly, the conceptual discussion, the second discussion in the model, is also an inductive discussion. The application discussion, the third type in the model, is a deductive discussion, or one that moves from a scientific concept back to student experience. Framing, conceptual, and application discussions can be further distinguished by the types of discourse moves employed, by the amount of preparation required, by the grouping strategies employed, and by the accountability strategies needed. In the chapters that follow, each will be described in detail.

Using the Bow Tie to Create New Discussions

As a conceptual tool, the bow tie model can help teachers understand and manipulate their classroom discourse. It is intended to help teachers locate opportunities for new discussions within teaching units and to recognize the strategies needed to create each type of discussion. The bow tie can also provide a common language that enables teachers from a variety of disciplines to share their experiences, thus enabling the kind of practice-based discussions that sustain professional growth and stimulate the reflective power of teachers (for a detailed description of a professor who implemented the bow tie model, see Henning, Nielsen, & Hauschildt, 2006).

The written reflections of teachers who have used the bow tie model will be presented in each of the following three chapters. As indicated by the description of the teacher above, teachers find the bow tie to be both a powerful and an easy to use tool.

What Teachers Need to Know

The purpose of this chapter was to introduce readers to the bow tie model, a conceptual tool that can help teachers identify the most likely locations within a unit to create a more open discourse. To fully understand the relationships described by the bow tie, it is important to have mastered the concepts introduced in earlier sections of the book, such as the differences between more convergent (closed) and divergent (open) discourse moves, how to move discussions along an either inductive or deductive path, and how to influence student participation through preparation and accountability strategies.

The three chapters that follow this one will provide detailed descriptions of how to construct framing, conceptual, and application discussions. Each chapter will be organized to describe the preparation, grouping, and accountability strategies needed to create each type of discussion. The types of discourse moves associated with each discussion will also be described. An example unit from a seventh grade mathematics classroom will provide illustrations of each of these discussion components.

Application Discussion

The chapters in the first part of the book addressed the components governing discussion-based teaching. They included teacher questioning, student responses, teacher follow up moves, how to create a discussion, how to guide discussion, how to keep students involved, and how to support culturally and linguistically diverse students. Briefly review these elements and then discuss how you could use these strategies for converting teacher centered lessons into discussion-based lessons.

Activities

1. Design a teaching unit to include all three of the discussion types introduced in this chapter. Provide a brief description of your discourse moves, preparation and grouping arrangements, and accountability strategies. In the following three chapters, you will explore each of these discussions in more depth, and you will be asked to add more details to your design.

Study Group Activities

2. Bring your unit designs to a teacher study group meeting and compare your strategies. Identify the discussions you plan as inductive or deductive, describe your preparation, grouping, and accountability strategies. Then, describe some of the discourse moves you anticipate making and the types of responses you anticipate from students.

3. Implement the unit plan you designed. Audio or videotape your discussions, then analyze them in your study groups.

nine
Creating the Framing Discussion

You have encountered framing discussions at the beginning of each chapter throughout the book. In this chapter, you will learn how to create your own framing discussion. Below, a ninth grade English teacher describes how she will lead a framing discussion to begin a unit on mental health. In the first part of her plan, she describes how the unit has typically begun in the past. As you read her plan, pay careful attention to what she changed and the strategies she plans to use as part of the framing discussion. After you finish reading, answer the following questions.

Framing Discussion

1. How did the teacher connect the lesson to her students' previous knowledge?
2. What kind of preparation were students given before the discussion?
3. What kinds of accountability strategies were used?
4. What kinds of discourse moves did the teacher anticipate?
5. Is this an inductive or a deductive discussion?
6. How could you take a similar approach to creating a discussion in your classroom?

Description of Lesson/Unit

The purpose of this plan is to devise a way to open a segment of discourse related to a novel unit for my ninth grade language arts students. I refer to this unit as a novel case study (NCS) because students pick novels from a select group of books that deal with teen characters who struggle with stress, moral issues, peer or familial crisis, health problems, etc.

Prior to introducing the novels, we read a short story that opens with a fourteen-year-old boy facing charges for shooting his abusive father. The story fosters a lot of meaty discourse about the character's motives, situation, and alternatives. In addition, students often debate the guilt or innocence of the teenager. While students are eager to argue their points, I try to steer them to offer textual evidence as support. The primary purpose of using this story is to give us a common frame of reference, for example, to use as we discuss issues relating to the NCS (since all students do not read the same NCS books).

The lesson I would like to work on opening up is my introduction to the topic of mental health. Typically, I will give lesson notes in an overview titled, "What is mental health?" I give a definition for mental health and list some characteristics of mentally healthy individuals, factors that can negatively affect a person's mental health, and how a person's health may fluctuate from day to day based on their environment and circumstances. I explain how we'll be thinking about the mental health of characters in literature, and I give an overview of each NCS book, outlining some of the bigger issues or topics so students can decide which books are right for them.

Current Discourse: Participant Framework

In this lesson, there is very little (student) discourse. The lesson, and book talks which follow, center on teacher talk, with some time toward the end of class for students to peruse books and ask questions about authors and titles. The closest framework that fits this lesson would be Inquiry–Response–Evaluation (IRE); however, even that is very limited. Overall, student discourse on this day is minimal at best.

Restructuring Plan for More Open Discourse

Typically, we have very thoughtful, open discourse once the students have selected their books (forming small groups reading the same title). Students are eager to share their reactions, as well as discuss and evaluate the mental health of characters in their books. However, I would like to find out what students know or think about mental health *at the start* of the unit, *before* they select a book or begin to read.

Since many students may have a difficult time with the term "mental health," I think it will be important to start with something they can relate to personally. Beginning with writing might be the best, nonthreatening way to start a dialogue. Also, using a phrase like "stressed out" might be easier for them to relate to and understand. A possible prompt could be, "Describe a recent time when you were stressed out. What caused this stress? How did you deal with the situation? If possible, try and list some steps you may have gone through—for example: 'First I cried a lot and called my best friend, but after talking to her, I got really angry and then I . . .,' etc. This can be a private entry, or you can choose to share it with others in here."

At this point, every student would be participating, even if it is through a short written piece for me. Because some people may have private stories, I think sharing in small groups initially may be the best way to get students talking. Still, I would explain that they could refer to a part of their entry or all of it—whatever they are comfortable sharing. Students will be sitting at round tables along with people they have been working with for some time, so hopefully it will feel like a safe, nonthreatening place to share something personal.

After some time for small groups talking, I would move to large group discussion. First, I would share my own experience about a recent stressful experience. Then, I would open it up for more people to share their stories with the entire group. As students share, I would try to listen, and occasionally offer support through reformulating or restating comments or asking questions for clarification and examples. Mentally, I would need to note how student examples will fit my lesson notes on mental health—the more I can tie their individual stories and experiences to the definition and characteristics in the lesson, the better.

Expected Discourse

My hope is that, when students get the opportunity to talk about their thoughts, ideas, and feelings about mental health, as a class we'll be able to deal with some preconceived notions they hold that might stem from T.V., hearsay, or friends and family. In addition, however, we may find some students have first-hand experience to share, which can shed light on the subject and demystify it a bit. I think once students understand that they, too, have a level to their own mental health, it is easier for them to understand and identify with each other as well as characters they encounter in the books. This kind of discussion would include elaboration, since much of what we talk about could be personal opinion or personal experience. Students would most likely offer explanations to defend their opinions or arguments. I also think that questions would be a big part of the discourse, as we determine a working definition for mental health and applicable characteristics.

Introduction

The teacher above uses several key strategies for changing a teaching unit that began with a lecture to a unit that begins with a discussion. First, she designs a writing activity to prepare her students for the discussion. The activity is intended to stimulate her students' thinking and help them make connections with their previous experiences. Having them write down their ideas also serves as an informal accountability strategy. In addition, she has created a prompt that will elicit divergent student responses (describe a time you were "stressed out"), thus increasing the chances that there will be a high level of participation. In anticipation that her students will be able to elaborate on their personal experiences, she plans on guiding the discussion with reformulations and restatements. In summary, this teacher has given thoughtful consideration to the numerous and complex interactions that constitute a framing discussion.

Framing discussions take place at the very beginning of a single lesson or a teaching unit, usually before any new ideas have been introduced. Typically, the teacher asks questions that elicit information or opinions based on the previous experience of students, whether it is knowledge acquired through their everyday experiences or their previous schooling. As illustrated in the teacher reflection above, the framing discussion can serve multiple purposes. First, it can elicit a high level of student participation by engaging students in a discussion that is relevant to their previous knowledge. Thus, students need little preparation in order to participate. Second, by eliciting the relevant knowledge of students, the discussion can set the stage for the learning that will follow. The framing discussion is an inductive discussion, i.e., a discussion that leads from previous student experience toward a new concept or some kind of new learning. As such, it provides an opportunity to introduce new concepts in natural, rather than technical, language. Third, the framing discussion provides an excellent opportunity to assess the current knowledge of students and inform subsequent teaching strategies.

The purpose of this chapter is to help you design your own framing discussions. Accordingly, the following sections will fully describe and illustrate the type of preparation and group work, accountability strategies, discourse moves, and one-on-one support associated with framing discussions. Examples from framing discussions in a seventh grade mathematics classroom will also be provided.

Preparation and Group Work for Framing Discussions

Since framing discussions are located within the students' previous experiences, little preparation and few or no materials are needed to begin the discussion. Framing discussions can be started by simply posing a question or presenting a problem to students. Similarly, the grouping arrangements are more likely to be organized on a temporary or more informal basis, e.g., temporary pairings like think–pair–share or buzz groups (see chapter 7 for descriptions). The small group discussions preceding the larger class framing discussion could help build relationships in anticipation of more challenging academic activities. In either case, the small group discussion will give students a chance to brainstorm, express their ideas in a low risk environment, and to hear other ideas.

Providing Individual Help during the Framing Discussion

Providing individual guidance during group work will often include helping students brainstorm and generate new ideas. The teacher's questions are likely to be open ended and intended to help students make connections with their previous knowledge. This approach is directly related to the purposes of the framing discussion, which are to maximize student participation and to assess the knowledge base of students.

Accountability Strategies for the Framing Discussion

The accountability strategies needed for the framing discussion are more informal than formal. Formal accountability strategies are not usually needed because framing discussions usually occur very early in the unit, and the discussion is often rooted in students' previous knowledge. To encourage student participation during framing discussions, more informal strategies are often appropriate, such as recording student responses as part of a participation grade, creating positive peer pressure, using numbered heads, or assigning someone to report out from a small group conversation. Other examples of informal accountability strategies would include having your students evaluate their participation on an index card, cold calling, or giving bonus points for participating. The more stimulating the topic and the more inviting the classroom atmosphere, the fewer accountability strategies will be needed.

Discourse Moves Associated with the Framing Discussion

Effective framing discussions are characterized by less teacher talk, more student talk, more wait time, more student-to-student interaction, and more student control of the direction of the discussion. A framing discussion often begins with a very broad question that enables a wide range of responses from students of all ability levels. Their responses will reveal much about what interests them, what is most important to them, and the level of detail to which they are attending.

Teachers should strive not to provide too much guidance by asking leading questions, especially early in the discussion. Exerting too much control too early may preclude important insights that could lead to effective teaching strategies. Instead, teachers should initially allow for a broad exploration of the discussion topic to better assess their students' existing knowledge base. Inevitably, student responses will begin to dwindle, thus providing an opportunity for the teacher to ask follow up questions to further probe and guide student thinking toward the lesson objectives. As the discussion continues to unfold, teachers may further guide student thinking through elaborations and reformulations.

Framing Discussion Example

The example framing discussions presented below were taken from Ms. Brady's seventh grade classroom composed of twenty-one students, including thirteen boys and eight girls, with a wide range of abilities. Sixteen students were Caucasian, two were African American, and three were Asian. The purpose of the unit, which was entitled *Filling and Wrapping* (Lappan, Fey, Friel, Fitzgerald, & Phillips, 1998), was to develop strategies for finding the surface areas and volumes for cubes, prisms, cylinders, cones, and spheres; to discover relationships between these geometrical forms; and to reason about problems involving these geometrical forms. The unit required a total of nine class sessions over a three-week period. The class met two days per week in a "blocked" session for ninety minutes, and one day per week for forty-five minutes in an "unblocked" session. During the unit, Ms. Brady's classes engaged in discussions that were designed using a bow tie model. Examples of conceptual and application discussions from Ms. Brady's class will be discussed in the chapters following this one (Henning & Balong, 2005).

The example seventh grade mathematics unit began with three framing discussions, which took place over the first two class sessions of the unit. In all three of the framing discussions for this unit, the teacher's goal was to establish a relationship between the form and function of objects. Each of these discussions began within the previous personal experiences of the students. Their high level of knowledge enabled students to contribute diverse responses from multiple perspectives. All three framing discussions were initiated by posing a problem to the class, as reflected in the questions below:

1. Why are there differences in the shape of ice cream containers?
2. How does the form of shoes conform to their function?
3. Can you explain how the forms of objects in this room conform to their function?

Preparation and Group Work

For the initial framing discussion, the teacher used several strategies to prepare her students for the discussion. First, the students were asked to use an index card to sketch the last package from which they ate ice cream. Underneath the sketch, they had to explain the reason why the container had that shape. After a few minutes of whole group discussion, the teacher allowed the class a brief time to brainstorm in small groups of four. During the brainstorming sessions, the students wrote their ideas on their index cards, while the teacher walked around the room interacting with the small groups and individual students.

The preparation for the second and third framing discussions did not include small group work. These discussions were preceded by short activities in which students were asked to make observations and draw conclusions. During the second framing discussion, students moved around the room, examining their classmates' shoes for the relationship between their form and function. They brainstormed answers on their index card, exchanged ideas for a brief period of time, and then discussed as a whole class. In the third and final framing discussion, the students were asked to write down the relationship between the form and function of objects in the room before discussing as a whole class.

Accountability Strategies

The accountability strategies employed by Ms. Brady were informal and were primarily focused on encouraging student engagement. At the end of each of the three discussions, the students were asked to reflect on their participation by evaluating their contribution to the discussion on their index card, which they turned in to the teacher. They were also asked to write down observations on their index cards and sticky notes, which they later used during the framing discussions. Even with informal accountability strategies, minimal preparation, and only a limited time to interact within groups, participation was widespread during the discussion because the students' experience with and knowledge about the topic was high.

Discourse Moves for Framing Discussions

The teacher began the discussion by asking students about the shape of the container for their favorite ice cream. As students hypothesized about why ice cream is packaged in the different shaped containers, a variety of shapes were named during the discussion, including cylinder, rectangular prism, and cone. The discourse during these discussions was characterized by a high ratio of student to teacher talk. The teacher gave a relatively small number of cues, gave a low number of explanations, and made only a few procedural and management comments. The purpose was to provide minimal guidance as students explored their current understanding of the relationship between shape and function. Eventually, this discussion led to others that incorporated more mathematical ideas, such as volume and surface area.

Below is an excerpt from the first framing discussion. The discourse is characterized by relatively brief teacher elicitations and relatively extended student responses. The teacher opens the discussion with a very broad, open-ended question to begin the discussion. Her comments are brief and primarily intended to encourage further student responses. The students give relatively lengthy responses, based primarily on their previous knowledge.

Ms. Brady:	Okay! A lot of you already have some good ideas, so all I want you to do is share your ideas with each other, okay? Share your ideas with each other. Remember that I would like to see you contributing today. And some of you I've already heard, almost all of you, I didn't talk to each and every one, have some idea of why things are shaped . . . are the way they are as far as ice cream containers, so who feels they want to start? Who feels like . . . Kevin, go ahead.
Tony:	I think they have different containers to fit people's needs because like that one on the end behind, that's like for a person who wants some ice cream on their own and they like have that. And like the gallon, whatever in the box, rectangular prism size is for bigger families or whatever and it's just like . . . yeah . . . different people's needs.

Ms. Brady:	So, multiple packages to fit different needs. All right, Chuck, go ahead.
Chuck:	Well, those, um . . . like the cylinder boxes and those others um . . . those are used a lot by Haagen-Dazs, and Ben & Jerry's, and Blue Bunny and those are really big and well known companies, but like you'll see Hy-Vee ice cream in the square ones and think the little . . . well, those aren't square . . . the rectangular prism boxes are a little cheaper than just the hard ones. But the circular, well some of these, are easier to use because there's no corners for the ice cream to get stuck on.
Ms. Brady:	Oh! I've never thought of the corner things.
Chuck:	Um . . . we thought the freezer space . . .
Ms. Brady:	Wait. Make sure everybody's giving you their attention and respect . . . go ahead.
Chuck:	The freezer space because some people have a freezer and some people have a smaller one. We thought that, the gallon one, you would want to bring home a gallon in a box, like a big box because gallons take a lot of room. And we thought the small one was made like that was because it's like if you want to buy ice cream like that they make it more expensive because they don't sell it in that one then they'd make more money off this one because if you had five people, you'd probably have to buy two or three of those things. One for each person maybe, or like one for every two persons and then and they're more expensive so that they people make more money than off the other two with discounts.
Ms. Brady:	Okay. What else? Sam did you have?
Sam:	No.
Ms. Brady:	No? You guys had a lot more ideas when I went around. What else? Brittany? What did you guys have?
Brittany:	Um . . . we think that it costs more to make different kinds of shapes like the circular one, it like costs more. But then the plastic, er . . . the box, it might cost less because it doesn't take a lot of effort to make it.

In this excerpt, the teacher provides very little guidance. Her main purpose at this early point of the discussion is to elicit student participation, so she lets the student responses determine the direction of the discussion. Too much guidance too early can inhibit student responses. Teachers who are too quick to ask leading questions or to follow up on specific student responses miss an opportunity to enable student creativity and assess student thinking. It is better to wait until student responses begin to dwindle and the discussion begins to lose momentum before taking subtle control of the discussion's direction through probing questions and carefully crafted follow up moves.

The excerpt below is intended to illustrate the gradual change in teacher discourse moves that can occur a framing discussion. In this excerpt from a later part of the same discussion, Ms. Brady has begun to exert more influence over the discussion's direction. For example, she affirms student answers in her first two comments; repeats and elaborates in her second comment; asks probing questions in her third and fourth comments; reformulates a student answer in her fifth comment; and rejects a student answer and offers an explanation in her sixth comment.

Ms. Brady (1):	Right. Did anybody come up with a . . . I heard a couple reasons, which are all very good reasons. [*Confirmations*] Did anybody come up with any other reason of why it seems like the cheaper ones are in the rectangle, but the more expensive ones are in the cylinder, and the very expensive ones are in this shape which we didn't name yet? [*Elicitation*] What is this shape? Anybody know the name of this one?
Justin:	Semi-triangular cylinder.
Ms. Brady (2):	Semi-triangular cylinder. [*Repetition*] I think that's the best name I've ever heard for it! [*Confirmation*] It's not the mathematical name, but it's probably the one that people would definitely recognize. [*Elaboration*] So that's good, Justin. [*Confirmation*] Anybody else have an idea of what the name for this one is? [*Elicitation*] I'm going to use Justin's because that's the most descriptive, okay? [*Procedure*]
Carey:	It's just a smaller cylinder.
Ms. Brady (3):	But isn't a cylinder . . . what's not cylindrical about it? [*Elicitation—Probing question*]
Carey:	It has an angle.
Ms. Brady (4):	What's not cylindrical about it, Alex? [*Elicitation—Probing question*]
Alex:	Well, it tilts in instead of staying straight up the side.
Ms. Brady (5):	Okay, so it tilts in a little bit, [*Reformulation*] so the top circle and the bottom circle are . . . [*Elicitation*]
Ramona:	Then a big gallon wouldn't be a cylinder either.
Ms. Brady (6):	Huh? Right, not quite. [*Rejection*] This is actually called a frustum of a cone. So I want you to picture that this would come back to a cone, right? If it kept going down it could be a cone. So it's like a cone that has been cut off, okay? So, it's actually called a frustum of a cone. [*Explanation*] Sherry? Did you guys . . . did you come up with any other good reason of why less expensive to more expensive? [*Elicitation*] And all the other things about fitting people's needs . . . um . . . freezer space have all been important. [*Confirmation*]

What the Teacher Needs to Know

With an understanding of the purpose and component parts of a framing discussion, you can redesign your teaching units in a way that converts lectures to discussions. For example, a photography teacher in one of my graduate classes wanted to change his opening lesson on camera operation from a lecture on the parts of a camera to a discussion. A discussion on the parts of a camera would not have worked because his students would have lacked the knowledge to answer any questions. To create a discussion, the topic had to be framed within the students' existing knowledge base.

Therefore, I suggested that he show the students two contrasting photographs, each of them taken using different settings on the camera (see "Responding to an Observation" in chapter 5). The students could discuss the two pictures in small groups and then have one member of the group summarize their discussion. During the large group discussion, the teacher could gradually lead his students to an awareness of how the camera settings influenced the quality of the images they had seen. Later in the unit, after he has begun teaching the camera settings, the teacher could use this initial discussion to make connections between the various camera settings and the resulting quality of the photographs. Thus, the initial discussion could serve as a reference point throughout the entire unit.

The framing discussion provides teachers with an opportunity to maximize student participation, assess the current level of student knowledge, and establish a foundation for the new learning that will follow. To be successful at creating a framing discussion, the teacher must know their students' interests and the relationship between their previous knowledge and the content to be covered. That knowledge can lead them to framing a question that is broad enough to elicit student responses but focused enough to provide a pathway to new concepts. Finally, teachers must be familiar with the discourse moves that will enable them to guide the discussion from the students' previous knowledge toward the learning objectives.

Application Discussion

Reexamine the teacher discussion plan you read at the beginning of the chapter. Discuss the types of changes she made in the lesson to open up the discourse. Consider her discourse moves, preparation and grouping strategies, her accountability strategies, and the direction of the discussion. Rank in order the relative importance of these changes when redesigning a lesson.

Activities

1. Think of a picture or find a story that could be used to begin a framing discussion in your subject area. Since this is a framing discussion, the picture or graph you choose should start a discussion with very little preparation; the story you tell

should require no more than a few minutes. Explain how you will use the picture or story to begin your discussion.

2. Design a framing discussion for an existing unit using one of the following approaches: responding to a problem, responding to an observation, or responding to a reading. Incorporate your opening question, the concept you will be teaching, and some of the discourse moves you anticipate. As part of your design, describe the preparation, grouping strategies, and accountability strategies that will be part of the assignment. In addition, describe your and your students' anticipated discourse moves. If you do not have an existing unit of instruction, design a framing discussion for a new unit that you plan to teach.

3. Implement the framing discussion you designed, collect audio or videotape data, create a research question, and analyze the participant frameworks.

Study Group Activities

4. Bring your plan for a framing discussion to the study group discussion and share ideas.

5. Write a reflection paper based on your framing discussion data and compare your data with other members of the study group.

ten
Creating the Conceptual Discussion

Framing Discussion

In the reflection paper below, a teacher describes a conceptual discussion he led in his industrial technology classroom. As you read his reflection, identify the strategies he used to restructure the lesson into a conceptual discussion. After you finish reading, answer the following questions.

1. How does the teacher make connections between the students' previous knowledge and the conceptual knowledge he wants them to learn?
2. What kind of preparation were students given before the discussion?
3. What kinds of accountability strategies were used?
4. What kinds of discourse moves did the teacher anticipate?
5. Is this an inductive or a deductive discussion?
6. Do the changes the teacher makes in the discussion lead to a more student centered or teacher centered discourse?
7. How could you take a similar approach to creating a discussion?

Nature of Activity/Discussion

The activity or discussion that I would like to focus on for this paper is related to the development of a woodworking project and the classroom discourse that takes place during this development.

Current Classroom Discourse Related to this Activity

Much of the class time associated with the development of a practical hands-on project, such as the creation of a woodworking project, is in the form of lecture/demonstration by the teacher and then application by the student. The unit usually starts out with me informing the students about proper techniques for designing, planning, machine safety, proper manufacturing processes, and then the assigning of a project that applies all of the above. This discussion is very closed in the sense that I demonstrate/explain to the students the procedures for an activity, and then the students try to replicate the procedures on their own projects. Demonstrations on particular machines and processes are once again teacher centered, as is the giving of information to the students. There is not much class discussion during the instruction phase of the unit.

The problem that I see with this type of classroom interaction is that most students can duplicate the initial, teacher chosen project, but cannot apply the information to the next project that is student chosen. Transfer of information to a new activity is very limited.

Restructuring of Activity

In the traditional sense, it is very difficult to apply the discussion model that was discussed in our class to my classroom environment. I do not have much classroom time dedicated to class discussion. Much of the classroom time is dedicated to the students working on their individual projects. As stated above, any type of teacher/class discussion comes in the form of short verbal instructions on how to perform a given task. Therefore, when analyzing the use of the discussion model that we studied, my classroom is very heavy in the conceptual and application phases. The following plan will be what I consider an attempt at opening up the discourse in my classroom by having a wider "framing" aspect of the discussion model that will facilitate better understanding and student transfer of knowledge toward new applications.

The first step in the restructuring of this activity is to have the students discover and construct the knowledge of designing, planning, and construction of a practical project and move away from me depositing this knowledge into the student through the use of lecture/demonstration. I would start the unit by grouping the students by fours and providing the students with supplies such as scraps of various types of wood, hand tools, various types of fasteners (screws, nails, glue) and finishes. My framing of the discussion would come in the form of a statement such as "Your group is to build a device to hold these four books (I would have four different sizes of books available). The supplies are at your group's bench."

I would hope with this type of statement that the "framing" of the discussion would give the groups of students an opportunity for an open discussion in solving the problem at hand. I know this type of participant structure is not a whole class discussion that I am attempting to change, but I do think this is an open approach to getting the students discussing the problem, analyzing different solutions, and better engaging in their learning.

Criteria for evaluation of total student response would be the following. Each group would have to journal answers to the following questions. Each member in the group would be responsible for one of the four questions and reporting the recorded information to the rest of the class. The questions would be:

1. List the different procedures performed on the project.
2. For each procedure listed, explain why the procedure was attempted.
3. List the different skills or knowledge needed to complete the project.
4. Analyze the completed project for the following: appearance, function, durability, etc.

Within the different responses, I would imagine the groups would come up with statements related to the formal concepts or lessons that I would be teaching or demonstrating to the students. I would think that many of the projects would lack any type of proper woodworking joinery with the exception of the pounding of nails into the boards to keep pieces together. The finish of the project would not be adequate due to lack of sanding or materials preparation. The projects may not fit together correctly due to improper tool usage or the inability to cut "square" boards. Procedures would have to be repeated or redone due to lack of planning.

Using the journaling and adequate analysis/reflection of their final project I feel there would be many concepts that could now be discussed in the conceptual phase of our discussion model. Also, with the students' experiences in creating their group project, they now have a connection between their past knowledge and the need to learn new ideas.

During the conceptual phase of the discussion model, I would then be instructing the class on the importance of different concepts or objectives related to woodworking. These concepts would include: planning, machine usage, the importance of using different woodworking joints, manufacturing techniques such as sanding, cutting, applying finishes, and the importance of general skills such as measuring. This part of the unit would be very "closed" as I would be doing a lot of lecturing and/or demonstrating. Hopefully, the students would then be able to make connections or transfer knowledge from their group projects to the proper techniques that I would be teaching them.

The final phase of the discussion model is the application phase. In my lesson, the application phase would be a new project that each student would complete. With the knowledge and experience gained from the group project and my teaching of proper techniques, I believe the students would have a better understanding of how to plan, design, and create an adequate woodworking project. They would be able to transfer the information learned to a new setting.

Reflection

I know this method of applying the discussion model we learned in class is a little more nontraditional than in a class that uses class discussion frequently. In my classes, we just do not have much time dedicated to class discussion. Therefore, I feel that applying the model to a larger scale and focusing on a time frame larger than just a single class discussion is more appropriate for me.

Basically, I would like to try a new way of introducing woodworking to the students. The participant framework discussed in this paper gets the students involved in the learning process a lot quicker. Instead of the students sitting and being lectured to early in the term, the students become engaged learners a lot quicker. With the initial project, the students will have some kind of past knowledge to link the new conceptual knowledge to. Structuring the class into groups creates an environment that will give the students support in co-constructing knowledge and the ability to discuss.

Introduction

Like the framing discussion, the conceptual discussion is an inductive discussion, i.e., it always begins with previous student experience and moves toward new concepts. But while similar in this regard, there are significant differences between the two types of discussions. Framing discussions are the initial discussions in the unit. They are begun with very little preparation, and their main purpose is to engage students with the topic, to elicit and assess their current level of knowledge on the topic, and to create a mindset for future lessons. At the conclusion of a framing discussion, students will probably have been partially, but not fully, introduced to a new concept.

In contrast, conceptual discussions occur after the framing discussion in the bow tie, and the purpose is to introduce students to new information, ideas, or concepts. The conceptual discussion usually requires more preparation than a framing discussion and is often preceded by exposing students to new information through lecture, reading, or activities. New information is needed in order to lift students to new levels of conceptual understanding.

The new activity is the key design element in the conceptual discussion plan described above. This activity resembles, but is significantly different than, the activity described at the opening of the previous chapter. Like the framing discussion, the students are asked to reflect on an experience and discuss it together in small groups as preparation for the large group discussion. However, the purpose of the writing activity at the beginning of chapter 9 was to elicit student knowledge based upon their previous experiences of being "stressed out." That activity did not involve acquiring a new experience. In contrast, the activity described above adds to student experience by requiring students to solve a problem (building a woodworking project) within a context that is located closer to the curriculum goals. The experiences that students gain from this activity can provide additional pathways to new concepts, ideas, or procedures to be learned later. Later in the unit, as new procedures are introduced, they can be preceded by a discussion that refers back to the activity described above. For example, when the teacher introduces the procedures for squaring a board, he can begin the lesson by asking his students to describe their experiences during the initial activity. Then, through a series of questions and answers, he can move his students to a more principled understanding of the procedures.

Proximity to the subject matter is what distinguishes the conceptual discussion from the framing discussion. The framing discussion uses previous student experience to preassess student knowledge, elicit student participation, and set the stage for the lesson. The conceptual discussion creates new experiences to introduce new concepts and vocabulary. The purpose of this chapter is to fully describe and illustrate conceptual discussions so that you can better design your own. Accordingly, the following sections will characterize the type of preparation and group work, accountability strategies, discourse moves, and one-on-one support associated with conceptual discussions. Examples from conceptual discussions in a seventh grade mathematics classroom will also be provided.

Preparation and Group Work for the Conceptual Discussion

The conceptual discussion moves from the students' previous experience toward new learning, i.e., it is an inductive discussion. As the discussion introduces more unfamiliar ideas, it becomes harder for students to elaborate on them. Therefore, to achieve a high level of student participation during a conceptual discussion, a significant amount of preparation is needed. It could involve engaging in a series of activities, working individually or in groups on a project, making extended observations, or completing a series of readings. Students will be able to contribute to a conceptual discussion to the degree that they possess relevant information or experience.

The need for extended preparation may mean that students will spend more time working in groups together. If groups stay together longer, they will necessarily require more planning in regards to the division of tasks, accountability strategies, and collaborative interactions. For example, you may want to designate a more formal role to each member of the group, such as facilitator, reporter, and recorder. Holding students accountable may include more formal strategies, such as taking a test or receiving a rubric score on a group project. Since the students will be developing ideas together over an extended period of time, you may also want to give more consideration to teaching collaborative skills and to the compositions of groups in regard to both social and academic skills.

Providing Individual Help During the Conceptual Discussion

In contrast to the framing discussion, individual support in preparation for a conceptual discussion may require helping students uncover key factual information. These facts will be needed during the large group discussion in order to establish a shared understanding among students and a basis for drawing conclusions, i.e., moving inductively from experience to new concepts. For example, while providing help during small group work in her unit on surface area and volume, Ms. Brady asked a number of probing questions and followed up by confirming student answers. The primary purpose of the exchanges between teacher and students was often to ensure that the mathematical calculations were done correctly.

These more convergent or closed exchanges between teacher and student supported a more open large group discussion, during which students justified and defended their choice of particular solution paths. For example, in the transcript excerpt below, the students were working in small groups to find surface area and volume using wooden blocks as manipulatives. The students were asked to find a preferred solution method, record it on an index card, and explain it in a follow up discussion. During this preparatory activity, the teacher moved around the room checking the accuracy of her students' calculations, thus enabling them to have greater confidence in their explanations. In the transcript excerpt below, the teacher is talking to a small group of students about the steps they used to solve the problem.

Ms. Brady:	Do you remember how to find surface area or do you need help? [*Elicitation*]
Antoine:	You find the one side and then you multiply by two. You find the other side and you multiply by two and then you add them.
Ms. Brady:	Okay. You were ... that's very quick, okay ... [*Confirmation*] but I don't know if ... I got it, but I want to make sure that everybody has it, okay? So, that was fast. So, ... Do you need help? Can you go on to the next one? Okay, I'll be right there. Let's check it. Let's check this one. Sam, Sam ... quieter, please. All right, now check the (inaudible). Sam, you can help out, too. [*Procedure*] Do you remember? [*Elicitation*]
Sam:	Six.
Ms. Brady:	And how did you get six? [*Elicitation*]
Sam:	There's six on top.
Ms. Brady:	Oh, good, good, good. So, that's a good start. [*Confirmation*] Six squares on top, which means you want to find the same thing for each face, for each of the faces, so (laughter) you have six into [*Cue*] ... how many on this side? How many? [*Elicitation*]
Sam:	Sixteen.
Ms. Brady:	How did you get sixteen? [*Elicitation*]

Sam:	I counted all these and then I added it and then I timesed it like this, right there.
Ms. Brady:	So you added all those squares. [*Reformulation*] Was Justin trying to help? Justin, have you been trying to help? Thank you very much, I appreciate that, okay? [*Procedure*]

The discourse between teacher and student was relatively closed during this small group activity. The teacher inquired of students whether they needed help, asked numerous questions as a way of checking on student progress, and made many evaluative comments when following up on student responses. There were few reformulations or repetitions, and no recaps, perhaps because those are moves that can better be associated with whole class discourse. There is less reason to repeat or recap for emphasis when dealing with one or just a few students.

Accountability Strategies for the Conceptual Discussion

Accountability strategies in conceptual discussions address dual concerns. The first is student engagement. To promote participation, employ informal accountability strategies such as reporting from groups, having students write a written reflection on participation, assigning individual roles to each group member, having students report out from their groups, or creating group structures such as jigsaw or numbered heads. These types of accountability strategies are intended to motivate students to stay focused on the task and to contribute to the discussion.

The second function of accountability strategies in conceptual discussions would be to assess new learning. Since a primary purpose of conceptual discussions is to introduce new concepts, more formal accountability strategies are also needed, such as a test, a paper, a project, or some kind of other well structured outcomes. These strategies would determine whether students acquired the primary information associated with the learning objectives for the unit. More formal accountability strategies become increasingly relevant later in the unit as students come closer to attaining the unit learning goals.

Discourse Moves Associated with the Conceptual Discussion

Of the three discussion types—framing, conceptual, and application—the conceptual discussion is the most teacher guided. This is acceptable for two reasons. First, student thinking will benefit from teacher scaffolding because the concepts are new and likely difficult. Second, there will be other opportunities to create a more open discourse within the unit (e.g., framing and application discussions). More convergent discourse moves (e.g., question, brief student response, and evaluative follow up) are unacceptable only when they constitute the only teacher approach to classroom discourse. They are entirely appropriate when teachers employ convergent discourse moves to achieve a worthwhile purpose, e.g., to establish a common factual foundation or to lift student understanding. As a conceptual tool, the bow tie can help teachers visualize an idealized pattern of open and closed discourse that delineates a place for each without excluding the advantages of the other.

Since learning new concepts often requires conforming to a specific technical vocabulary and a well defined set of relationships, the teacher is more likely to reject a student answer during the conceptual discussion than during either the framing or the application discussions. Compared with framing and application discussions, student responses are briefer, there is likely to be a lower ratio of student to teacher talk, less interaction among students, and more scaffolding by the teacher. The teacher is also more likely to give explanations, reformulate student comments, recap information for students, and ask probing questions that lead students step by step to the concept. In addition, the teacher is more likely to cue students (give hints or direction) during a conceptual discussion than during a framing discussion. The increased teacher direction indicates a greater emphasis on requiring students to conform their thinking to fit a more convergent discussion, in this case conforming to mathematical concepts.

The phase of the teaching unit associated with conceptual discussions would be the most likely place that teachers would choose to forgo a discussion altogether, perhaps opting for a dialogue that closely resembles the IRE participant framework (recall question, convergent answer, and evaluative follow up). In some cases, the learning goals might be more efficiently achieved by directly dispensing information or providing students with time to investigate the concept individually as a prelude to an application discussion.

Conceptual Discussion Example

In the example seventh grade mathematics unit from Ms. Brady's classroom, the three framing discussions were followed by four conceptual discussions. Like framing discussions, conceptual discussions are inductive discussions, intended to lead students from their experience toward a new concept. Unlike in framing discussions, the students were given much more preparation before conceptual discussions through activities and group work.

Preparation and Group Work

The preparation for the conceptual discussions was more structured and extended than the preparation for the framing discussions. The first two conceptual discussions were preceded by an activity titled "Packaging Blocks." The students were asked to arrange twenty-four blocks into as many different rectangular prisms as possible. As part of the assignment, students were required to find the dimensions, the surface area, and provide a sketch of each rectangular prism. They were also required to make a written recommendation identifying the combination of blocks needed to create a package with the least surface area.

This was an extended activity over two class periods, for which the teacher provided considerable individual support. The students worked in groups of three, and rotated the roles of recorder, builder, or verifier. The teacher moved around from group to group giving help as needed. During the first discussion, the students explained their solutions to the "Packaging Blocks" problem. During the second discussion, they were asked to explain their hypothesis for obtaining the smallest surface area. The second discussion was preceded by a brief time to consult with their group members.

For the third conceptual discussion, the topic shifted to differentiating rectangular prisms from cones, cylinders, and other geometric shapes. The students were given a geometric shape and asked to move into one of two groups, either prisms or nonprisms, depending on the shape they were holding. In preparation for the third conceptual discussion, the students worked in pairs to solve warm up problems on finding surface areas and volumes. Partners were rotated with each new problem. To facilitate the movement of students as they changed partners, the desks were arranged in two semicircles. Students in the inside semicircle rotated in an opposite direction to the students in the outside semicircle.

The fourth conceptual discussion was a question and answer session used as a review in preparation for completing an applied project. The purpose of the review was to make sure the students understood the mathematical concepts well enough to complete the application project. Since this was a review session, the preparation for this discussion was the accumulation of ideas from the previous activities and discussions.

Accountability Strategies

Several informal accountability strategies were used during the first two conceptual discussions. One approach was the use of numbered heads. The students numbered themselves by counting off, and the teacher rolled dice to randomly determine who explained their answers to problems. During the discussion, the teacher checked comprehension by asking students to give a thumbs up if they understood, thumbs to the side if they were unsure, and thumbs down if they didn't understand at all. When they turned in their problems, they put a star, a check, or a minus next to each one. The star indicated they could do the problem without help, the check indicated they needed help to get started, and the minus indicated complete uncertainty about how to proceed. They were also required to write down definitions on their paper at different points during the discussion.

During the third conceptual discussion, two accountability strategies were employed. The first was an informal strategy: students were asked to write down their definition of a prism. The second was a more formal strategy: students took a quiz on the material during the following class period. The problems on the quiz tested the students' ability to use formulas to find surface areas and volumes. Accountability during the fourth conceptual discussion, which was primarily a review in preparation for an application activity, consisted of answering the verbal questions posed by the teacher.

Discourse Moves

In contrast to the framing discussion, conceptual discussions are characterized by much shorter student responses, more support from the teacher, and a greater emphasis on conforming to established mathematical concepts. In the following excerpt from a conceptual discussion during Ms. Brady's unit on surface area and volume, the students explain their answers to practice problems. The teacher's discourse moves are identified in brackets following the comment.

Gabrielle:	Um, the surface area for that one is eighty-eight, but on one of the sides you're going to have to multiply twenty-four by two.
Ms. Brady:	Um-hum—and that's . . . [*Confirmation*]
Gabrielle:	Forty-eight.
Ms. Brady:	And then you have to multiply that by two. [*Elaboration*]
Gabrielle:	Yeah!
Ms. Brady:	Yeah, very good! [*Confirmation*] Anybody else want to say it differently? Larry? [*Elicitation*]
Larry:	Since this is the long one, it's not the longest one, but it's . . .
Ms. Brady:	The longest one would be one by one by forty-eight. [*Elaboration*]
Larry:	Forty-eight. Yeah. This is longer than that and less cubed, cubical or whatever, however . . .
Ms. Brady:	Less cubical? [*Elicitation*]
Larry:	Yeah.
Ms. Brady:	I like that. [*Confirmation*]
Larry:	However you say it. And so it's going to be longer so it's going to . . . it's going to have more surface area.
Ms. Brady:	Everybody okay with that? Is there any one that would be actually . . . yes, this is bigger . . . is there any one that would have a smaller surface than four by two by six? [*Elicitation*] I want you to talk with your partner only about that. [*Procedure*] Is there any one that would be smaller than four by two by six? [*Elicitation*] Remember last time, Larry just hinted at it, it's the one that's closest to a cube if you can get there. Closest to a cube. [*Recap*]

There are several indicators in this transcript excerpt that Ms. Brady is providing considerable support and guidance in these interactions. Her discourse moves contain a lot of questions and confirmations, both indicators that she is pursuing definite objectives in the discussion. She also provides guidance through the use of elaborations, which add more information to the discussion. Finally, she makes the most extended comment in this excerpt, which suggests a higher ratio of teacher to student talking.

What the Teacher Needs to Know

The conceptual discussion serves an important purpose by introducing students to concepts that increase the power and efficiency of their thought processes. Therefore, it is highly appropriate to recognize that convergent discourse moves serve an important role in a classroom. On the other hand, even the relatively convergent, closed discourse moves of the conceptual discussion can be opened up when preceded by an activity that is structured to promote reflection. As suggested previously, the key to more open discourse lies in preparing students for discussion through an activity and small group work.

The conceptual discussion offers several opportunities to teachers. Carefully designing a conceptual discussion provides a way for students to discover the conceptual knowledge in a topic rather than receiving it passively. This could enable increased student participation and more in-depth learning on the part of students. The teacher must know how to construct a task that will allow students to discover the concept inductively. The teacher must also know how to reconceptualize the topic in a way that allows them to imagine how a student would discover that knowledge in a classroom context. This requires an in-depth understanding of both the content and the discrete discoveries made by students as the learning unfolds. These "aha" moments are difficult to remember because most of us don't have the capacity to be fully aware of how we are learning as we learn. Thus, it requires considerable insight on the part of the teacher to imaginatively reconstruct this process.

Application Discussion

Reexamine the teacher's reflection located at the beginning of the chapter. Discuss the types of changes he made in the lesson to open up the discourse. Consider his discourse moves, preparation and grouping strategies, his accountability strategies, and the direction of the discussion. Rank the relative importance of these changes in relationship to each other in order to successfully redesign the lesson.

Activities

1. Create an activity in your subject area that could lead to a conceptual discussion. Describe how you would use this activity as a basis for the discussion.
2. Design a new conceptual discussion for an existing unit. As part of your design, describe the preparation, grouping, and accountability strategies that will be part of the assignment. In addition, describe the discourse moves that you anticipate you will make and the responses you anticipate from your students. If you do not have an existing unit of instruction, design a conceptual discussion for a new unit that you plan to teach.

3. Implement the conceptual discussion you designed, collect audio or videotape data, and analyze your discourse moves.

Study Group Activities

4. Bring your plan for a conceptual discussion to a study group discussion and share ideas.
5. Write a reflection paper on your conceptual discussion data and compare your findings with other members of the study group.

eleven

Creating the Application Discussion

Framing Discussion

Throughout the book, you have been engaging in application discussions at the end of each chapter. In this chapter, you will learn how to create your own application discussion. Below, a teacher describes how she created an application discussion in her seventh grade science classroom. As you read her reflection, try to identify the type of strategies the teacher used to create the application discussion. After you finish reading, answer the following questions.

1. How were students asked to apply their knowledge during this discussion?
2. What kind of preparation were students given before the discussion?
3. How do the activities preceding this discussion differ from those in the framing and conceptual discussions?
4. What kinds of questions did the teacher use to initially engage students in the discussion?
5. What kinds of discourse moves did the students make?
6. How does a discussion that asks students to apply new learning work differently than a discussion that leads students to new concepts?

Setting

The setting of this paper takes place in two seventh grade science classrooms. At the time, these seventh grade students were immersed in a Rock Unit. This unit's main objectives were to allow the students to come away with an understanding of the following: to understand that there are three main rock types, to identify each rock type based on observational characteristics, to describe how each of the three rock types is formed, to label a rock cycle chart in order to show their understanding of how one rock type can transform into another, and to use vocabulary that is representational of the three types of rocks.

At the time of this tape recording, the students were about two weeks into their unit. They had learned that there are three types of rocks. The students had taken notes, participated in activities, and discussed in a large group setting the different characteristics of each of the three types of rocks. Finally, at this point in the unit, they had become aware of how each of the three types of rocks is formed. This paper will discuss a small group activity of identifying rocks as the three different types.

Participants

This paper discusses two conversations held in two different seventh grade science classes taught by the same teacher. The first of the two classes is actually the second science class taught during the day, and consequently falls the period before lunch. This class is made up of twenty-six students, thirteen are female and thirteen are male. All of the students are of Caucasian descent. Of the three science classes taught, this class seems to have most of the upper level students (those who usually partake in the Program for Academic and Creative Talent [PACT] program). This was not done for the purpose of leveling students by ability, but rather by default of having a co-taught math and a co-taught science class during the day. Of those students who would fall into a more average ability level, there are two at the lower level and two students with an Individualized Education Plan (IEP).

The second of the two classes is the third, and last, science class of the day. It is the class period right after lunch. This class has an entirely different group of students. Again, in this class there are twenty-six students. There are, however, only eight males in this class. Of the twenty-six students, five are African Americans, and one is the only English language learner on our team—he is from India. In this class, there are only about four students who would fall into our PACT classes and thus be of an upper ability level. There are about nine students falling at an average level, ten who are at a low–average level and three with an IEP.

Purpose and Desired Outcome

The purpose of this lesson was for the students to have the opportunity to put into practice the notes that they had been taking over the last few days. It was also to give the students the chance to practice what they would eventually perform in their district hands-on assessment. The desired performance that I had envisioned for the students was that they would work together as a group to look at each rock individually and identify it as an igneous, metamorphic, or sedimentary rock. Using their notes, the book, and the discussion that we had during the last few days, the students should have been able to look at the physical characteristics of each rock and match them up with what a typical igneous, metamorphic, or sedimentary rock commonly has, while using the correct terminology.

During this discussion, students were to look at eight or nine different rocks and first sort them into groups based on their appearances. While doing this, the students were to fill out a rock study guide, which prompted them to ask questions such as the following: What traits make this rock igneous/sedimentary/metamorphic? What common characteristics do said rocks usually have? What does this rock look like? What does this rock feel like? What can this rock be compared to? How does this rock appear to have been formed? Using these sheets, not only did the students have a list of things they could ask themselves, but they also had an outline for the order in which they could do the tasks at hand. After identifying the rocks based on their physical characteristics, the students were to use a chart to assess themselves on whether they had correctly identified the rocks.

In order to prepare the students for this activity, we did a number of activities. There were two days spent specifically on each type of rock. Each of the two days consisted of a period of time in which notes were taken about the type of rock being discussed. Either following these notes or while taking the notes, a hands-on activity then took place (example: in order to demonstrate the two ways that sedimentary rocks are formed, we looked at and ate peanut butter and jelly sandwiches and then did the same with chocolate cookies). Finally, each second day was concluded with an individual practice in which the students had a homework piece where they were to discuss different aspects of the three types of rocks.

The strategies that were used to elicit student performance included allowing the students to work in small groups where they could communicate with each other about what they were thinking and using a worksheet to help guide them in their line of questioning. Along with this, I circled around the room during their discussions to help them when needed, observed their observation making, and asked questions when I saw fit. I also recommended at different times that the students should open up to their notes and use them as a guide in their discussions as well. These four things would not only enable the students to answer the questions on their homework sheet, but encourage them to use the different resources around the room to tap into their developing knowledge of rocks.

Assessment of Student Discourse

While my students were lacking in some areas, there were many other places where they made amazing conversation. Looking at the *Elaboration* criterion alone, my students did very well. I was extremely impressed with the way that they were able to give longer, more coherent answers as well as make arguments with supporting evidence. "We still haven't found out what this rock is." "That's metamorphic." "Where are the crystals?" "It does look kind of sedimentary too. It has sediments in it. It has natural cement too. Natural cement would have sediments in it."

Synthesis and *Analysis* are basically what this whole lab was based upon. The students were to examine the rocks and then apply the content they had been given to those rocks. They were able to make observations based on their experiences with the examples given on the different rocks (like peanut butter and jelly sandwiches and how that relates to layers, and the chocolate cookies in comparison to a rock with scattered sediments throughout). My students were able to ask very general questions as to the things that they were looking for while identifying the rocks. "What makes these rocks igneous?" "What makes these rocks sedimentary?" "Do you think this rock is made of one material or more than one material?" Finally, my students did well applying the current content that they had been given about the three types of rocks to the identification of actual rocks. I was impressed with the way they tried to use the different visuals that we had discussed to match each rock to a group. "Why is this igneous?" "Because it has air bubbles . . . this one does not . . . this one does." My students did a great job asking basic, but important questions for analyzing the different rocks that they were looking at.

The *Attitude* of my students is also something that I consider important when analyzing the conversations in my classroom. Under this heading, I looked for attributes such as enthusiasm, engagement, and willingness. With this in mind, I believe that my students were very successful in the area of *Attitude*. They were very enthusiastic about actually being able to touch rocks and observe them with hand lenses. The students truly enjoyed the opportunities to work with others in a small group. Not only were they able to engage themselves in their own participation, but they were also able to engage others who don't usually speak up as much in a large group setting by asking them questions. "Haley, do you think this has layers?" "No . . . yeah it does, look at the side Keegan." This unusual participation from my more shy students also indicates their willingness to participate as well.

Reflection

I remember thinking during this lesson that I was unsure of how I felt the outcomes would end. I didn't like the organization of this lesson at the time of it. Consequently, I know that next year when I have my students participate in this lab there will be different tasks for the students to complete. Next year, my students will also work on this lab at a later time during the unit. Making these changes will allow for more in-depth discussion as well as a better understanding of the concepts that I feel are important for this unit.

The objectives that I wanted met in this lesson were met by both of these groups. While they would have been more successful fulfilling these objectives even a week later in the unit, for the content and practice they had been given, they did well with it. The conversations that they held while identifying rocks were at a basic level for the new information that they had.

Introduction

The application discussion comes after the conceptual discussion in the bow tie model. It is a deductive discussion, which means it is preceded by learning new information and an application of that information. For example, in the teacher reflection above, the application discussion followed several days of learning about rock identification and was immediately preceded by an activity that required students to sort rocks into one of three categories. Activities that require students to use judgment lend themselves well to application discussions because they enable differing perspectives and the potential for argument. The application discussion gives students an opportunity to integrate their newly learned information into a real world setting, the third phase of the bow tie.

The teacher above also prepared students by giving them an opportunity to talk in small groups and by providing individual support. Because students must use newly acquired knowledge in unfamiliar settings, the application discussion requires the most preparation of the three discussion types for students to participate effectively. It is the last step in a cycle that begins with the students' lifeworld experience, then moves into some form of new learning, and concludes with an application of that learning in a real world setting.

The purpose of this chapter is to fully describe and illustrate application discussions. Accordingly, the following sections will characterize the type of preparation and group work, accountability strategies, discourse moves, and one-on-one support associated with application discussions. We will also continue with examples from Ms. Brady's classroom.

Preparation and Group Work for Application Discussions

The application discussion is most often associated with a series of activities or an extended project. These activities often provide subject specific experiences that students would not usually experience outside of school, e.g., debates, role playing, mock trials, scientific experiments, or applied mathematics. Activities are usually structured as relatively extended projects in which students may be given a chance to prepare in small groups. Therefore, more lesson planning in regards to the division of tasks, assigning roles, and accountability strategies would be appropriate. Encouraging cooperative behaviors is important, and so is scaffolding student performance through the use of goals, deadlines, checklists, and rubrics.

Providing Individual Help

Providing individual help in preparation for application discussions could serve multiple purposes. One approach would be to support student creativity. Application discussions often require students to generate creative solutions, thus teachers can provide individual support by asking divergent questions that support higher level thinking such as analysis, synthesis, and evaluation. This approach would be characterized by a more open dialogue in which the teacher would help students generate new ways to apply newly learned concepts. The opposite approach would be to provide more teacher guidance. In this case, the teacher would ask more leading and convergent questions to ensure an accurate use of the concept, as illustrated below in the transcript excerpt taken from Ms. Brady's seventh grade mathematics class. Ms. Brady is providing individual support to Abby as she works out a design for a ping pong ball package. Ms. Brady is checking to make sure Abby has correctly calculated the surface area and volume for her package design. The teacher's discourse moves are labeled in italics.

Ms. Brady:	Oh! Way to go! Look at that, Abby! Good job! [*Confirmation*] Did you calculate it all right? [*Elicitation*] Make sure you check that. [*Procedure*]
Abby:	I'm not sure because I still need help calculating. I just don't—I forget how to do (inaudible). Tiffany helped me on all of these and then this one.
Ms. Brady:	Do you have your note sheet? [*Elicitation*]
Abby:	No. I don't. I don't think so.
Ms. Brady:	Will you go look for it? [*Elicitation*]
Abby:	I tried to find it yesterday.
Ms. Brady:	And then I'll write down all the volume formulas if you don't have it. Right here! [*Procedure*]
Abby:	Well, it doesn't have all the formulas.
Ms. Brady:	Let's write it on here, okay? [*Procedure*] This is the volume of a sphere. The volume of a cone is right. That's the volume of a pyramid, that's the volume of a sphere. So volume equals two/thirds area of the base, which is pi, times the radius, times the radius times the height. [*Explanation*]
Abby:	So I would do two/thirds times . . .
Ms. Brady:	What's pi? [*Elicitation*]
Abby:	Um . . . the rad . . . the 3.14.
Ms. Brady:	Right. [*Confirmation*] Times your radius . . . [*Elaboration*]
Abby:	Which would be um . . . two.
Ms. Brady:	Two times your radius [*Reformulation*] and then how high would this be? [*Elicitation*]
Abby:	Four.
Ms. Brady:	Yep! You've got it! [*Confirmation*] And this is the little fraction for right there. [*Elaboration*]

This interaction was a typical example of Ms. Brady's interactions as she moved around the classroom helping students. She spent a very brief time with each student she helped, quickly checking to see if they were on task and then checking their mathematical calculations. In general, she provided support for their understanding of the concepts relevant to surface area and volume, as indicated by the high ratio of teacher to student talk and by her use of elicitations, confirmations, elaborations, and explanations in her interaction with Abby.

Accountability Strategies for the Application Discussion

The purpose of application discussions is to extend student understanding of specific concepts by applying them in real world settings. As part of these discussions, students are asked to exercise their judgment and decision making capabilities. This kind of work is best evaluated through some kind of performance-based assessment such as a rubric. Assessment could occur through some kind of project, a written paper, a multistep problem on a test, or essay questions on a test. These assessments may complement rather than replace the test. Like the framing and conceptual discussions, it may also be desirable to use more informal accountability strategies, as well as a more immediate form of motivation.

Discourse Moves Associated with the Application Discussion

Both the teacher and the student participate extensively during the application discussion. This is in contrast to a framing discussion, which focuses primarily on the student, and the conceptual discussion, which requires more teacher guidance. Students are more likely to make more extended comments during an application rather than a conceptual discussion because they can draw on two sources of knowledge: newly acquired concepts from the conceptual discussion and their practical knowledge of the everyday world. These dual sources of information combined with extensive preparation provide a high potential for student participation. Even students with an uncertain mastery of the new concept can draw on more familiar information from their life experience to make an extended comment.

Similar to conceptual discussions, teachers must still provide considerable scaffolding during the application discussion, as students struggle to apply new vocabulary and concepts in an applied setting. They will still need to provide a high number of cues to their students, although they may use fewer recaps, reformulations, and explanations in comparison to conceptual discussions. However, student comments during an application discussion are likely to be more extended than conceptual discussions, although they are not as likely to be as extended as those made during a framing discussion, which is rooted in the students' most familiar experiences.

Application Discussion Example

Near the end of the example seventh grade mathematics unit, the teacher led two application discussions. The purpose of the application discussions was to apply the newly acquired mathematical concepts to a real world setting. The first application discussion followed an activity in which students were required to design a soft drink can. The students were encouraged to discover the most economical container as determined by surface area and volume. The second application followed an activity in which students were required to design a package to market ping pong balls. The students were encouraged to consider various design factors such as surface area, volume, cost of packaging materials, and aesthetic appeal.

Preparation and Group Work

The first application discussion took place after the completion of a project in which students worked in pairs to design a soft drink can. Students were required to sketch their soft drink can, label the dimensions, and calculate the volume. Like the conceptual discussion, the application discussion was preceded by significant preparation time, during which the teacher assisted students as they worked with their partner. The discussion began with the partners explaining their project design to the whole class. Much of the discussion that followed consisted of asking for and giving justifications for the design, which were primarily based on mathematical criteria, e.g., the greatest volume for the least cost.

The second application discussion also took place after the completion of a project on the final day of the unit. For this project, students worked in pairs to design and construct a package for ping pong balls. Before beginning, the teacher shared with students the rubric for the project, which consisted of both mathematical and real world criteria (e.g., cost, appeal, stackability, appearance on the shelves).

The project for the second discussion was more complex than the first one and was preceded by more preparation. As students worked to complete the project, the teacher assisted students over two extended help sessions. One of the two discussions was devoted exclusively to practice problems on finding surface area and volume so that student project calculations would be more accurate.

Accountability Strategies

Numerous informal accountability strategies were employed during the application discussion. For example, students were encouraged to explain and defend their project design, as well as question their classmates about their designs. They were also encouraged to write down and ask questions about their classmates' designs as a way of encouraging student-to-student interactions. They also had to respond to written questions for the purpose of justifying their design, in regards to both real world and mathematical criteria. A more formal accountability strategy was the use of a rubric to grade their final project.

Discourse Moves

Two excerpts from an application discussion are provided below, during which the students explain their design features for a package of ping pong balls. In these excerpts, Ms. Brady encourages more student-to-student dialogue by encouraging other students to write down and ask questions about key features of the design, e.g., cost, appeal, volume, and surface area. Both teacher and students are very active in these excerpts. Ms. Brady uses a variety of discourse moves, including elicitations, confirmations, repetitions, cues, and providing for student questions. For their part, the students are able to give extended responses in response to queries on their package design. Ms. Brady's discourse moves are labeled in italics.

Ms. Brady:	The flower one. [*Repetition*] Let's see. All right. So right now, you guys are going to be writing down questions for it. [*Procedure*] Okay, tell us about your package. [*Elicitation*] So you're going to write down the question that you might have over that package, okay? So I need you guys to think about it. [*Procedure*] So Cassandra or Amanda, I'll let either one of you tell us about your heart package. Or not about your heart one, the flower one, that's the one you choose, right? [*Elicitation*]
Amanda:	The flower box is a big box. It's great because it can hold many ping pong balls. It has good (inaudible) also for stackability. It's pretty big, it's not big enough that it's hard to stack. It's also flat so it can be easily stacked. This could be high on the list of (inaudible) also. It holds a lot of balls. It is neat because it is a flower, it's big and it's plain cool.
Ms. Brady:	It is plain cool. [*Repetition*] Do you know how many balls it holds in it? Did you calculate that or did you not calculate that part? No? Okay. What questions do you guys have? Kind questions, okay? [*Elicitation*] And if you're not sure you always can say, "Well, we still need to—we're still looking into that." You know we're looking into that. [*Procedure*] Okay, Sam. [*Elicitation*]
Sam:	How did you find the volume and surface area for that flower thing?
Amanda:	Well, we got with the graph and then we put the graph paper over it and then we counted how many boxes the graph paper would cover on the flower.
Ms. Brady:	All right. [*Confirmation*] What other questions? Bob?
Bob:	How much does it cost?
Sarah:	This package is really expensive. It's $42.35.
Ms. Brady:	So my follow up to that would be, do you think—I will let you know that our costs for these packages were a little bit higher because the actual cost per square centimeters that was recommended to me was

a fractional cent, and I didn't want a whole lot of time—not that it would have been too difficult for you guys—but I didn't want a whole lot of time spent on that, and so I rounded it to the nearest penny, which just made it one cent per square. So I mean, if your package is solid and it costs a lot that is part of it. [*Cue*] So, let's see Amanda and Cassandra, right? Um . . . did you decide that . . . why did you decide . . . obviously you knew the cost was big. Was there something that you thought, well the cost can be big because why. [*Elicitation*]

Amanda:	It can hold a lot of ping pong balls and . . .
Ms. Brady:	Okay. That's a good answer. [*Confirmation*] What was the highest thing on your—if you had to take stackability, cost, or appeal, which one do you think that you rated the highest? [*Elicitation*]
Cassandra:	Appeal.
Ms. Brady:	Appeal. [*Repetition*] All right. Very good. [*Confirmation*] Any other questions for Cassandra and Amanda? [*Elicitation*]

In the excerpt above, Amanda and Cassandra are able to elaborate when asked questions about their package design. But their use of mathematical justifications is somewhat limited; their primary justification for the design is based on appeal. In the second excerpt below, the students are also able to elaborate on their package design with more emphasis on the mathematical features of their design.

Ms. Brady:	Okay. Who did I say next? Bob? Ah, Bob! [*Elicitation*]
Bob:	Okay, this is my smallest cube. I just made cubes because cubes have small surface areas for their volume so I was worried about cost a lot.
Ms. Brady:	Okay. [*Confirmation*]
Bob:	Trying to have a low cost. So then this one holds eight ping pong balls. It costs $3.47. It's 7.6 centimeters by 7.6 centimeters. It's surface area is 346 square centimeters. And the volume is 438.976 cubic centimeters.
Ms. Brady:	All right. [*Confirmation*]What questions do you have for Bob? Okay, Brett? [*Elicitation*]
Brett:	Why did he choose a box and not like a prism?
Bob:	I chose a cube because they have a really small surface area. Because we were working with the real cube—centimeter cubes and then whenever all the dimensions were all close together then it had the smallest surface area so I did cubes so then it would cost less.

The two excerpts above illustrate the difference in mathematical knowledge between Cassandra and Amanda in the first transcript and Bob and Brett in the second transcript. Bob and Brett's greater use of mathematical vocabulary and concepts indicates a better understanding of surface area and volume. However, Amanda and Cassandra are still able to participate because they can elaborate on real world criteria for the ping pong packages, such as aesthetic appeal.

What Teachers Need to Know

Like the conceptual discussion, the key to creating an application discussion is the activity that precedes it. The activity must apply a newly learned concept in a real world setting in a way that requires judgment on the part of the student. As the students exercise their judgment, they must use both conceptual and real world criteria. Processing them both together helps them to better integrate and retain the concept.

The application discussion offers several possibilities for teachers. It provides the teacher with an opportunity to evaluate how well students have integrated the conceptual knowledge into their lifeworld. It also provides an opportunity to assess the change in student dialogue by comparing the application discussion to the framing and conceptual discussions. Through the assessment of application discussions, teachers can see to what degree their students can apply new vocabulary and concepts in a real world setting. To successfully lead an application discussion, the teacher must be familiar with both the concept and how to apply it. This requires more extensive knowledge than simply understanding the concept. In addition, the teacher must be able to create or find suitable application problems that will maximize student engagement and understanding.

Application Discussion

Reexamine the teacher's reflection located at the beginning of the chapter. Discuss the types of changes she made in the lesson to open up the discourse. Consider her discourse moves, preparation and grouping strategies, her accountability strategies, and the direction of the discussion. Rank the relative importance of these changes in relationship to each other in order to successfully redesign the lesson.

Activities

1. Create an activity in your subject area that could lead to an application discussion. Describe how you would use this activity as a basis for the discussion.
2. Redesign an existing unit to include an application discussion. As part of your design, describe the preparation, grouping, and accountability strategies that will be part of the assignment. In addition, describe the discourse moves that you anticipate you will make and the responses you anticipate from your students. If you do not have an existing unit of instruction, design an application discussion for a new unit that you plan to teach.

3. Implement the application discussion you designed, collect audio or videotape data, and analyze the participant frameworks.

Study Group Activities

4. Bring your plan for an application discussion to the study group discussion and share ideas.
5. Write a reflection paper on your application discussion data and compare your data with other members of the study group.

part five
Analyzing Discussions

The final chapter of the book describes several techniques for videotaping classroom interactions and then analyzing them in teacher study groups. Carefully analyzing your application of the techniques discussed in this book will maximize their potential effectiveness. A subsidiary benefit of collecting videotapes is their potential usefulness as part of a portfolio, professional development plan, or career plan. Videotapes or transcripts derived from videotapes can provide compelling evidence of a teacher's ability to meet state and national teaching standards.

twelve
Collaborating in a Teacher Study Group

Framing Discussion

In this chapter, you will learn how to analyze discussions in a teacher study group. Before you begin reading, take a few minutes to discuss the benefits and challenges of collaborating in a teacher study group. Use your past experiences with teacher study groups to answer the questions below.

1. If you have already engaged in a collaborative conversation with other teachers, share some of the benefits you found in collaboration. What benefits can you imagine beyond what you have experienced?
2. If you have had past experiences with collaborative conversations, what has made them effective or ineffective?
3. Do you have any concerns about sharing data (student work, observational data, audiotapes) from your classroom?
4. How could interactions within a study group be constructed to address these concerns?

Introduction

The purpose of this chapter is to show how analyzing classroom interactions in a teacher study group can help teachers to improve their practice. Increasingly, teacher collaboration is seen as a means for improving student achievement, facilitating professional development, improving school improvement processes, and effecting educational change. In addition, collaborating in a teacher study group can heighten teachers' powers of observation, increase their insight into student performance, and multiply their discussion strategies within a nonthreatening atmosphere that maintains an appropriate balance of comfort and challenge.

As teacher study groups have become more widely utilized, various educators have made recommendations for establishing and maintaining viable teacher study groups. This chapter will draw on their recommendations for collecting audio and/or videotapes of classroom discourse, establishing a teacher study group, and moving through a collegial discussion of classroom discourse in a systematic and unthreatening way. Specific topics include managing time, establishing group norms, analyzing data, and facilitating interactions among group members.

Benefits of Audio and Videotaping

Videotaping makes it possible to directly analyze teacher and student interactions. Recording classroom interactions on audio and videotape fully preserves them so the teacher researcher can replay and observe them over and over, thus enabling a much more complex analysis. Using videotapes preserves more information than audiotapes, which can be a significant advantage. The meaning of words is often heavily dependent on their context, and it is sometimes difficult to determine the meaning of a specific classroom interaction without a visual image—even when the lesson has been recently taught. For an even closer analysis, verbal interactions from the video and audiotapes can be transcribed into transcripts. Close analyses of the transcripts or repeated viewings of the videotapes are ways of slowing down classroom interactions so they can be analyzed in more depth.

Limitations of Videotaping

However, there are some limitations to collecting and analyzing audio and videotaped data. While most teachers have access to video and audiotaping equipment, it can be unavailable at inconvenient times. Taping can also require some supplies (tapes or cassettes) and a certain amount of technical expertise to operate the equipment. In addition, audio or video recorders can malfunction, due to either an equipment failure or operator error, and it is likely that you will experience both at one time or another. Regardless, most of these limitations can be overcome without undue difficulty, given that you are willing to make the extra effort to learn and practice the techniques.

Another limitation of videotaping classroom actions is artificial behavior, whether in the form of highly scripted presentations by the teacher or stiff, contrived behavior on the part of the students (Tochon, 1999). Therefore, it is important to collect data in a way that facilitates normal and natural classroom behaviors. The best approach may be simply to turn on the camera and let it run. The longer the camera is running, the more likely your students will get used to it or even forget about it. In addition, recording much more than is needed will ensure capturing more varied and more authentic discourse interactions. It may even reveal some unexpected and overlooked gems in lessons previously considered unexceptional. If not, lessons that don't live up to expectations need not be shared. Deciding whether to share a video should always be left to the discretion of the individual teacher.

Collecting Videotapes

Therefore, I suggest that readers don't try to target specific, showpiece lessons, but simply begin videotaping. Lessons that already involve discussions or lessons for which teachers would like to incorporate more discussion would be equally valuable. You will also have to make some decisions whether you audio or videotape the whole class, a group of students, or an individual. Starting with individual students or a small group of students may make it easier to become acclimated to data collection. Even after you have become more experienced, you may choose to use audiotape under certain circumstances, e.g., when the videotaping equipment is less available or when a less intrusive means of recording conversations may be preferred, like recording small group conversations.

When you begin audio or videotaping, try to place the equipment in a location that will not distract the participants (the students or teachers) yet is close enough to clearly record what is being said. Often it is better to place the camera closer to the students than the teacher, because the teacher usually projects much better than the students. Since the students are harder to hear, consider placing the recording equipment farther away from the teacher and closer to the students. However, when teachers are helping individual students or working in small groups, their voices may not record well over background noise. In this case, attaching a small microphone or placing the tape recorder very close to the group would be helpful. If a tape recorder is placed with a small group, it should be located in the middle of the action as close to the students as possible. Otherwise, background noise from other group interactions may make it very hard to discern what the students said from the audiotape.

When videotaping, someone is needed to operate the camera. There are several possibilities. First, study team members could visit each other's classrooms to videotape. A second option may be a student aide or a technician who is familiar with the equipment and available at the right time. A third option is to use a volunteer student from the class being videotaped. This was immensely popular with one of my classes, and I earned the enduring loyalty of a difficult student by letting him run the camera.

Regardless of who operates the camera, equipment failures and operator errors are inevitable. They can be reduced, however, by reviewing the tapes after each session to check for technical difficulties, operator mistakes, and to make sure the equipment has been positioned in a location that ensures the participants can be heard. There is nothing more discouraging than recording a sequence of lessons and then finding out later they are not audible. If the videotaping is successful, then it is often prudent to make a back up copy so that a particularly worthwhile lesson isn't lost.

Before audio or videotaping, consult with the principal about existing policies in the school district. When speaking with the principal, emphasize the benefits of videotaping for your teaching. Be clear as to how you will secure the tapes to protect the students from potential embarrassment. Be honest about how the tapes will be used and how you will share what you are doing with parents.

Transcribing the Tapes

Videotaping classroom interactions can be taken a step further by transcribing the tapes. There are several advantages to creating a transcript from the videotape. Typing out the classroom interactions sentence by sentence will make you very familiar with their contents. Furthermore, it is a way to create a permanent record that can be analyzed at length and in considerable depth for specific patterns. Conversely, it enables the reader to scan several pages of transcript very quickly for the purpose of detecting larger patterns.

The primary disadvantage to using transcripts is the time it takes to create them; generally four times longer than watching a videotape. Part of the difficulty is interpreting what has been said. Those who listen closely to people talking find they do not speak in the carefully worded sentences that are printed in books. They pause, they speak in bursts, they shift to a different thought in midsentence, they leave their sentences and their thoughts unfinished, and often they depend on visual cues as a substitute for words. So it can be very slow work to precisely capture the hurried and sometimes messy interactions that occur in a classroom setting. Two ways to shorten this lengthy process are to (a) pay someone else to transcribe the data, perhaps with funding obtained through a grant, or (b) limit the transcription to selected portions of the most interesting classroom interactions, perhaps episodes that you would like to include in your professional portfolio or career plan.

Forming the Teacher Study Group

When analyzing videotape data, members of a teacher study group must establish a productive culture for analyzing data (Cochran-Smith & Lytle, 1999). The following sections will treat the following aspects of establishing such a culture: managing time, establishing group norms, discussing the data systematically, and facilitating the discussion.

Managing Time

Time is always a scarce resource for teachers and can serve as a significant barrier to the successful implementation of a teacher study group (Cochran-Smith & Lytle, 1999;

Little, Gearhart, Curry, & Kafka, 2003). To begin a teacher study group, enough time must be allotted to meet for at least an hour once or twice a month. If the interval between meetings is longer than a month, the study group will probably lose momentum. Too much time will be spent trying to recall what happened at previous meetings at the expense of moving forward in a productive fashion. It is best that the meetings occur during the school day or as part of regular school activities, so that other concerns, such as extracurricular responsibilities or family obligations, don't cause absences or the cancellation of meetings. The second step in organizing a teacher study group is planning a series of meetings with a specific, year long focus.

Establishing Group Norms

Little et al. (2003) have suggested that a second significant barrier is concern for personal comfort and collegial relationships. It is crucial that study team members trust and support one another. Watching videotapes of yourself or your colleagues teaching may be the least comfortable form of analyzing data. Often study team members may find it hard to watch themselves or to comment on the teaching of a colleague.

Teachers are generally not as familiar with examining and discussing videotaped data, which involves a form of conversation with which they have often had little experience. In addition, the teacher's actions are often the focus of videotaped data. So, by sharing audio or videotapes with other teachers, study group members are exposing themselves to the scrutiny and judgment of others. When a team member feels a heightened sensitivity to potential criticism, it is critical the group interacts in a nonthreatening way.

Therefore, a primary task when organizing a teacher study group is to establish the norms for conducting the conversation. Group norms are the procedures that govern the interactions among group members, such as how study team members manage their time, how they talk to one another, and how they structure the meetings. They are the single most important factor in determining the group's harmony, efficiency, and productivity. It is even more important to set ground rules that increase the comfort level when engaged in more risky group interactions, such as commenting on videotapes of each other's teaching.

Reducing Risk

The first and most effective way to reduce the risk of sharing classroom interactions is to give study team members control over what they show their peers. No one should be obliged to share any episode with which they feel uncomfortable. When study team members know that others will only see their most successful and effective teaching, it can substantially reduce their anxiety about videotaping and sharing their teaching.

Easing into the Discussion

There are several possible approaches to easing into a discussion of videotaped classroom events. One approach would be for the study group to begin with less risky forms of data sharing, such as analyzing lesson plan questions, charting student participation, or recording wait time. This would also allow study group members more time to collect and select relevant video segments, would provide some time to practice their conversational skills in the study group and to develop trust among group members. Finally, they could select a very brief segment of videotape to share with the study team. Later, they could show longer segments or they may want to keep the video segments relatively brief. Viewing protracted segments of discourse can be very time consuming and can often fail to serve a specific purpose. The final step would be to share a videotape of their teaching with the entire study group without editing. Each study team should decide the level of sharing that they feel is appropriate.

Avoid Making Snap Judgments

Another way to reduce risk in a teacher study group is to avoid making snap judgments concerning other study group members. The less evaluative the conversation, the safer it will feel. Therefore, it is important to remember that the ultimate purpose of study group discussions is to improve your teaching: it is not to evaluate the teaching of other study team members. Trying to understand the relationship between teacher and students' discourse moves will have a much greater impact on your growth as a teacher than trying to decide whether or not a colleague made an appropriate decision. When study group members stay focused on finding ways to improve their own instructional strategies, it is much easier to maintain a nonevaluative and supportive position toward other group members.

Structuring the Discussion

Structuring the discussion among study group members can also reduce the feeling of risk and discomfort. In a structured discussion, the study group articulates a clear purpose, targets specific phenomenon to observe (e.g., participation patterns, wait time, levels of questions), and keeps the conversation focused on those observations. Observations and comments about the teacher or students should always address the purpose of the analysis. Comment on any other matters only if invited to do so by the host teacher. Even then be very cautious in your comments and limit them to objective and factual statements about what was observed. Following this form of observational etiquette makes it less risky for teachers to share their classroom interactions.

A structured conversation is also time efficient. Within the hour or so that study team members have to examine their classroom interactions, they must establish and follow a focused agenda or the time will quickly be squandered without accomplishing very much of value. Using time wisely also means that individual meetings must be carefully planned and executed. Following a well defined set of procedures for analyzing data provides a means for organizing individual meetings, for keeping the meetings focused, and for managing the process.

A third benefit of a structured discussion is better data analysis. Analyzing data is a systematic process that occurs in discrete steps. Study team members should (a) be aware of the thinking that needs to be done at each of these steps, (b) be able justify the decisions made at each step of analysis, and (c) be willing to make their thinking public so that it can be critiqued. A four-step approach to structuring your data analysis is recommended in this book: (1) establishing the background information related to the data, (2) making observations about the data, (3) explaining or interpreting the data, and (4) generating new strategies and a plan for action.

Background Information

The first step in the analysis is to establish the necessary background information for the study. This could include information about the teacher's purpose, the participants, the setting, and the source of data.

1. The teacher's purpose could either be related to teaching, i.e., the objective for the lesson, or the research, i.e., the particular problem she is investigating.
2. The participants in a study of classroom discourse will usually be the students. The kind of information that is relevant to an inquiry related to classroom discourse could include their grade level, their gender, their ethnicity, or their ability levels. Other possible participants could also include teachers, administrators, and parents.
3. The setting will generally refer to the classroom, school, or possibly community environment. It could include physical descriptions, a description of the psychological environment, or descriptions of other environmental factors.
4. Data collection methods will generally refer to the ways the data (such as lesson plans, student writing, classroom observations, and audio or videotapes) was collected.

The information above should be explicitly stated before moving to the next phase of the analysis for three reasons. First, it is an important part of communicating within the teacher study group. Without understanding the grade level of students, the ability level of the students, the school environment, or the data collection methods, other study group members will not be able to ask effective and stimulating questions or reach significant insights. Second, teaching and learning always occur in specific locations under specific conditions. Knowing the gender, age, or ability level of students can often have a profound effect on the conclusions that are drawn from a set of data. It is also helpful to understand the purposes of the teacher, what she was trying to accomplish, and what she anticipated would happen during the lesson. Finally, it can also be helpful to know what kind of data was collected and how it was collected. As discussed earlier, different insights can be gained from analyzing videotapes than from analyzing lesson plans. As is true of every step of the process, the thoroughness with which study team members attend to the details will have an impact on the conclusions they can draw from the next phases of the discussion.

Observations

In the observation phase of the discussion, the study group examines the data together. As discussed previously, the data could include teacher lesson plans, samples of student writing, observations of classroom interactions, or audio and videotapes of classroom interactions. Observations are made while watching the videotapes, reading the transcripts, or reading a discussion plan or a teacher reflection written about the discussion. Observations about the teacher's discourse moves could include the type of questions asked, the wait time, and the teachers' follow up moves in response to student comments. Observations about the students' talking could include the length and quality of student responses, the amount of student-to-student interaction in the discussion, student questions about the content, and the response patterns of students.

The primary purpose of this step in the analysis is to make and record as many relevant observations about the data as possible. To increase the number and quality of observations, teacher researchers must make a concerted effort to look at the data in new ways and to examine more closely what had previously seemed trivial. This is vital to the discovery of new information. Otherwise, we are likely to simply see what we have always seen, or to disregard potentially valuable information. So, when making observations, systematically comb through the data to find what has been previously ignored. Making more observations during this step of the process increases the possibility of gaining more insight during the analysis phase.

As you make your observations, try to withhold judgment and be impartial. Typically, we human beings tend to see what we value as important or what we are conditioned to see and, once a judgment or a decision is made, thinking stops. Thus, one of the goals of a study group analysis is to withhold judgment as long as possible to consider different ways of seeing, different ways of interpreting what is seen, and different courses of action. It requires a conscious decision to be self-disciplined enough to withhold judgment and consider other possibilities before drawing a conclusion.

Interpretations

The purpose of the interpretation phase of the discussion is to integrate your individual observations into larger patterns of relationships. In this part of the analysis, the study group members closely examine the observations they made previously for patterns and relationships. For instance, what conclusion could you draw from the following three observations made from a videotape of an eighth grade history discussion?

1. The teacher asked primarily factual questions.
2. Student responses tended to be brief.
3. There was little student-to-student interaction.

The pattern in these observations is consistent with a discussion that was heavily guided by the teacher. Identifying patterns will not always be as easy as this simple example. It is likely that the observations from the data you collect will be far more complex. Thus, it will be necessary to make an avid search for meaning in your data. Following are three suggestions for finding meaningful patterns in your data.

Make Comparisons

Try to find a comparison in your data or, better yet, plan for a comparison before collecting your data. For example, compare two different teachers with different styles, two different students with different ability levels, or two ways to ask questions in the same setting. The possibilities are endless. By comparing and contrasting, we can often trigger new insights.

Combine and Recombine Data

Combine and recombine the observations in different ways. For instance, in a group of seven observations, examine them as a group of five and two or a group of four and three, or six and one. Look at each new grouping to see if a pattern is revealed by the new combination. This process can be particularly interesting when data is collected from multiple sources. Integrating your findings about the types of questions asked during a discussion with wait time data, response patterns, and the amount of elaboration in student responses may yield more insight than any single source of data. For example, the teacher may be asking divergent questions, but as she only allows a very brief wait time, there is little elaboration and only high achievers are volunteering.

Try Different Conceptual Frames

Examine the data with a variety of conceptual frames. In this case, "conceptual frames" refers to a set of preexisting relationships as defined by a theory or hypothesis. One example would be the taxonomies of educational objectives from the previous chapters. When analyzing the types of questions asked by the teacher, use a variety of taxonomies. Using a different lens to interpret the same set of data can spark new insights. Other conceptual frames would include the concept of wait time, response patterns, and participant frameworks (see Part I).

Just as you tried to multiply your observations in the previous phase of the discussion, in this phase of the discussion, try to multiply your interpretations. Consider as many different ways to connect and explain the data as you possibly can. The objective of data analysis is not to find a single truth; the purpose is to better understand the complex interrelationships governing teacher and student interactions and to use that understanding to improve teaching strategies in the next phase of the discussion.

Design a Plan

One of the primary purposes of analyzing classroom interactions in study teams is to develop decision making skills in the classroom. In this step of the analysis, you should use your interpretations of the data to devise new strategies for improving your classroom interactions. Try to generate as many alternative strategies as possible, then select the most promising one(s) for implementation. The advantage of developing multiple strategies is twofold. First, keeping your mind open to a variety of possibilities may prevent a premature negative judgment regarding a potentially effective strategy. Initially, it is important to generate possibilities; later, you can select among the most promising approaches. Second, no single approach to teaching will ever be effective because of the widely varying contexts and interactions that are a part of teaching. Therefore, it is always helpful to have additional strategies on hand.

Four approaches to developing new strategies include:

1. through an analysis of student work, e.g., examining student writing, student speaking, or observing student behavior;
2. by sharing strategies among teachers;
3. through searching and reading through the educational literature;
4. through professional inservice.

Facilitating the Discussion

The group may operate more effectively if one person is designated as a facilitator in order to set the agenda and keep the group on task. Effective facilitators should be knowledgeable and skilled enough to directly teach communication and analytical skills to other group members. Yet the facilitator must also be adept at shifting to a nondirective, more democratic style of leadership when needed. According to Little et al. (2003), the facilitator must maintain a balance between creating comfort and challenge. In other words, a part of the facilitator's role is not to let group members become too complacent in their thinking.

Study groups might want to consider rotating the role of facilitator among group members because serving as a facilitator offers several benefits. First, it offers another teacher leadership opportunity, which various studies have shown to be associated with increased student achievement, professional development opportunities, and overall school improvement. Second, using the discourse skills needed to facilitate teacher study groups provides valuable practice for leading classroom discussion.

To stimulate the interactions among study team members, three specific conversational moves have been suggested by Langer, Colton, and Goff (2003): pausing, paraphrasing, and probing.

1. Pausing is simply waiting and thinking before speaking. The facilitator or any other group member is trying to understand first, trying to be understood second. It is important to listen carefully to others, to remain nonjudgmental so that you do not rule out new ideas without due consideration, and to inquire for the purpose of learning.
2. Paraphrasing is rephrasing what you have heard in order to make sure you understood correctly. Using this technique could save you from wasting time spent in misunderstanding. It could also help you clarify your assumptions or the unspoken premises that lie underneath what you are saying.

3. Probing is when you ask a series of questions to clarify what the other person is saying. This technique can help another person better articulate what they are trying to say. Sometimes what they are saying can be clarified with examples. This can enhance shared understanding.

Pausing to understand is very closely related to wait time; rephrasing is very similar to revoicing or reformulating student comments; and probing is very similar to asking follow up questions in a classroom.

Asking Good Questions

To facilitate the study team's understanding of the background information, the facilitator or other study team members could pose questions to the teacher who is presenting the data. The purpose of these questions is to probe for additional details concerning the context of the study. Questions that could be asked during the discussion to help clarify the background information could include:

GOALS

1. What were your goals for these interactions?
2. What instructional strategies did you use to reach these goals?
3. What was the context of the lesson?
4. What did you hope would happen during the lesson?

OBSERVATIONS

5. What do you see in this sample of student writing?
6. How would you summarize these tallies of classroom interaction?
7. What do you observe in these interactions?

INTERPRETATIONS

8. What might explain why the student is performing this way?
9. What do these interactions tell you about the effect of the instructional strategies you used?

DESIGN NEW STRATEGIES

10. What is a logical next short term goal for making these interactions more effective, and why do you think it's an appropriate choice?
11. What instructional strategies will you try, and why do you think they will work?
12. What kind of data will you bring to the next study group?
13. What is still puzzling to you? What questions do you have?

What Teachers Need to Know

Teacher study groups can provide important practice for modeling discussion skills in a classroom. Effective study group conversations require the establishment of group norms, a skilled facilitator, and a structured approach to analyzing the data. Group norms should include a nonjudgmental disposition and skill with appropriate conversation moves such as pausing, paraphrasing, and probing. The collaborative and inquiry skills involved for participating in a teacher study group are similar to the ones that students should learn through discussion. Therefore, engaging in inquiry through a teacher study group can help teachers become better role models for inquiry and better discussion leaders.

Application Discussion

Create and record a set of group norms for your study group. Address time management, participation, and the group focus by answering the questions in each of those categories given below. You may want to use the accompanying examples for reference. The examples listed below are to facilitate the discussion: each group should determine its own norms.

Time

Questions
- What is our beginning and ending time?
- Will we start and end on time?
- How will we use our time?

Examples
- Start on time; end on time.
- Set and honor realistic time lines.

Participation

Questions
- How will we encourage everyone's participation?
- Is it okay not to participate?
- When sharing individual student work, what is the role of study group participants?
- How will we encourage listening?
- How do we encourage sharing of ideas? How do we support experimentation with new ideas?

Examples
- Seek to understand before being understood.
- Criticize ideas, not members.
- Support each other's experimentation.
- Build on others' ideas.
- Engage in open and honest communication.
- Withhold judgment.

Focus

Questions

- What should be the focus of our conversation?
- How might the group keep the conversation focused?

Examples

- Focus on issues of teaching and learning related to recent student work (Langer et al., 2003, p. 45).

Activities

1. Locate a videotape of teacher and student interactions of someone outside of your group. Share all the background information related to the video. Select five or ten minutes of videotape to watch. Discuss the interactions in the video in two distinct stages. First, state what you have observed very carefully. Second, offer as many explanations for what is happening as possible. Then, after you have created several possible explanations, discuss what additional information you would need to know more about the classroom interactions. Make sure you practice pausing, paraphrasing, and probing when you talk with each other.

2. Videotape your teaching, preview it, and select a five-minute episode to share with your teacher study group. Before sharing it with the group, write down all the relevant background information, such as the grade level, the subject area, the purpose of the lesson, and the purpose for watching this tape.

Study Group Activities

3. The composition of study groups will vary from school to school. For instance, at one school, a teacher study group could consist of teachers who all share the same grade level or subject area. At another school, the study group could be composed of teachers from a variety of grade levels or from different subject areas. Discuss the advantages and disadvantages of each situation. Regardless of which one you might initially favor, try to create lists of equal length. Then, after you have finished creating comparable lists, examine the advantages and limitations and discuss which one is more favorable to your situation and how you will compensate for the limitations you have identified.

4. Share your five-minute teaching videotape with the study group. Practice moving through the steps of the analysis by sharing the background information, by making observations, and by generating as many explanations of the events as possible during the analysis.

For Further Reading

Introduction

The full reference for each of the works given below is provided in the references at the end of the book.

For more about the persistence of recitation, see Hoetker and Ahlbrand (1969), Stodolsky et al. (1981), Goodlad (1984), Conner and Chalmers-Neubauer (1989), Alvermann and Hayes (1990), and Nystrand, Gamoran, Kachur, and Prendergast (1997).

For more about the relationship between discourse, learning, and the construction of scientific theory, see Vygotsky (1978, 1986), Nelson et al. (1987), Simons (1989), Prelli (1989), Gross (1990), Ernest (1998), and McCloskey (1998).

For more about the general benefits of discussion-based teaching, see Gall and Gall (1976, 1990).

For using discussion to promote democratic values, see Lasker (1949), Bridges (1979), and Dillon (1994).

For using discussions to improve reading comprehension and English classes, see Nystrand et al. (1997), Applebee, Langer, Nystrand, and Gamoran (2003), Nystrand (2006), Kahn (2007), and VanDeWeghe (2007).

For increasing tolerance, students' belief that they can have an impact on the political system, and the level of civic participation after high school, see Hahn (1991), Hess and Posselt (2002), Avery (2002), and Andolina, Jenkins, Zukin, and Keeter (2003).

For promoting conceptual change in science classes by encouraging students to voice their ideas, defend them, and negotiate knowledge claims in a way that resembles discourse in the scientific community, see Posner, Strike, Hewsen, and Gertzog (1982) and Beeth and Hewsen (1999).

For the importance of promoting a mathematic discourse, see Davis (1996), the Principles and Standards endorsed by the National Council of Teachers of Mathematics (2000), and Wood, Williams, and McNeal (2006).

For more on different approaches to discussion, see Flanders (1970), Haroutunian-Gordon (1991), Saunders, Goldenberg, and Hamann (1992), Burbules (1993), and Applebee (1996).

Chapter 1

For more on taxonomies of educational objectives, see Bloom et al. (1956), Anderson and Krathwohl (2001), and Marzano and Kendall (2007).

Strategies for asking questions have been extensively treated in the literature. Here are a few suggestions: Dillon (1988, 1990), Walsh and Sattes (2005), and Wilen (1987).

Chapter 2

For more on thinking skills, see Schiever (1991) and Beyer (1997).

For more on wait time, see Rowe (1986).

For more on what determines the quality of student talking, see van Boxtel and Roelofs (2001).

Chapter 3

For more on the IRE (Inquiry–Response–Evaluation) or IRF (Inquiry–Response–Feedback) pattern, what Cazden (2001) called the "default" structure, see Bellack et al. (1965), Sinclair and Coulthard (1975), Mehan (1978, 1979, 1982), and Macbeth (2003).

For more questioning strategies for following up on student responses, see Dantonio and Beisenherz (2001).

For more on types of teacher follow up moves, see Mercer (1995, 2000).

Chapter 4

For more on larger patterns of discussion, see Roby (1988) and Wilen (1990).

Chapter 5

For more specific information on how discussions are constructed within specific subject areas, consult the practitioner journals listed below. Many of the references given throughout the chapter were taken from these journals and refer to descriptions of discussions as described by practitioners in their specific subject area:

Social Education
The Social Studies
English Journal
Science Education
Mathematics Teaching in the Middle School

For more on teaching mathematics through the use of narrative, see Laubenbacher and Pengelley (1998) and Thiessen (2004).

Chapter 6

For more on managing conflict and speaking respectfully to students, see Gordon (2003) and Charles (2005).

For more on providing one-on-one support, see Lepper et al. (1997).

For more on the importance of relationship building, see Noddings (1992) and Sidorkin (2002).

Chapter 7

For more on culturally congruent teaching, see Ladson-Billings (1994), Delpit (1995), Gay (2000), and Barrera and Corso (2003).

Chapter 8

For a previous discussion of the bow tie, see Henning (2004).

For an analysis of the bow tie in a professor's classroom, see Henning et al. (2006).

Chapter 12

For more on constructing and leading teacher study groups, see Cochran-Smith and Lytle (1999), Langer et al. (2003), Little et al. (2003), and Langer and Colton (2005).

For more on how teacher collaboration is seen as a means for improving student achievement facilitating professional development, improving school improvement processes, and effecting educational change, see Jenlink and Carr (1996), Darling-Hammond (1999), Horn (2000), Britt, Irwin, and Ritchie (2001), Poetter and Badiali (2001), DeBruin-Parecki and Henning (2002), and Joyce and Showers (2002).

For more on the role of videotaping in teacher study groups, see Tochon (1999).

For more on teacher leadership, see Smylie and Denny (1990), Poetter and Badiali (2001), and Beachum and Dentith (2004).

References

Adams, R., & Biddle, B. (1970). *Realities of Teaching.* New York: Holt, Rinehart, & Winston.

Alvermann, D., & Hayes, D. (1990) Classroom discussion of content reading assignments: An intervention study. *Reading Research Quarterly, 24,* 305–335.

Amit, M., & Klass-Tsirulnikov, B. (2005) Paving a way to algebraic word problems: Using a nonalgebraic route. *Mathematics Teaching in the Middle School, 10* (5), 271–276.

Anderson, L. W., & Krathwohl, D. (eds.) (2001) *A Taxonomy for Learning, Teaching, and Assessing: A Revision of Bloom's Taxonomy of Educational Objectives.* New York: Longman.

Andolina, M. M., Jenkins, K., Zukin, C., & Keeter, S. (2003) Habits from home, lessons from school: Influences on youth civic engagement. *PS: Political Science and Politics, 36* (2), 275–280.

Appalachia Educational Laboratory (1994) *Questioning and Understanding to Improve Learning and Thinking (QUILT): the Evaluation Results. A Proposal to the National Diffusion Network (NDN) Documenting the Effectiveness of the QUILT Professional Development Program.* ERIC Document Reproduction Service No. ED403230. Charleston, WV: Appalachia Educational Laboratory.

Applebee, A. N. (1996) *Curriculum as Conversation: Transforming Traditions of Teaching and Learning.* Chicago, IL: University of Chicago Press.

Applebee, A. N., Langer, J. A., Nystrand, M., & Gamoran, A. (2003) Discussion-based approaches to developing understanding: Classroom instruction and student performance in middle and high school English. *American Education Research Journal, 40* (3), 685–730.

Aschner, M. J., Gallagher, J. J., Perry, J. M., and Afsar, S. F. (1961) *A System for Classifying Thought Processes in the Context of Classroom Verbal Interaction.* Urbana, IL: University of Illinois.

Austin, R. A., & Thompson, D. R. (1997) Exploring algebraic patterns through literature. *Mathematics Teaching in the Middle School, 2* (5), 274–281.

Avery, P. (2002) Teaching tolerance: What the research tells us. *Social Education, 66* (5), 270–275.

Barrera, I., & Corso, R. M. (2003) *Skilled Dialogues: Strategies for Responding to Cultural Diversity in Early Childhood.* Baltimore, MD: Paul H. Brookes Publishing.

Beachum, F., & Dentith, A. M. (2004) Teacher leaders creating cultures of school renewal and transformation. *Educational Forum, 68* (3), 276–286.

Beeth, M. E., & Hewsen, P. W. (1999) Learning goals in an exemplary science teacher's practice: cognitive and social factors in teaching for conceptual change. *Science Education, 83* (6), 738–760.

Bell, K. (2002) Using moot courts in the classroom. *Social Education, 66* (1), 41–45.

Bellack, A. A., Kliebard, H. M., Hyman, R. T., and Smith, F. L., Jr. (1966) *The Language of the Classroom.* New York: Teachers College Press.

Berliner, D. C. (1984) The half full glass! A review of research on teaching. In N. Pl. Hosford (ed.) *Using What We Know about Teaching* (p. 51–77). Alexandria, VA: Association for Supervision and Curriculum Development.

Beyer, B. K. (1997) *Improving Student Thinking: A Comprehensive Approach.* Boston, MA: Allyn and Bacon.

Billings, E., & Beckman, C. (2005) Children's literature: A motivating context to explore functions. *Mathematics Teaching in the Middle School, 10,* 470–478.

Bintz, W. P., & Moore, S.D. (2003) Using literature to teach factorials. *Mathematics Teaching in the Middle School, 8,* 461–465.

Bloom, B., Englehart, M., Furst, E., Hill, W., & Krathwohl, D. (1956) *Taxonomy of Educational Objectives: The Classification of Educational Goals. Handbook I: Cognitive Domain.* New York: Longmans, Green.

Bridges, D. (1979) *Education, Democracy, & Discussion.* Atlantic Highlands, NJ: NFER Publishing.

Britt, M. S., Irwin, K. C., & Ritchie, G. (2001) Professional conversations and professional growth. *Journal of Mathematics Teacher Education, 4,* 29–53.

Brookfield, S. D., & Preskill, S. (2005) Keeping discussion going through creative grouping. In S. D. Brookfield & S. Preskill (eds.) *Discussion as a Way of Teaching: Tools and Techniques for Democratic Classrooms,* 2nd edn. San Francisco: Jossey-Bass.

Burbules, N. C. (1993) *Dialogue in Teaching: Theory and Practice.* New York: Teachers College Press.

Cazden, C. B. (2001) *Classroom Discourse: The Language of Teaching and Learning,* 2nd edn. Portsmouth, NH: Heinemann.

Chappell, M., & Thompson, D. R. (2000) A raisin in the sun: Fostering connections with a classic movie. *Mathematics Teaching in the Middle School, 6* (4), 222–225, 233.

Charles, C. M. (2005) *Building Classroom Discipline,* 8th edn. New York: Longman.

Cheng, L. (1996) Enhancing communication: Toward optimal learning for limited English proficient students. *Language, Speech, and Hearing Services in Schools, 28* (2), 347–354.

Cochran-Smith, M., & Lytle, S. L. (1999) Relationships of knowledge and practice: Teacher learning in communities. *Review of Research in Education, 24,* 249–305.

Coker, D. (1988) The Asian students in the classroom. *Education and Society, 1* (3), 19–20.

Cole, R., & Williams, D. (1973) Pupil responses to teacher questions: Cognitive level, length, and syntax. *Educational Leadership Research (Suppl.),* 142–145.

Conner, J. W., & Chalmers-Neubauer, I. (1989) Mrs. Schuster adopts discussion: A four-week experiment in an English classroom. *English Education, 21,* 30–38.

Corbett, E. P. J., & Connors, R. J. (1999) *Classical Rhetoric for the Modern Student,* 4th edn. New York: Oxford University Press.

Cuban, L. (1984) *How Teachers Taught: Constancy and Change in American Classrooms, 1890–1980.* New York: Longman.

Dallimore, E. J., Hertenstein, J. H., & Platt, M. B. (2004) Classroom participation and discussion effectiveness: Student-generated strategies. *Communication Education, 53* (1), 103–115.

Dantonio, M., & Beisenherz, P. C. (2001) *Learning to Question, Questioning to Learn: Developing Effective Teacher Questioning Practices.* Needham Heights, MA: Allyn and Bacon.

Dantonio, M., & Paradise, L. V. (1988) Teacher question–answer strategy and the cognitive correspondence between teacher questions and learner responses. *Journal of Research and Development in Education, 21* (3), 71–75.

Darling-Hammond, L. (1999) Teacher learning that supports student learning. *Educational Leadership, 55* (5) 6–11.

Davis, B. (1996) *Teaching Mathematics: Toward a Sound Alternative.* New York: Garland Publishing.

DeBruin-Parecki, A., & Henning, J. E. (2002) Using reflective conversations as a tool for constructing meaningful knowledge about classroom practice. *Catalyst for Change, 31* (3), 16–20.

Delamont, S. (1983) *Interaction in the Classroom,* 2nd edn. New York: Methuen.

Delpit, L. (1995) *Other People's Children: Cultural Conflict in the Classroom*. New York: The New Press.

Delpit, L., & Dowdy, J. K. (2002) *The Skin That we Speak: Thoughts on Language and Culture in the Classroom*. New York: The New York Press.

Demi (1997) *One Grain of Rice: A Mathematical Folklore*. New York: Scholastic Press.

Dillon, D. R. (1989) Showing them that I want them to learn and that I care about who they are: A micro-ethnography of the social organization of a secondary low-track English-reading classroom. *American Educational Research Journal, 26* (2), 227–259.

Dillon, J. T. (1987) The multidisciplinary world of questioning. In W. W. Wilen (ed.) *Questions, Questioning Techniques, and Effective Teaching* (p. 49–66). Washington, DC :National Education Association.

Dillon, J. T. (1988) *Questioning and Teaching: A Manual of Practice*. New York: Teachers College Press.

Dillon, J. T. (1990) Conducting discussions by alternatives to questioning. In W. W. Wilen (ed.) *Teaching and Learning through Discussion: The Theory, Research, and Practice of the Discussion Method*. Springfield, IL: Charles C. Thomas.

Dillon, J. T. (1994) *Using Discussion in Classrooms*. Philadelphia, PA: Open University Press.

Edwards, D. & Mercer, N. (1987) *Common Knowledge*. London: Methuen/Routledge.

Ernest, P. (1998) *Social Constructivism as a Philosophy of Mathematics*. Albany, NY: SUNY Press.

Feng, J. (1994) Asian-American children: What teachers should know. ERIC Digest. Urbana, IL: ERIC.

Flanders, N. A. (1970) *Analyzing Teacher Behavior*. Reading, MA: Addison Wesley.

Foster, M. (1989) It's cooking now: A performance analysis of the speech events of a Black teacher in an urban community college. *Language in Society, 18* (1), 1–29.

Gall, J. P., & Gall, M. D. (1990) Outcomes of the discussion method. In W. W. Wilen (ed.) *Teaching and Learning through Discussion: The Theory, Research, and Practice of the Discussion Method* (p. 25–44). Springfield, IL: Charles C. Thomas.

Gall, M. D. (1971) The use of questioning in teaching. *Review of Educational Research, 40,* 707–721.

Gall, M. D. (1984) Synthesis of research on teachers' questioning. *Educational Leadership, 42,* 40–47.

Gall, M. D. (1985) Discussion methods of teaching. In T. Husen & T. N. Postlethwaite (eds.) *International Encyclopedia of Education* (Vol. 3, p. 1423–1427). Oxford: Pergamon Press.

Gall, M. D., & Gall, J. P. (1976) The discussion method. In N. L. Gage (ed.) *The Psychology of Teaching Methods*. The seventieth-fifth yearbook of the NNSE, part I (p. 166–216). Chicago, IL: University of Chicago Press.

Gall, M. D., & Gillet, M. (1980) The discussion method in classroom teaching. *Theory into Practice, 19* (2), 98–103.

Gall, M. D., & Rhody, T. (1987) Review of research on questioning techniques. In W. W. Wilen (ed.) *Questions, Questioning Techniques, and Effective Teaching* (p. 23–48). Washington, DC: National Education Association.

Gall M. D., Ward, B. A., Berliner, D. C., Cahen, L. S., Winne, P. H., Elashoff, J. D., & Stanton, G. C. (1978) Effects of questioning techniques and recitation on student learning. *American Educational Research Journal, 15,* 175–199.

Gallas, K. (1994) *The Languages of Learning: How Children Talk, Write, Dance, Draw, and Sing their Understanding of the World*. New York: Teachers College Press.

Garcia, R. L. (2005) *Teaching for Diversity*, 2nd edn. Bloomington, IN: Phi Delta Kappa International.

Gay, G. (2000) *Culturally Responsive Teaching: Theory, Research, & Practice*. New York: Teachers College Press.

Gee, J. P. (1989) The narrativization of experience in the oral style. *Journal of Education, 171* (1), 75–96.

Gibson, C., & Jung, K. (2002) *Historical Census Statistics on Population Totals by Race, 1790 to 1990, and by Hispanic Origin, 1970 to 1990, for the United States, Regions, Divisions and States*. U.S. Bureau of the Census. Retrieved May 6, 2007 from http://www.census.gov/population/ www/socdemo/race.html

Good, T. L. (1970) Which pupils do teachers call on? *The Elementary School Journal, 70* (4), 190–198.

Good, T. L., Slavings, R. L., Harel, K. H., & Emerson, H. (1987) Student passivity: A study of question asking in K-12 classrooms. *Sociology of Education, 60,* 181–199.

Goodlad, J. (1984) *A Place called School*. New York: McGraw-Hill.

Gordon, T. (2003) *Teacher Effectiveness Training*. New York: Three Rivers Press.

Greene, T. (1954) The art of responsible conversation. *Journal of General Education, 8,* 34–50.

Gross, A. G. (1990) *The Rhetoric of Science*. Cambridge, MA: Harvard University Press.

Guyer, R. L., Dillon, M. L., Anderson, L., & Szobota, L. (2000) Bioethics cases and issues: Enrichment for social sciences, humanities, and science courses. *Social Education, 64* (7), 410–414.

Habermas, J. (1984–87) *The Theory of Communicative Action*, trans. by T. McCarthy. Boston, MA: Beacon Press.

Hahn, C. (1991) Controversial issues in social studies. In J. P. Shaver (ed.) *Handbook of Research on Teaching and Learning in Social Studies* (p. 470–480). New York: Macmillan Publishing Company.

Hall, W. S., Reder, S., & Cole, M. (1979) Story recall in young Black and White children. Effects of racial group membership, race of experimenter, and dialect. In A. W. Boykin, A. J. Franklin, & J. F. Yates (eds.) *Research Directions of Black Psychologists* (p. 253–265). New York: Russel Sage Foundation.

Haroutunian-Gordon, S. (1991) *Turning the Soul: Teaching through Conversation in the High School.* Chicago, IL: University of Chicago Press.

Heath, S. B. (1982) What no bedtime story means: Narrative skills at home and school. *Language and Society, 11,* 49–76.

Heath, S. B. (1983) *Ways with Words: Language, Life, and Work in Communities and Classrooms.* Cambridge: Cambridge University Press.

Henning, J. E. (2004) The "bow tie": A conceptual tool for opening up classroom discourse. *Curriculum and Teaching Dialogue, 6* (1), 59–67.

Henning, J. E. (2005) Leading discussions: Opening up the conversation. *College Teaching, 53* (3), 90–94.

Henning, J. E., & Balong, M. (2005) The rhythm of open and closed discourse: A design-based study of classroom talk. Paper presented at The Annual Meeting of the American Educational Research Association, Montreal, Quebec.

Henning, J. E., & Lockhart, A. (2003) Acquiring the art of classroom discourse: A comparison of teacher and preservice teacher talk in a fifth grade classroom. *Research for Educational Reform, 8* (3), 46–57.

Henning, J. E., Nielsen, L. E., & Hauschildt, J. A. (2006) Implementing case study methodology in critical care nursing: A discourse analysis. *Nurse Educator, 31* (4), 153–162.

Herrera, S. G., & Murry, K. G. (2005) *Mastering ESL and Bilingual Methods: Differentiated Instruction for Culturally and Linguistically (CLD) Diverse Students.* Boston, MA: Pearson.

Hertz-Lazarowitz, R., & Calderon, M. (1993) *Children's Writing about Learning in the Bilingual Cooperative Integrated Reading and Composition (BCIRC) Project.* Baltimore, MD: Johns Hopkins University, Center for Research on Effective Schooling for Disadvantaged Students.

Hess, D., & Marri, A. (2002) Which cases should we teach? *Social Education, 66* (1), 53–59.

Hess, D., & Posselt, J. (2002) How high school students experience and learn from the discussion of controversial public issues. *Journal of Supervision and Curriculum, 17* (4), 283–314.

Hoetker, J., & Ahlbrand, W. P., Jr. (1969) The persistence of recitation. *American Educational Research Journal, 6* (2), 145–167.

Hoge, J. D., Stuart J., Foster, S. J., Nickell, P., & Field, S. L. (2002) Mandatory school uniforms: A debate for students. *Social Education, 66* (5), 284–291.

Holmes, T. (2005) The dropping of atomic bombs on Japan. *Social Education, 69* (4), 209–213.

Horn, R. A. (2000) *Teacher Talk: A Postformal Inquiry into Educational Change.* New York: P. Lang.

Howard, T. C. (1998) Pedagogical practices and ideological constructions of effective teachers of African American students. Unpublished doctoral dissertation, University of Washington, Seattle.

Hyman, R. T., & Whitford, E. V. (1990) Strategic discussion for content area teaching. In W. W. Wilen (ed.) *Teaching and Learning through Discussion: The Theory, Research, and Practice of the Discussion Method.* Springfield, IL: Charles C. Thomas.

Irvine, J. J., & York, D. E. (1995) Learning styles and culturally diverse students: A literature review. In J. A. Banks & C. A. M. Banks (eds.) *Handbook of Research on Multicultural Education* (p. 487–497). New York: Macmillan.

Irwin, A. R. (2000) Historical case studies: Teaching the nature of science in context. *Science Education, 84* (1), 5–26.

Jenlink, P. & Carr, A. A. (1996) Conversation as a medium for change in education. *Educational Technology, 36* (1), 31–38.

Jonassen, D. (1997) Instructional design models for well-structured and ill-structured problem-solving learning outcomes. *Educational Technology Research and Development, 45* (1), 65–94.

Jordan, C. (1985) Translating culture: From ethnographic information to educational program. *Anthropology & Education Quarterly, 16* (2), 105–124.

Joyce, B., & Showers, B. (2002) *Student Achievement through Staff Development*. Alexandria, VA: Association for Supervision and Curriculum Development.

Kahn, E. (2007) Building fires: Raising achievement through class discussion. *English Journal*, *96* (4), 16–18.

Kalman, R. (2004) The value of multiple solutions. *Mathematics Teaching in the Middle School*, *10* (4), 174–179.

Kindsvatter, R., Wilen, W., & Ischler M. (1996) *Dynamics of Effective Teaching*, 3rd edn. White Plains, NY: Longman.

Klinzing, H. G., & Klinzing-Eurich, G. (1988) Questions, Responses, & Reactions. In J. T. Dillon (ed) *Questioning and Discussion: A Multidisciplinary Study* (p. 212–239). Norwood, NJ: Ablex.

Kochman, T. (1981) *Black and White Styles in Conflict*. Chicago, IL: University of Chicago Press.

Krashen, S. (1982) *Principles and Practice in Second Language Acquisition*. Oxford, UK: Pergamon Press.

Labov, W. (1972) *Language in the Inner City: Studies in the Black English Vernacular*. Philadelphia, PA: University of Pennsylvania Press.

Ladson-Billings, G. (1994) *The Dreamkeepers: Successful Teachers of African American Children*. San Francisco: Jossey-Bass Publishers.

Lange, B. (1982) ERIC/RCS report: Questioning techniques. *Language Arts*, *59*, 180–185.

Langer, G. M., & Colton, A. B. (2005) Looking at student work. *Educational Leadership*, *62* (5), 22–26.

Langer, G. M., Colton, A. B., & Goff, L. S. (2003) *Collaborative Analysis of Student Work: Improving Teaching and Learning*. Alexandria, VA: Association for Supervision and Curriculum Development.

Lappan, G., Fey, J., Friel, S., Fitzgerald, W., & Phillips, E. (1998) *The Connected Mathematics Project*. White Plains, NJ: Dale Seymour Publications.

Lasker, B. (1949) *Democracy through Discussion*. New York: The H. W. Wilson Company.

Laubenbacher, R., & Pengelley, D. (1998) *Mathematical Expeditions: Chronicles by the Explorers*. New York: Springer-Verlag.

Lawrence, A. (1999) From the giver to the twenty-one balloons: Explorations with probability. *Mathematics Teaching in the Middle School*, *4* (8), 504–509.

Lawrence, A., & Hennessy, C. (2002) *Lessons for Algebraic Thinking. Grades 6–8*. Sausalito, CA: Math Solutions Publications.

Lee, C. (1991) Big picture talkers/words walking without masters: The instructional implications of ethnic voices for an expanded literacy. *Journal of Negro Education*, *60* (3), 291–304.

Lee, C. (1993) *Signifying as a Scaffold to Literary Interpretation: The Pedagogical Implications of a Form of African-American Discourse*. NCTE Research Report No. 26. Urbana, IL: National Council of Teachers of English.

Lepper, M. R., Drake, M. F., & O'Donnell-Johnson, T. (1997) Scaffolding techniques of expert human tutors. In K. Hogan & M. Pressley (eds.) *Scaffolding Student Learning: Instructional Approaches and Issues* (p. 18–144). Cambridge, MA: Brookline Books.

Little, C. (1999) Geometry projects linking mathematics, literacy, arts, and technology. *Mathematics Teaching in the Middle School*, *4* (5), 332–335.

Little, J. W., Gearhart, M., Curry, M., & Kafka, J. (2003) Looking at student work for teacher learning, teacher community, and school reform. *Phi Delta Kappan*, *84* (3), 184–192.

Lubienski, S. T. (2000) A clash of social class cultures? Student experiences in a discussion-intensive seventh grade mathematics classroom. *The Elementary School Journal*, *100* (4), 377–403.

Macbeth, D. (2003) Hugh Mehan's *learning lessons* reconsidered: On the differences between the naturalistic and critical analysis of classroom discourse. *American Educational Research Journal*, *40* (1), 239–280.

Marzano, R. J. (1993) How classroom teachers approach the teaching of thinking. *Theory into Practice*, *32* (3), 154–160.

Marzano, R.J., & Kendall, J.S. (2007) *The New Taxonomy of Educational Objectives*, 2nd edn. Thousand Oaks, CA: Corwin Press.

Mathis, J. B. (2001) Respond to stories with stories: Teachers discuss multicultural children's literature. *The Social Studies*, *92* (4), 51–60.

Matsuda, M. (1989) Working with Asian family members: Some communication strategies. *Topics in Language Disorders*, *9* (3), 45–53.

Maus, J. (2005) Every story tells a picture. *Mathematics Teaching in the Middle School*, *10* (April), 375–379.

McCloskey, D. N. (1998) *The Rhetoric of Economics*, 2nd edn. Madison, WI: University of Wisconsin Press.

McDonnell, M. (2002) Making a case for the case study method. *Social Education*, *66* (1), 68–69.

Mehan, H. (1978) Structuring school structure. *Harvard Educational Review*, *48* (1), 32–64.

Mehan, H. (1979) *Learning Lessons: Social Organization in the Classroom*. Cambridge, MA: Harvard University Press.

Mehan, H. (1982) The structure of classroom events and their consequences for student performance. In P. Gilmore & A. Glatthorn (eds.) *Children In and Out of School: Ethnography and Education* (p. 59–87). Washington, DC: Center for Applied Linguistics.

Mercer, N. (1995) *The Guided Construction of Knowledge: Talk amongst Teachers and Learners*. Clevedon, UK: Multilingual Matters.

Mercer, N. (2000) *Words & Minds: How We Use Language to Think Together*. New York: Routledge.

Michaels, S. & Cazden, C. (1986) Teacher–child collaboration on oral preparation for literacy. In B. Schieffer (ed.) *Acquisition of Literacy: Ethnographic Perspectives*. Norwood, NJ: Ablex.

Mills, S. R., Rice, C. T., Berliner, D. C., & Rousseau, E. W. (1980) The correspondence between teachers' questions and student answers in classroom discourse. *Journal of Experimental Education*, *48*, 194–204.

Mizell, L. (1998) Exploring primary sources: The ideal of liberty and the reality of slavery. *Social Education*, *62* (6), 350–351.

National Center for Educational Statistics (NCES) (2004a) *Racial/Ethnic Distribution of Public School Students*. Retrieved May 6, 2007, from http://nces.ed.gov/programs/coe/2006/section1/indicator05.asp

National Center for Educational Statistics (NCES) (2004b) *Language Minority School-Age Children*. Retrieved May 6, 2007, from http://nces.ed.gov/programs/coe/2006/section1/indicator07.asp

National Center for Educational Statistics (NCES) (2006) *Characteristics of the 100 Largest Public Elementary and Secondary School Districts in the United States: 2003–04*. Retrieved May 6, 2007, from http://nces.ed.gov/pubsearch/pubsinfo.asp?pubid=2006329

National Council of Teachers of Mathematics (2000) *Principles and Standards of School Mathematics*. Reston, VA: NCTM.

Nelson, J. S., Megill, L. A., & McCloskey, D. N. (eds.) (1987) *The Rhetoric of the Human Sciences: Language and Argument in Scholarship and Public Affairs*. Madison, WI: The University of Wisconsin Press.

Newton, P. (1999) The place of argumentation in the pedagogy of school science. *International Journal of Science Education*, *21*, 553–576.

Nieto, S. (1996) *Affirming Diversity: The Sociopolitical Context of Multicultural Education*, 2nd edn. White Plains, NY: Longman.

Nieto, S. (2002) *Language, Culture, and Teaching: Critical Perspectives for a New Century*. Mahwah, NJ: L. Erlbaum.

Noddings, N. (1984) *Caring, a Feminine Approach to Ethics & Moral Education*. Berkeley, CA: University of California Press.

Noddings, N. (1992) *The Challenge to Care in Schools: An Alternative Approach to Education*. New York: Teachers College Press.

Nystrand, M. (2006) Research on the role of classroom discourse as it affects reading comprehension. *Research in the Teaching of English*, *40*, 392–412.

Nystrand, M., Gamoran, A., Kachur, R., & Prendergast, C. (1997) *Opening Dialogue: Understanding the Dynamics of Language and Learning in the English Classroom*. New York: Teachers College Press.

O'Connor, M.C., & Michaels, S. (1996) Shifting participant frameworks. In D. Hicks (ed.) *Discourse, Learning, and Schooling*. Cambridge: Cambridge University Press.

Olneck, M. R. (2004) Immigrants and education in the United States. In J. A. Banks & C. A. M. Banks (eds.) *Handbook of Research on Multicultural Education*, 2nd edn. San Francisco: Jossey-Bass.

Ornstein, A. C. (1988) Questioning: The essence of good teaching. Part II. *NASSP Bulletin*, *72* (February), 72–80.

Palmer, J., & Burroughs, S. (2002) Integrating children's literature and song into the social studies. *The Social Studies*, *93* (2), 73–78.

Patchen, T. (2006) Engendering participation, deliberating dependence: Inner-city adolescents' perceptions of classroom practice. *Teachers College Record*, *108* (10), 2053–2079.

Phillips, S. U. (1972) Participant structures and communicative competence: Warm Springs children in community and classroom. In C. Cazden, V. John, & D. Hymes (eds.) *Functions of Language in the Classroom* (p. 370–394). New York: Teachers College Press.

Piestrup, A. M. (1973) *Black Dialect Interference and Accommodation of Reading Instruction in First Grade*. Monograph of the Language Behavior Research Laboratory. Berkeley, CA: University of California.

Pinker, S. (1994) *The Language Instinct*. New York: W. Morrow and Co.

Poetter, T. S., & Badiali, B. J. (2001) *Teacher Leader*. Larchmont, NY: Eye on Education.

Posner, G. J. Strike, K. A., Hewsen, P. W., & Gertzog, W. A. (1982) Accommodation of a scientific conception: Toward a theory of conceptual change. *Science Education*, *66* (2), 211–227.

Prelli, L. J. (1989) *A Rhetoric of Science: Inventing Scientific Discourse*. Columbia, SC: University of South Carolina Press.

Redfield, D. L., & Rousseau, E. W. (1981) Meta-analysis of experimental research on teacher questioning behavior. *Review of Educational Research*, *51*, 237–245.

Roby, T. W. (1988) Models of discussion. In J. T. Dillon (ed.) *Questioning and Discussion: A Multidisciplinary Study* (p. 163–191). Norwood, NJ: Ablex.

Rowe, M. B. (1986) Wait time: Slowing down may be a way of speeding up! *Journal of Teacher Education*, *37* (1), 43–46.

Sadker, D., & Sadker, M. (1985) Is the OK classroom OK? *Phi Delta Kappan*, *66* (5), 358–361.

Samson, G. E., Strykowsi, B., Weinstein, T., & Walberg, H. J. (1987) The effects of teacher questioning on students' achievement. *Journal of Educational Research*, *80*, 290–295.

Sauer, R., Popp, M., & Isaacs, M. (1984) Action zone theory and the hearing impaired student in the mainstreamed classroom. *Journal of Classroom Instruction*, *19* (2), 21–25.

Saunders, W., Goldenberg, C., & Hamann, J. (1992) Instructional conversations beget instructional conversations. *Teaching and Teacher Education*, *8*, 199–218.

Schiever, S. W. (1991) *A Comprehensive Approach to Teaching Thinking*. Needham Heights, MA: Allyn and Bacon.

Sidorkin, A. M. (2002) *Learning Relations: Impure Education, Deschooled Schools, & Dialogue with Evil*. New York: Peter Lang.

Simons, H. W. (ed.) (1989) *Rhetoric in the Human Sciences*. London: Sage Publications Ltd.

Sinclair, J. M., & Coulthard, R. M. (1975) *Towards an Analysis of Discourse: The English used by Teachers and Pupils*. London: Oxford University Press.

Slavin, R. E. (1995) *Cooperative Learning: Theory, Research, and Practice*, 2nd edn. Boston, MA: Allyn and Bacon.

Slob, W. H. (2002) *Dialogical Rhetoric: An Essay on Truth and Normativity after Post Modernism*. Dordrecht, The Netherlands: Kluwer.

Smith, S. N. (2004) Teaching for civic participation with negotiation role play. *Social Education*, *68* (3), 194–197.

Smith, F., Hardman, F., Wall, K., & Mroz, M. (2004) Interactive whole class teaching in the national literacy and numeracy strategies. *British Educational Research Journal*, *30* (3), 395–411.

Smylie, M. A., & Denny, J. W. (1990) Teacher leadership: Tensions and ambiguities in organizational perspective. *Educational Administration Quarterly*, *26* (3) 235–259.

Stodolsky, S., Ferguson, T., & Wimpelberg, K. (1981) The recitation persists, but what does it look like? *Journal of Curriculum Studies*, *13*, 121–130.

Strother, D. B. (1989) Developing thinking skills through questioning. *Phi Delta Kappan*, *71* (4), 324–327.

Stuart, J. F., Hoge, J. D., & Rosch, R. H. (1999) Thinking aloud about history: Children's and adolescents' responses to historical photographs. *Theory and Research in Social Education*, *27* (2), 179–214.

Suarez-Orozco, C., Suarez-Orozco, M., & Doucet, F. (2004) The academic engagement and achievement of Latino youth. In J. A. Banks & C. A. M. Banks (eds.) *Handbook of Research on Multicultural Education*, 2nd edn. San Francisco: Jossey-Bass.

Susskind, E. (1979) Encouraging teachers to encourage children's curiosity: A pivotal competence. *Journal of Clinical Child Psychology*, *8*, 101–106.

Swift, J. N. Gooding, C. T., & Swift, P. R. (1988) Questions and wait time. In J. T. Dillon (ed.) *Questioning and Discussion: A Multidisciplinary Study* (p. 192–211). Norwood, NJ: Ablex.

Thiessen, D. (2004) *Exploring Mathematics through Literature: Articles and Lessons for Prekindergarten through Grade 8.* Reston, VA: The National Council of Teachers of Mathematics.

Thompson, D. R., & Austin, R. A. (1999) Socrates and the three little pigs: Connecting patterns, counting trees, and probability. *Mathematics Teaching in the Middle School, 5* (November), 156–161.

Tochon, F. V. (1999) *Video Study Groups for Education, Professional Development, and Change.* Madison, WI: Atwood.

U.S. Bureau of the Census (2001) *Overview of Race and Hispanic Origin.* Retrieved May 6, 2007, from http://www.census.gov/population/www/cen2000/briefs.html#sr

U.S. Bureau of the Census (2005) *Language Spoken at Home.* Retrieved May 6, 2007, from http://factfinder. census.gov/servlet/STTable?_bm=y&-geo_id=01000US&-qr_name=ACS_2005_EST_G00_S1601&-ds_name=ACS_2005_EST_G00_

van Boxtel, C., & Roelofs, E. (2001) Investigating the quality of student discourse: What constitutes a productive student discourse? *Journal of Classroom Interaction, 36* (2), 55–61.

VanDeWeghe, R. (2007) What kinds of classroom discussion promote reading comprehension? *English Journal, 96* (3), 86–91.

Viiri, J., & Saari, H. (2006) Teacher talk patterns in science lessons: Use in teacher education. *Journal of Science Teacher Education, 17* (4), 347–365.

Vogler, K. (2004) Using political cartoons to improve your verbal questioning. *The Social Studies, 95* (1), 11–15.

Vogt, L., Jordan, C., & Tharp, R. (1987) Explaining school failure, producing school success: Two cases. *Anthropology & Education Quarterly, 18* (4), 276–286.

Vygotsky, L. (1978) *Mind in Society: The Development of Higher Psychological Processes,* trans. by M. Cole, V. John-Steiner, S. Scribner, & E. Souberman. Cambridge, MA: Harvard University Press.

Vygotsky, L. (1986) *Thought and Language,* trans. and edited by A. Kozulin. Cambridge, MA: M.I.T. Press.

Walsh, C.E. (1991) *Pedagogy and the Struggle for Voice: Issues of Language, Power, and Schooling for Puerto Ricans.* New York: Bergin & Garvey.

Walsh, J. A., & Sattes, B. D. (2005) *Quality Questioning: Research-Based Practice to Engage Every Learner.* Thousand Oaks, CA: Corwin Press.

Weinstein, C. S. (2007) *Middle and Secondary Classroom Management: Lessons from Research and Practice,* 3rd edn. New York: McGraw-Hill.

Wells, G. (1993) Reevaluating the IRF sequence: A proposal for the articulation of theories of activity and discourse for the analysis of teaching and learning in the classroom. *Linguistics and Education, 5,* 1–37.

Wierzbicka, A. (1991) Japanese key words and core cultural values. *Language in Society, 20* (3), 333–385.

Wilen, W. W. (ed.) (1987) *Questions, Questioning Techniques, and Effective Teaching* (p. 107–134). Washington, DC: National Education Association.

Wilen, W. W. (1990) Forms and phases of discussion. In W. W. Wilen (ed.) *Teaching and Learning through Discussion: The Theory, Research, and Practice of the Discussion Method.* Springfield, IL: Charles C. Thomas.

Wilen, W. W. (2004) Encouraging reticent students' participation in classroom discussions. *Social Education, 68* (1), 51–56.

Wilen, W. W., & Clegg, A. (1987) Effective questions and questioning: A research review. *Theory and Research in Social Education, 14,* 153–161.

Wineberg, S. S. (1991) On the reading of historical texts: Notes on the breach between school and academy. *American Educational Research Journal, 28,* 495–520.

Winne, P. H. (1979) Experiments relating teachers' use of higher cognitive questions to student achievement. *Review of Educational Research, 49,* 13–50.

Wood, T., Williams, G., & McNeal, B. (2006) Children's mathematical thinking in different classroom cultures. *Journal for Research in Mathematics Education, 37* (3), 222–255.

Zambo, R. (2005) The power of two: Linking mathematics and literature. *Mathematics Teaching in the Middle School, 10* (8), 394–399.

Zentella, A. C. (1997) *Growing up Bilingual: Puerto Rican Children in New York.* Oxford, UK: Basil Blackwell.

Index